SOMETHING Different ABOUT DAD

of related interest

The Complete Guide to Asperger's Syndrome
Tony Attwood
ISBN 978 1 84310 495 7 (hardback)
ISBN 978 1 84310 669 2 (paperback)

All Cats Have Asperger Syndrome
Kathy Hoopman
ISBN 978 1 84310 481 0

My Parent has an Autism Spectrum Disorder
A Workbook for Children and Teens
Barbara Lester
ISBN 978 1 84905 835 3

Siblings
The Autism Spectrum Through Our Eyes
Jane Johnson and Anne Van Rensselaer
ISBN 978 1 84905 829 2

Voices from the Spectrum
Parents, Grandparents, Siblings, People with Autism, and Professionals Share Their Wisdom
Edited by Cindy N. Ariel and Robert A. Naseef
ISBN 978 1 84310 786 6

SOMETHING Different ABOUT DAD

How to Live with Your Asperger's Parent

Kirsti Evans and John Swogger

Jessica Kingsley Publishers
London and Philadelphia

First published in 2011
by Jessica Kingsley Publishers
116 Pentonville Road
London N1 9JB, UK
and
400 Market Street, Suite 400
Philadelphia, PA 19106, USA

www.jkp.com

Library of Congress Cataloging in Publication Data
Evans, Kirsti.
  Something different about Dad : how to live with your Asperger's parent / Kirsti Evans and
John Swogger.
    p. cm.
  ISBN 978-1-84905-114-9 (alk. paper)
  1. Asperger's syndrome. 2. Parent and child. I. Swogger, John. II. Title.
  RC553.A88E943 2011
  616.85'8832--dc22
                          2010042493
British Library Cataloguing in Publication Data
A CIP catalogue record for this book is available from the British Library

ISBN 978 1 84905 114 9

Printed and bound in Great Britain by
MPG Books Group

for Rosie and Sonny

contents

Preface

This book is intended to be read by children aged approximately 7 to 15 years, who know and/or are living with an adult with Asperger Syndrome, whether diagnosed or not.

There has been a huge rise in the number of diagnoses of Asperger Syndrome in the United Kingdom in recent times. This has inevitably included adults who were previously overlooked and whose behaviour has been misunderstood.

Many of these adults have families – spouses, children and other relatives who live with the challenges Asperger Syndrome can present on a day to day basis. Through working with children and young people on the Autism Spectrum, I have come into contact with families where one or more of the adults also have an Autism Spectrum Condition or Asperger Syndrome.

I realised that there are few resources available to children and young people facing the unique challenges of living with an adult who is on the Autism Spectrum. So, we decided to develop this book and present it in a format accessible to a younger reader.

We would intend this book to be used either by a practitioner as a starting point for discussion with the child or young person, or as a stand alone resource for the child or young person to read by themselves.

Because there are currently more men with a diagnosis of Asperger Syndrome than women, this book focuses on what we think is quite a typical family set up. Of course, not every situation will reflect this model. However, the underlying issues regarding Asperger Syndrome are universal.

Kirsti Evans and John Swogger

Introduction

This book is for someone who has a parent or adult relative with Asperger Syndrome.

My name is **Kirsti** and I work with children and adults who have Autism and Asperger Syndrome. I wrote the book.

This is **John**, who works as a book and magazine illustrator. He helped me tell the stories in this book by drawing all the pictures.

Our book follows the story of Sophie and Daniel whose Dad, Mark, has Asperger Syndrome.

You might be reading this book to find out about your parent or adult relative, or you might just want to know more about Asperger Syndrome.

Perhaps, like Sophie and Daniel, you may not have noticed that your relative was "different" when you were younger, but maybe now you are starting to see that there is *"Something Different About Dad"*.

Whether or not you know for sure that the person you are thinking of has Asperger Syndrome, we hope this book will help. We hope it will help you answer some of the questions you might have and give you some ideas about how to deal with parents or other adults with Asperger Syndrome.

Kirsti and John

A Note on the Text

People in different parts of the world use different names and words for Autism and Asperger Syndrome. You may hear or come across names such as Autistic Spectrum Disorder and Asperger Syndrome, Autism, Kanner Syndrome, Classic Autism, High Functioning Autism, to name a few.

This is because people have differing ideas and understandings about what Autism and Asperger Syndrome actually are and what that means to individual people. Some people experience it as a disability; others see it as a different set of abilities.

For our book we have decided to use the terms Autism Spectrum Condition and Asperger Syndrome.

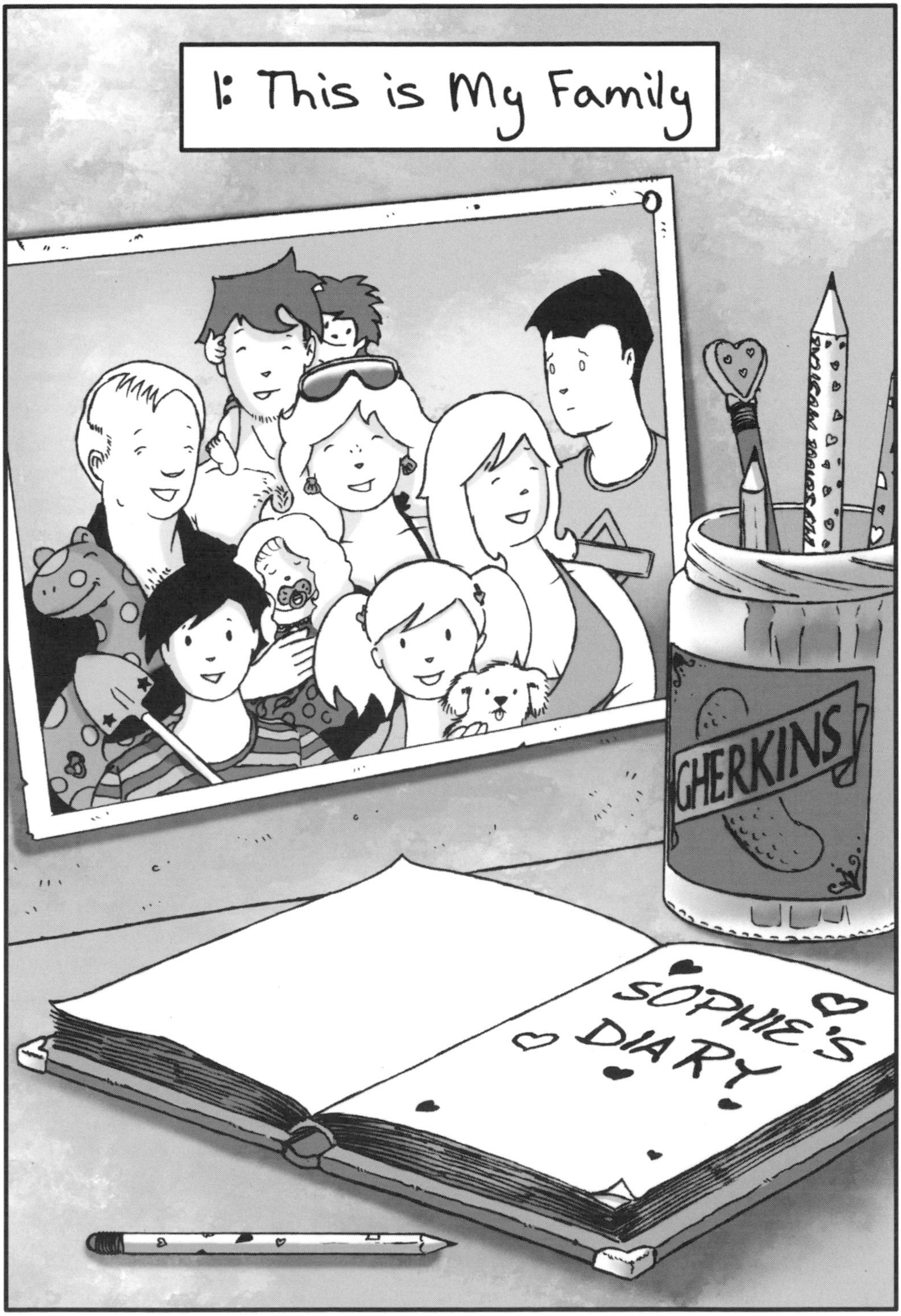
1: This is My Family
GHERKINS
SOPHIE'S DIARY

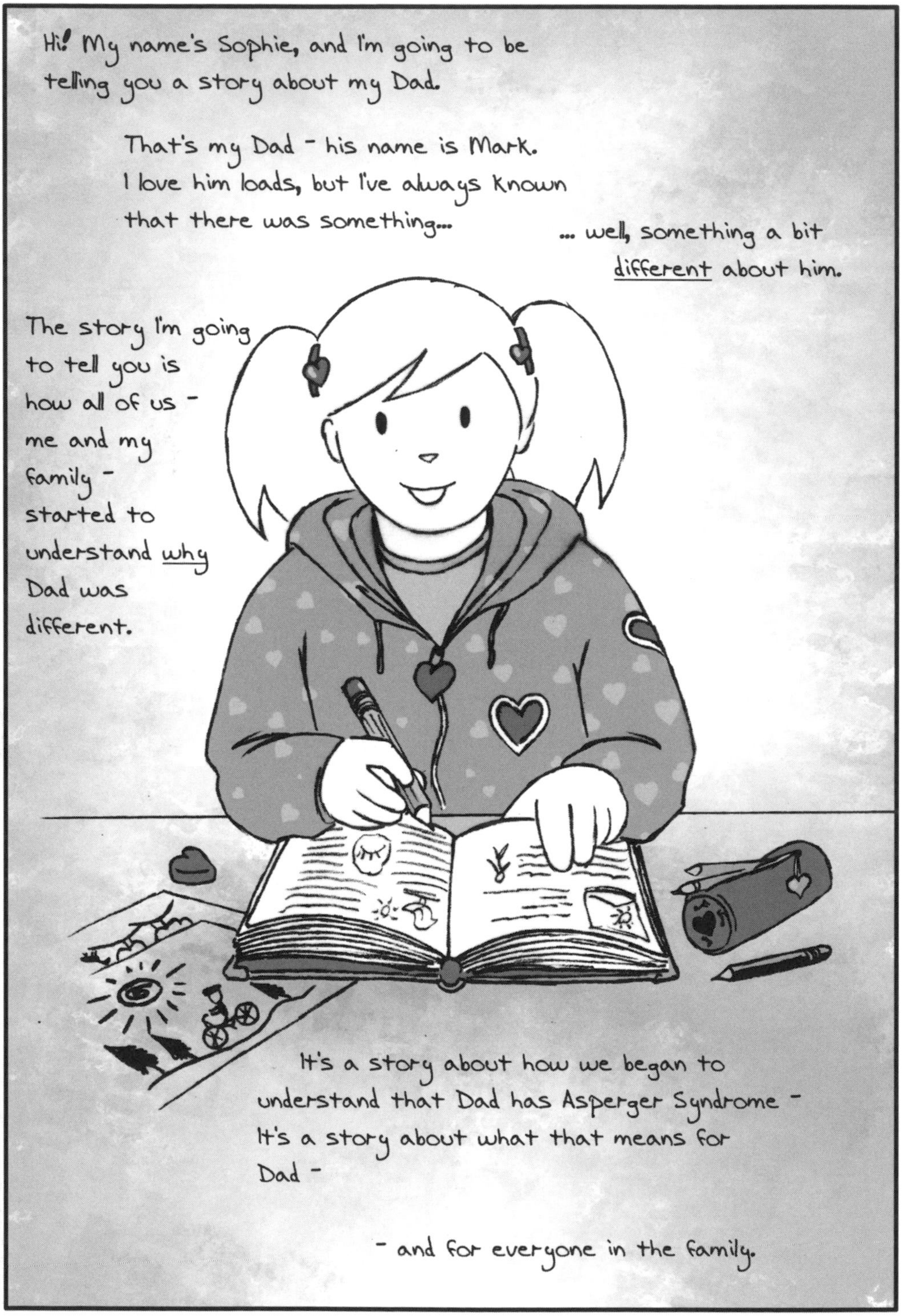
Hi! My name's Sophie, and I'm going to be telling you a story about my Dad.
That's my Dad - his name is Mark. I love him loads, but I've always known that there was something...
... well, something a bit different about him.
The story I'm going to tell you is how all of us - me and my family - started to understand why Dad was different.
It's a story about how we began to understand that Dad has Asperger Syndrome - It's a story about what that means for Dad -
- and for everyone in the family.

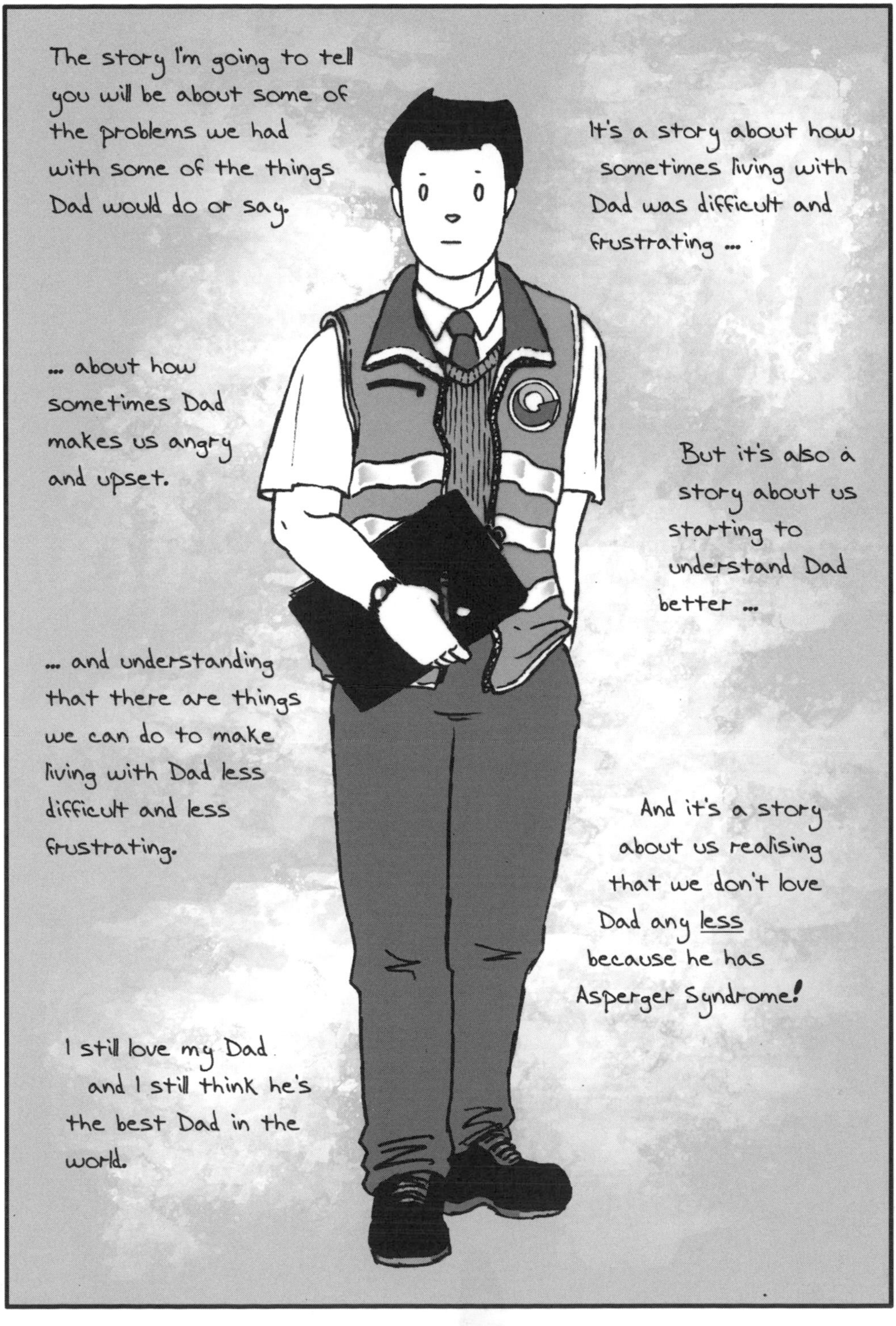
The story I'm going to tell you will be about some of the problems we had with some of the things Dad would do or say.
It's a story about how sometimes living with Dad was difficult and frustrating ...
... about how sometimes Dad makes us angry and upset.
But it's also a story about us starting to understand Dad better ...
... and understanding that there are things we can do to make living with Dad less difficult and less frustrating.
And it's a story about us realising that we don't love Dad any less because he has Asperger Syndrome!
I still love my Dad and I still think he's the best Dad in the world.

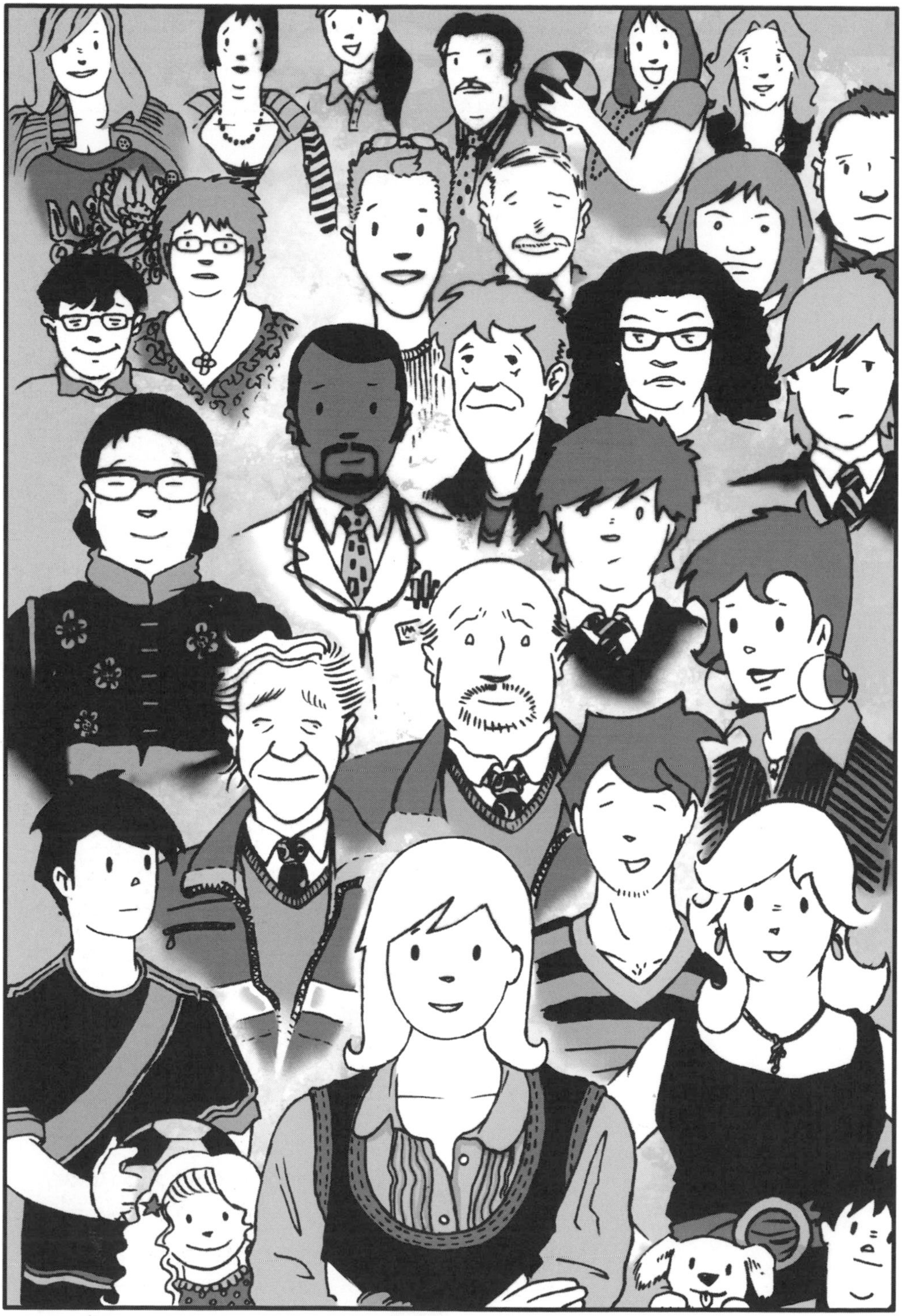

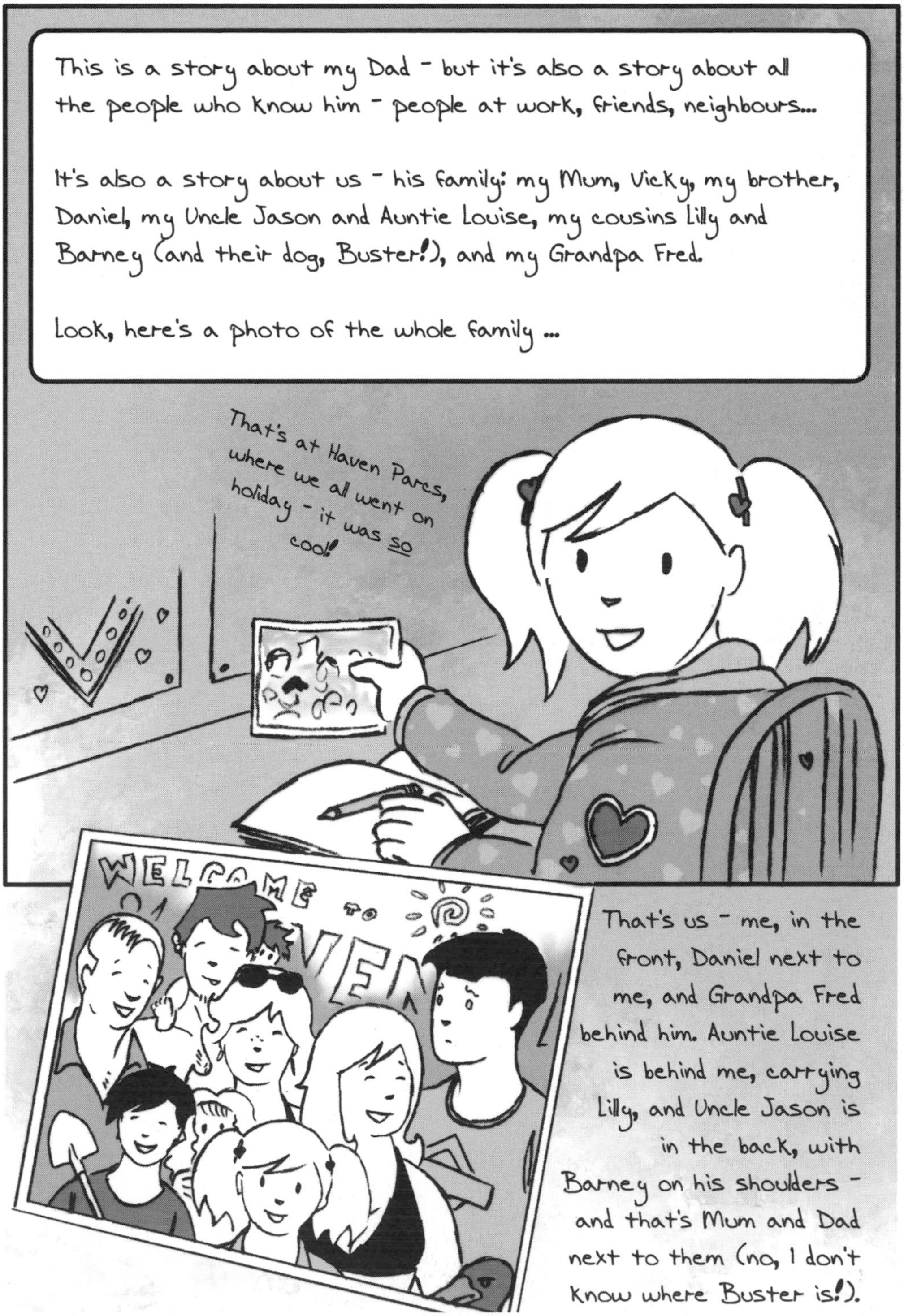
This is a story about my Dad – but it's also a story about all the people who know him – people at work, friends, neighbours...
It's also a story about us – his family: my Mum, Vicky, my brother, Daniel, my Uncle Jason and Auntie Louise, my cousins Lilly and Barney (and their dog, Buster!), and my Grandpa Fred.
Look, here's a photo of the whole family ...
That's at Haven Parcs, where we all went on holiday – it was so cool!
That's us – me, in the front, Daniel next to me, and Grandpa Fred behind him. Auntie Louise is behind me, carrying Lilly, and Uncle Jason is in the back, with Barney on his shoulders – and that's Mum and Dad next to them (no, I don't know where Buster is!).

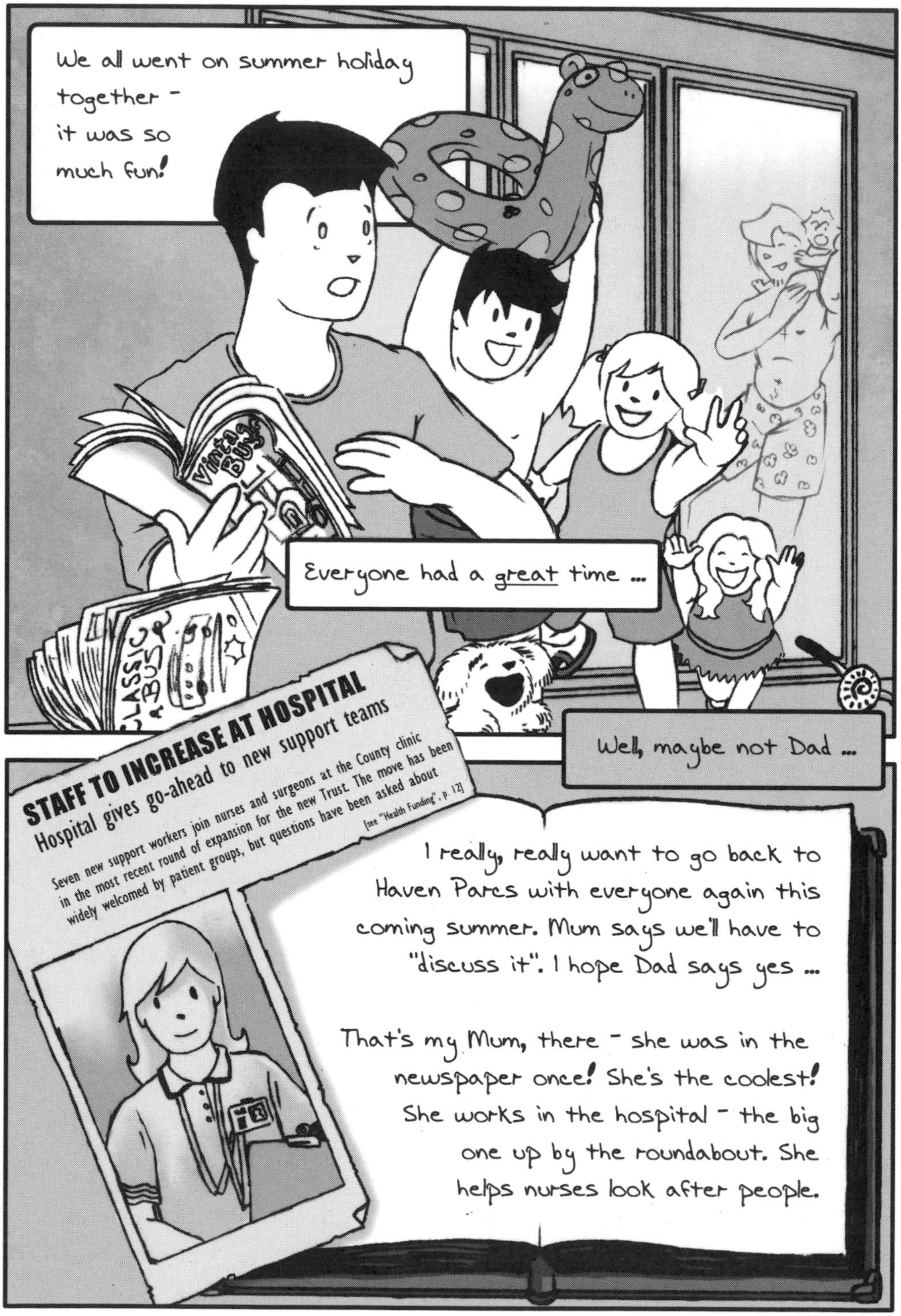
We all went on summer holiday together - it was so much fun!
Vintage Bus
Classic Bus
Everyone had a great time ...
Well, maybe not Dad ...
STAFF TO INCREASE AT HOSPITAL
Hospital gives go-ahead to new support teams
Seven new support workers join nurses and surgeons at the County clinic in the most recent round of expansion for the new Trust. The move has been widely welcomed by patient groups, but questions have been asked about
[see "Health Funding", p. 12]
I really, really want to go back to Haven Parcs with everyone again this coming summer. Mum says we'll have to "discuss it". I hope Dad says yes ...
That's my Mum, there - she was in the newspaper once! She's the coolest! She works in the hospital - the big one up by the roundabout. She helps nurses look after people.

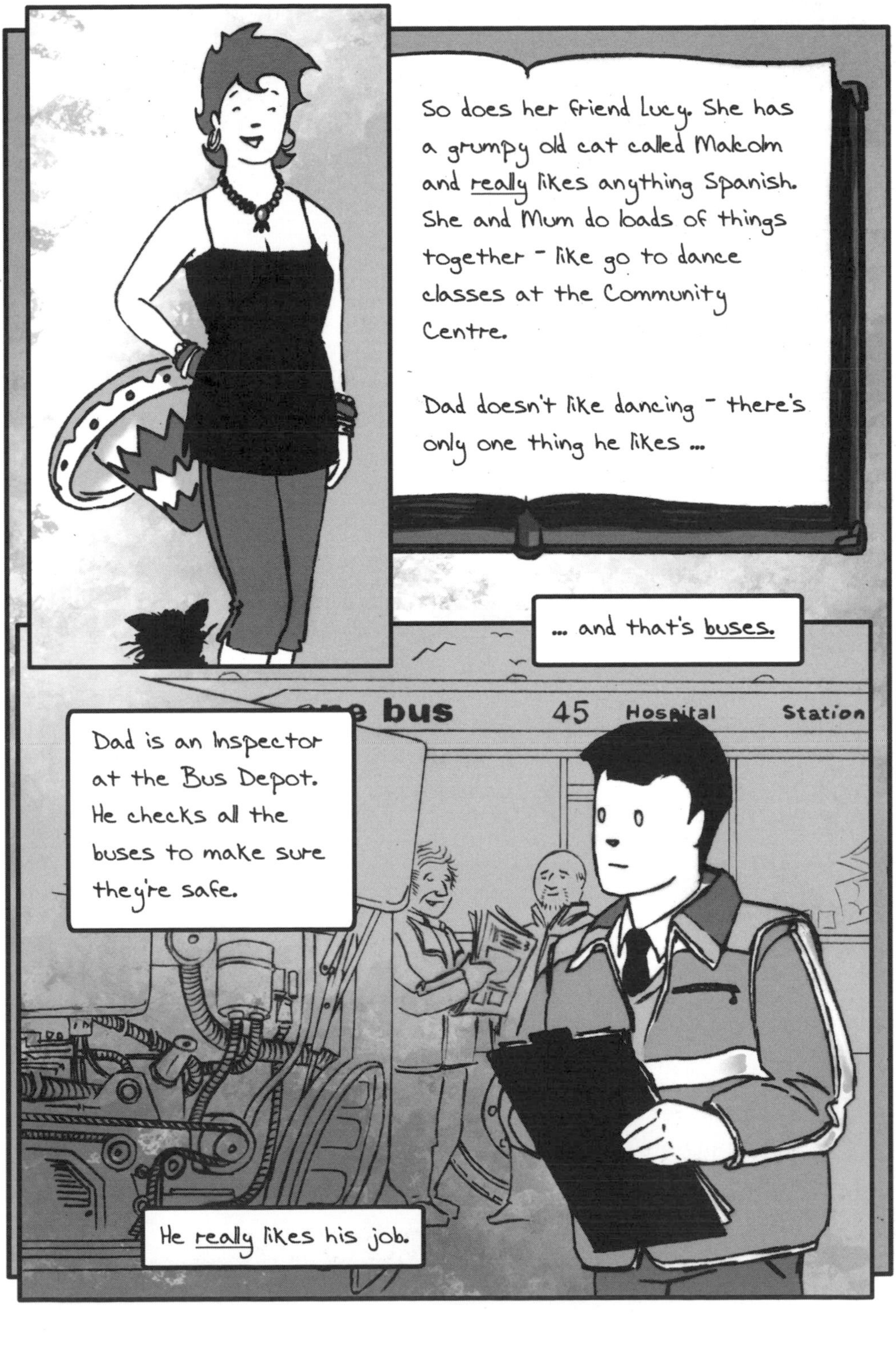
So does her friend Lucy. She has a grumpy old cat called Malcolm and really likes anything Spanish. She and Mum do loads of things together – like go to dance classes at the Community Centre.
Dad doesn't like dancing – there's only one thing he likes ...
... and that's buses.
one bus 45 Hospital Station
Dad is an Inspector at the Bus Depot. He checks all the buses to make sure they're safe.
He really likes his job.

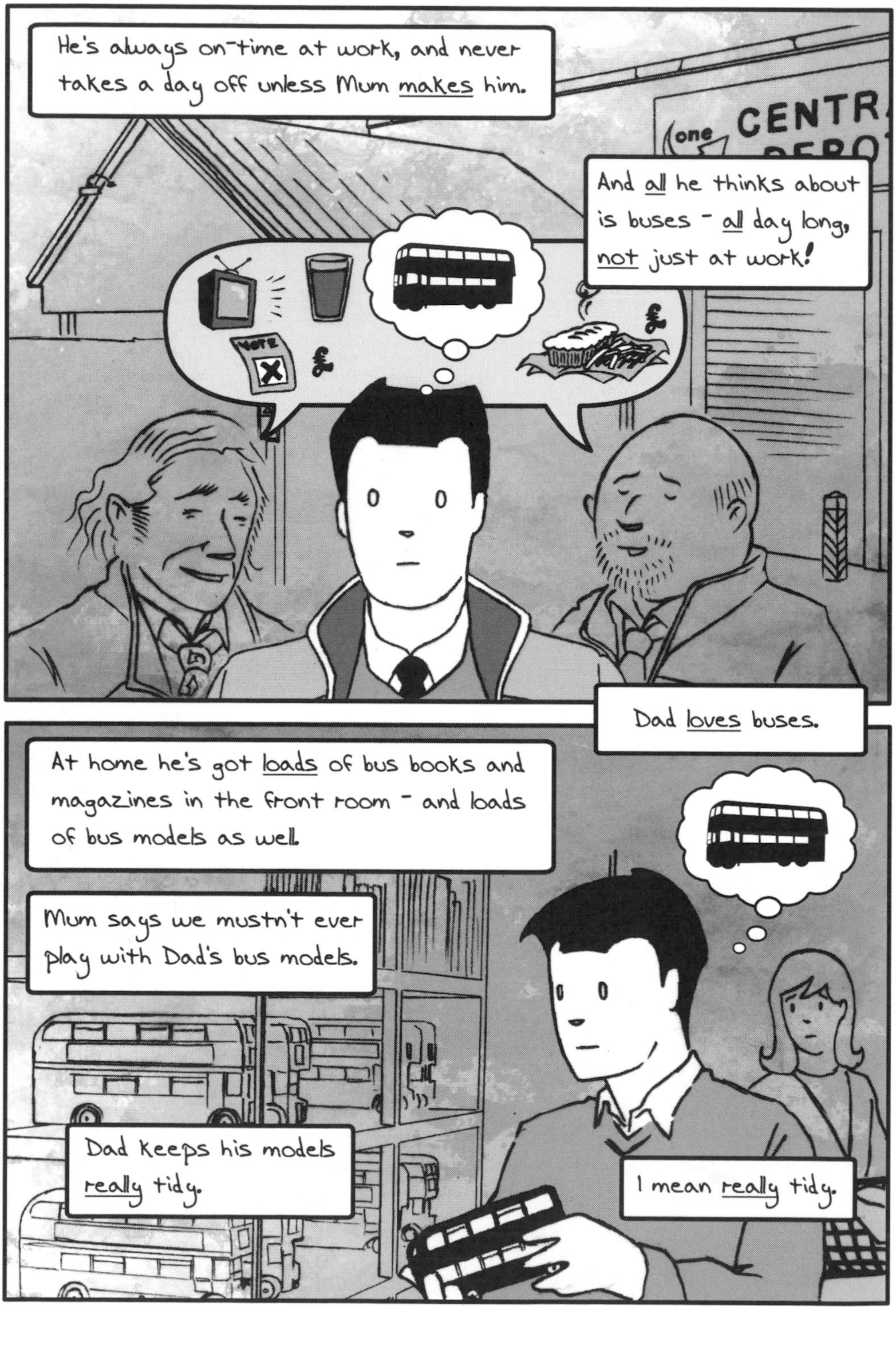
He's always on-time at work, and never takes a day off unless Mum makes him.
And all he thinks about is buses - all day long, not just at work!
VOTE
one CENTR
Dad loves buses.
At home he's got loads of bus books and magazines in the front room - and loads of bus models as well.
Mum says we mustn't ever play with Dad's bus models.
Dad keeps his models really tidy.
I mean really tidy.

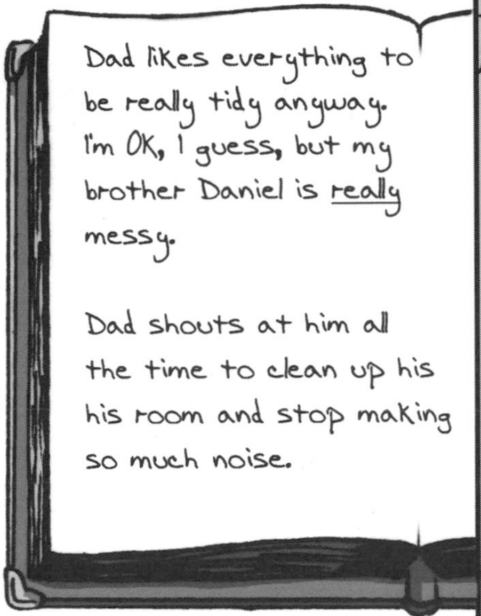
Dad likes everything to be really tidy anyway. I'm OK, I guess, but my brother Daniel is really messy.
Dad shouts at him all the time to clean up his his room and stop making so much noise.

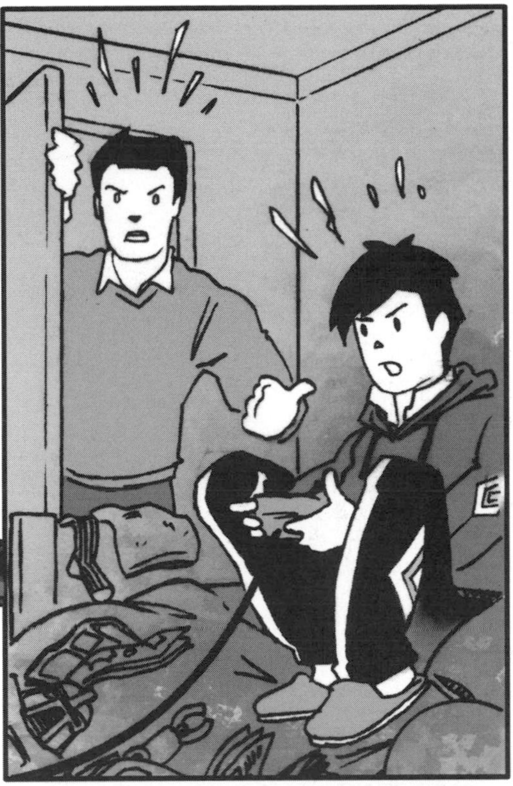

Daniel really, really likes football. He's dead good at it, too. He plays football video games, too.

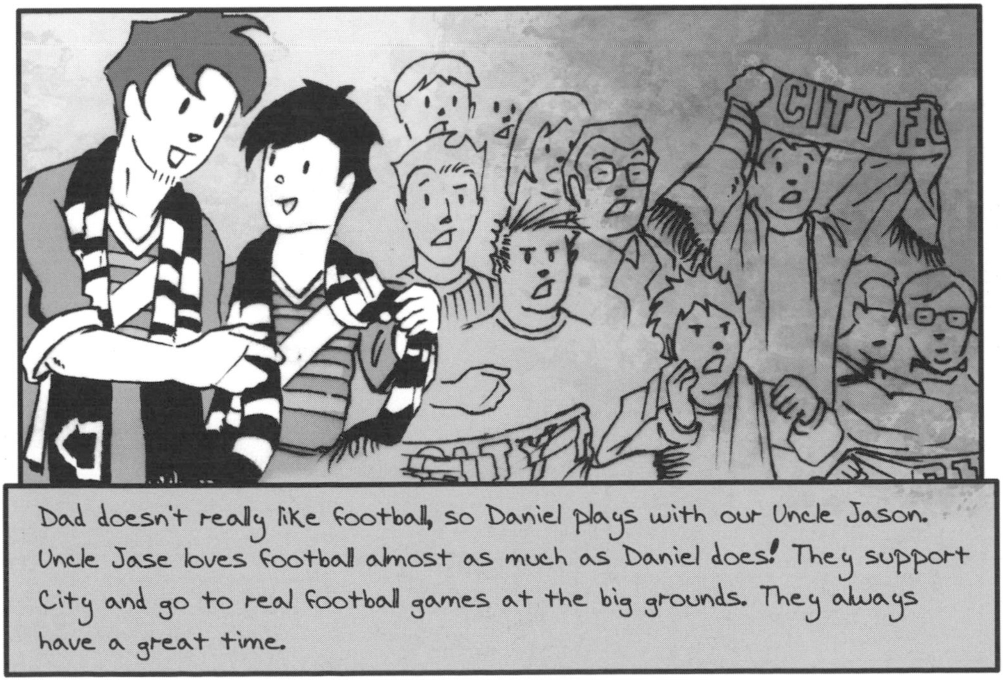
CITY F.C
CITY
Dad doesn't really like football, so Daniel plays with our Uncle Jason. Uncle Jase loves football almost as much as Daniel does! They support City and go to real football games at the big grounds. They always have a great time.

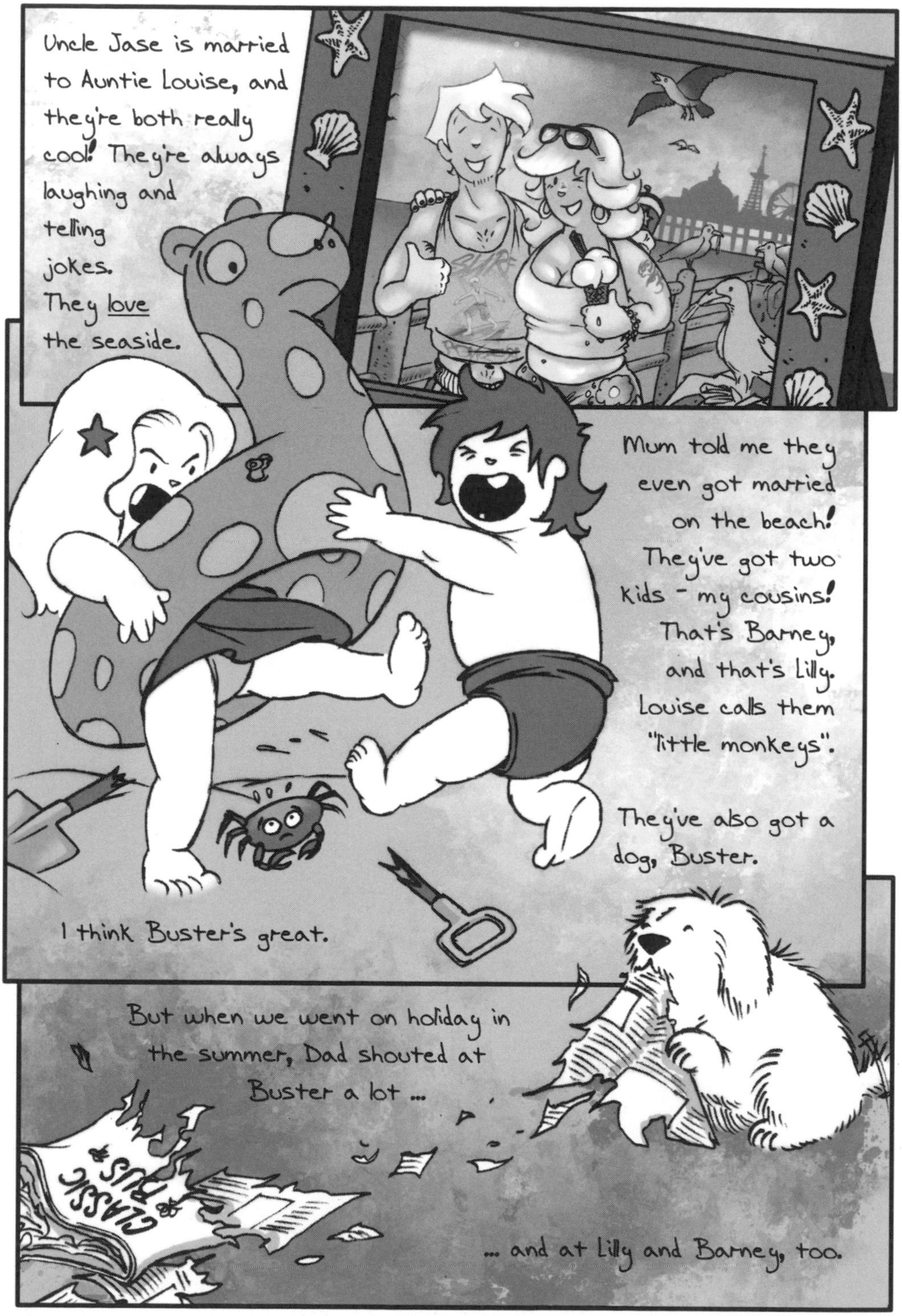
Uncle Jase is married to Auntie Louise, and they're both really cool! They're always laughing and telling jokes. They love the seaside.
Mum told me they even got married on the beach! They've got two kids - my cousins! That's Barney, and that's Lilly. Louise calls them "little monkeys".
They've also got a dog, Buster.
I think Buster's great.
But when we went on holiday in the summer, Dad shouted at Buster a lot ...
... and at Lilly and Barney, too.

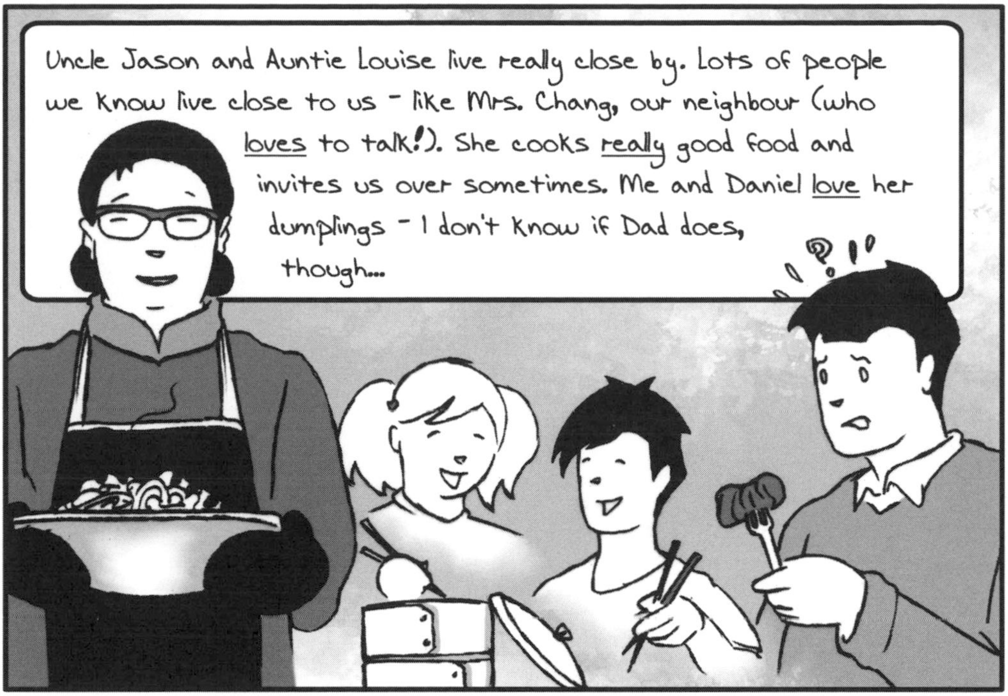
Uncle Jason and Auntie Louise live really close by. Lots of people we know live close to us – like Mrs. Chang, our neighbour (who loves to talk!). She cooks really good food and invites us over sometimes. Me and Daniel love her dumplings – I don't know if Dad does, though...
?!!

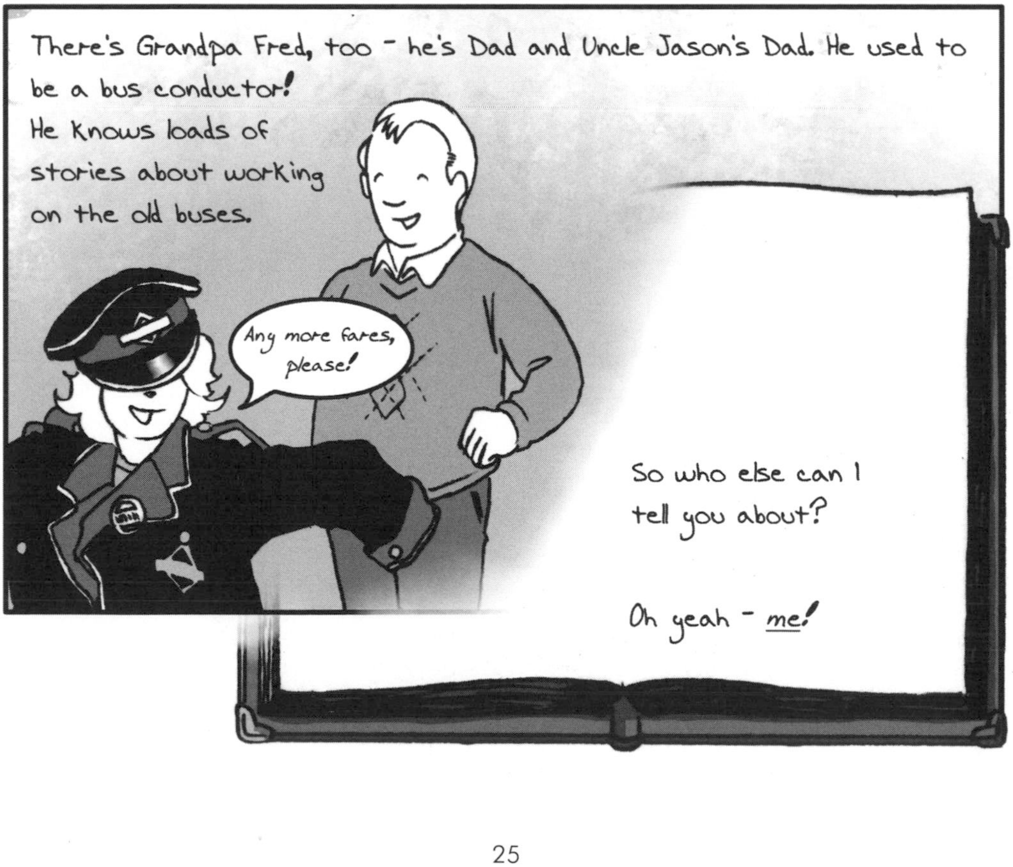
There's Grandpa Fred, too – he's Dad and Uncle Jason's Dad. He used to be a bus conductor!
He knows loads of stories about working on the old buses.
Any more fares, please!
So who else can I tell you about?
Oh yeah – me!

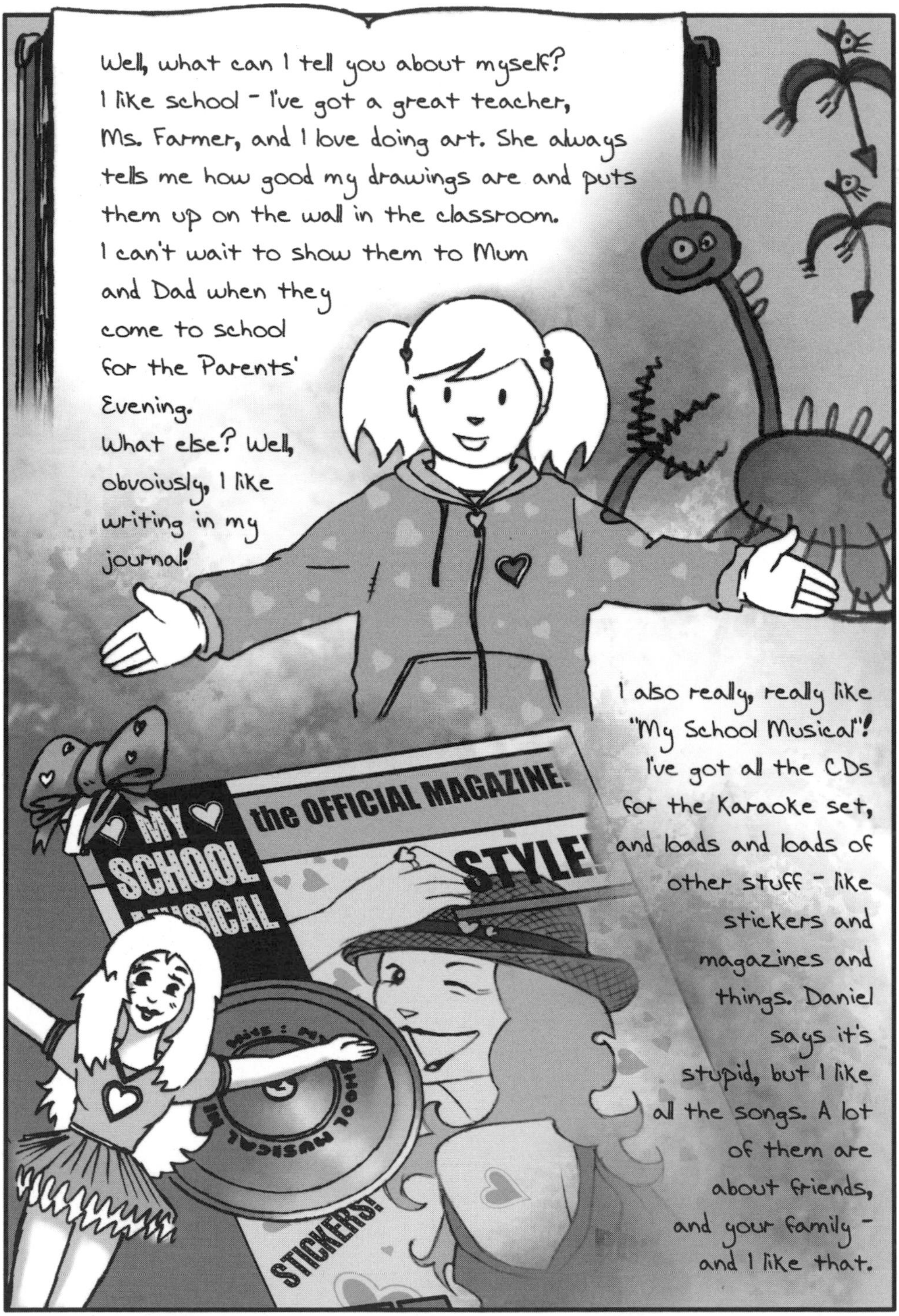
Well, what can I tell you about myself? I like school - I've got a great teacher, Ms. Farmer, and I love doing art. She always tells me how good my drawings are and puts them up on the wall in the classroom. I can't wait to show them to Mum and Dad when they come to school for the Parents' Evening.
What else? Well, obvoiusly, I like writing in my journal!
I also really, really like "My School Musical"! I've got all the CDs for the Karaoke set, and loads and loads of other stuff - like stickers and magazines and things. Daniel says it's stupid, but I like all the songs. A lot of them are about friends, and your family - and I like that.
MY SCHOOL MUSICAL
the OFFICIAL MAGAZINE.
STYLE!
STICKERS!

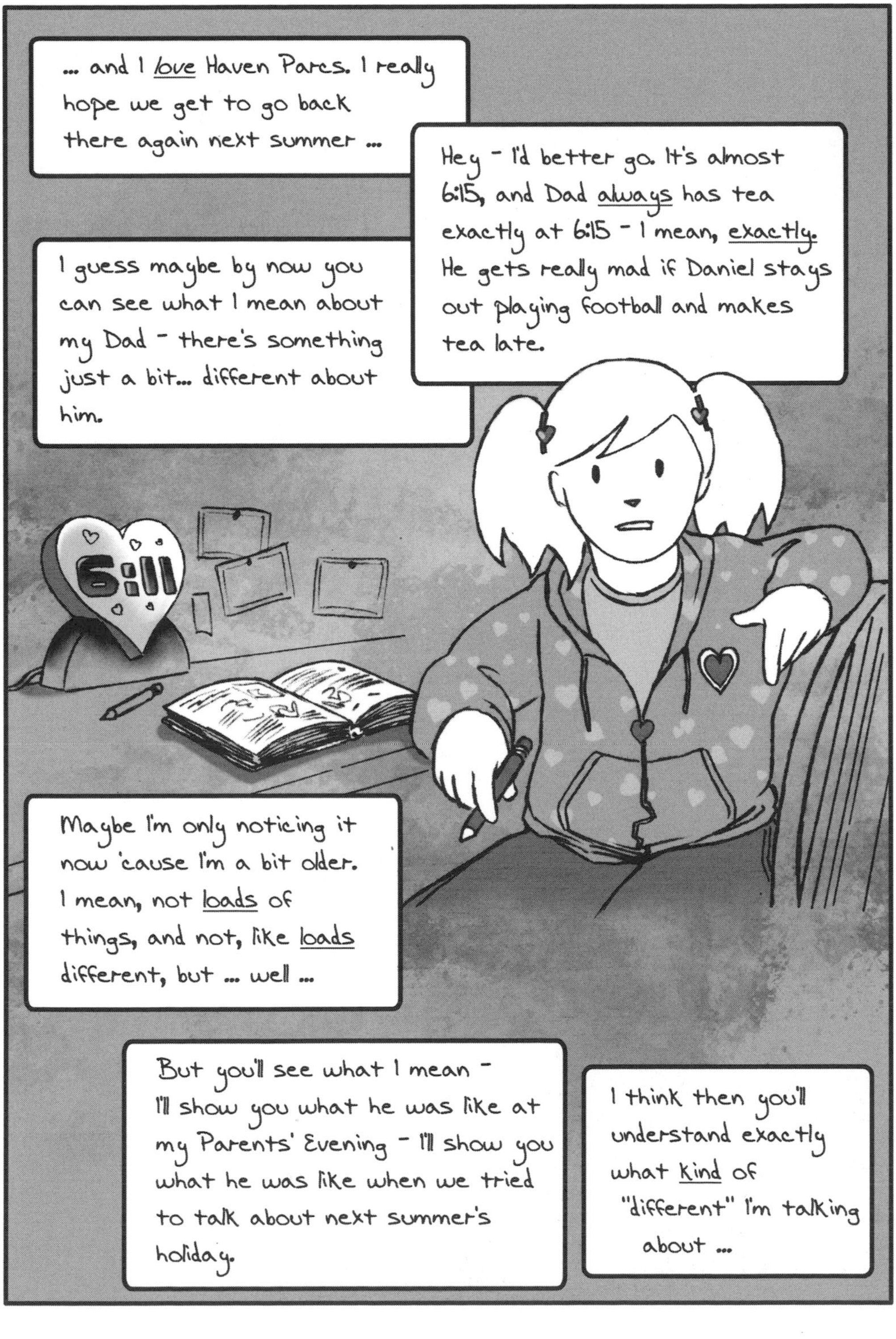
... and I love Haven Parcs. I really hope we get to go back there again next summer ...
Hey - I'd better go. It's almost 6:15, and Dad always has tea exactly at 6:15 - I mean, exactly. He gets really mad if Daniel stays out playing football and makes tea late.
I guess maybe by now you can see what I mean about my Dad - there's something just a bit... different about him.
6:11
Maybe I'm only noticing it now 'cause I'm a bit older. I mean, not loads of things, and not, like loads different, but ... well ...
But you'll see what I mean - I'll show you what he was like at my Parents' Evening - I'll show you what he was like when we tried to talk about next summer's holiday.
I think then you'll understand exactly what kind of "different" I'm talking about ...

Sophie has told us that her Dad has Asperger Syndrome.

Before we let Sophie tell us any more about her and her family, perhaps we'd better answer an important question ...

So what kind of "different" is Sophie talking about?

She's told us a little bit about her family, and about her Dad.

I think I can see what she's talking about - her Dad is very interested in buses, likes to have set times for things, and seems to get upset when things aren't as he would have them, or are unexpected.

Sophie says that she's maybe noticing these differences because she's getting a little older - both she and her brother Daniel are starting to grow up and change a bit themselves.

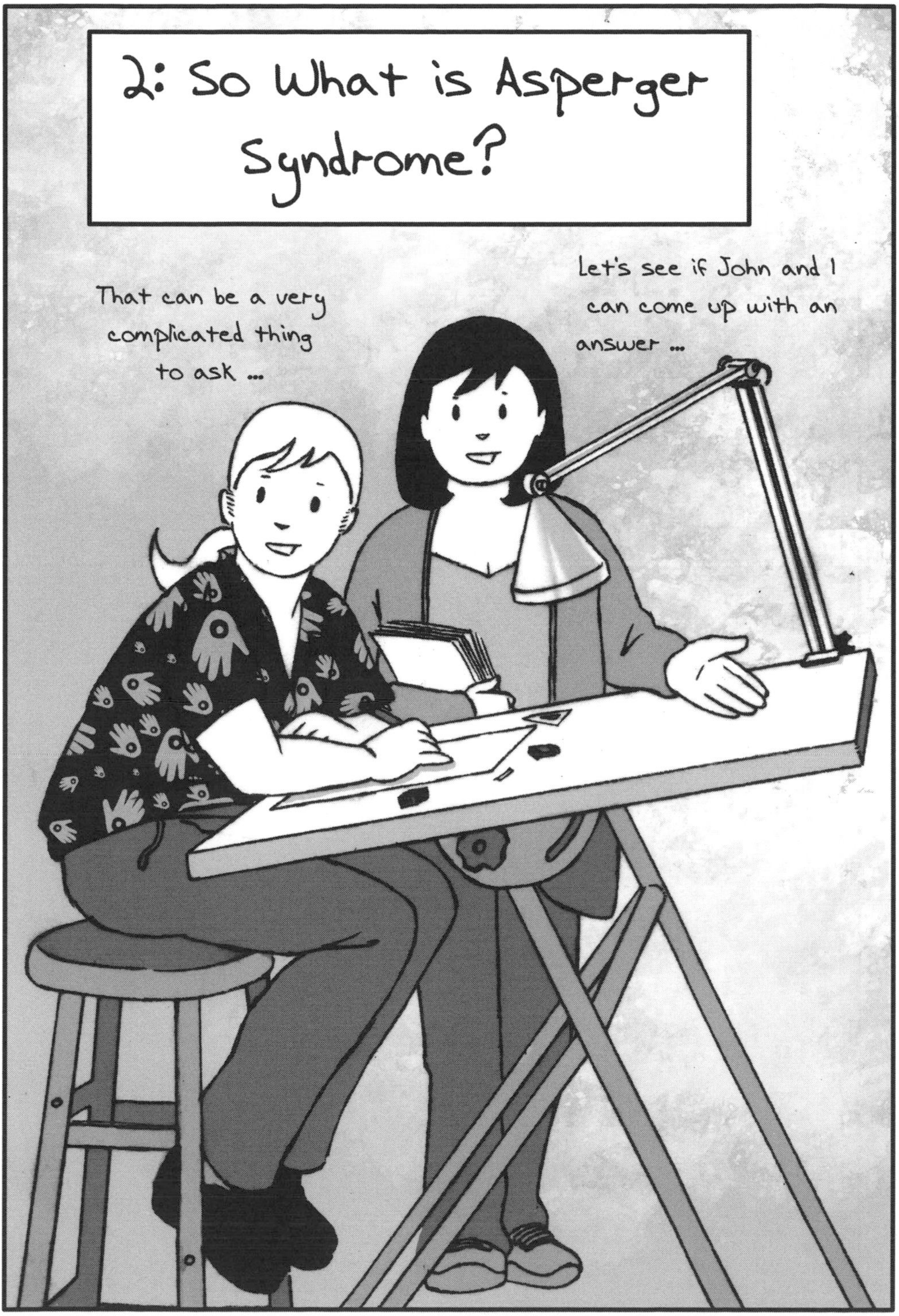
2: So What is Asperger Syndrome?
That can be a very complicated thing to ask ...
Let's see if John and I can come up with an answer ...

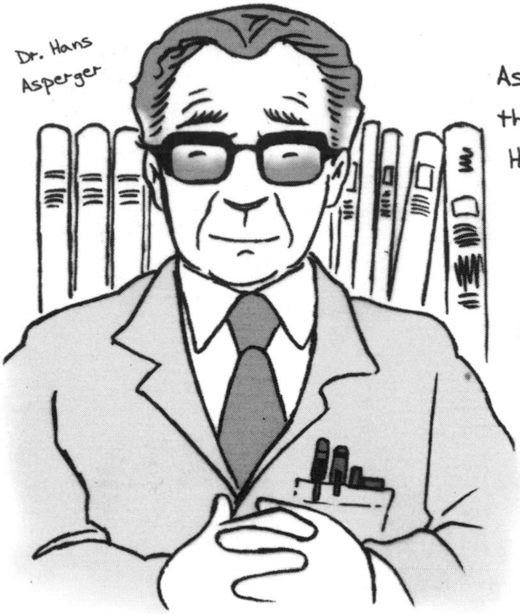
Dr. Hans
Asperger

Asperger Syndrome is named after the doctor who first identified it - Hans Asperger.

Sometimes it's also called *Asperger's Syndrome* and sometimes it's shortened to *AS*.

It's also seen as part of the *Autism Spectrum*, and you might hear it called *Autism Spectrum Condition* or something similar.

A lot of people are still not sure exactly what to call it, since it can be difficult sometimes to tell if someone's behaviour is a result of AS or something else.

We'll be using the terms Asperger Syndrome and AS in this book. But whatever name you give it, it's about behaving differently - but behaving differently in a particular way.

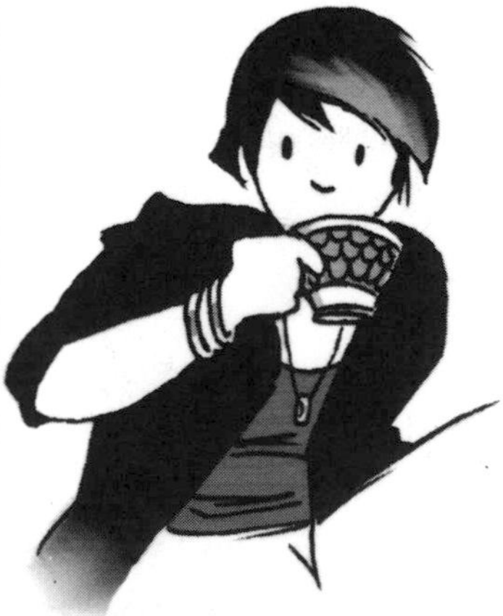

Lots of people can have Asperger Syndrome -

- some of them will know about it,

and some of them won't.

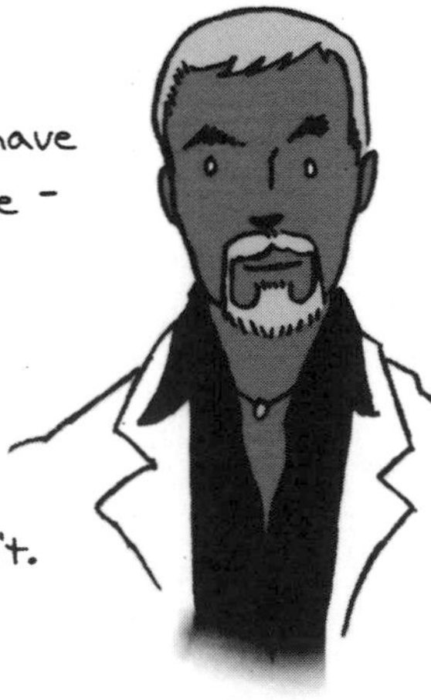

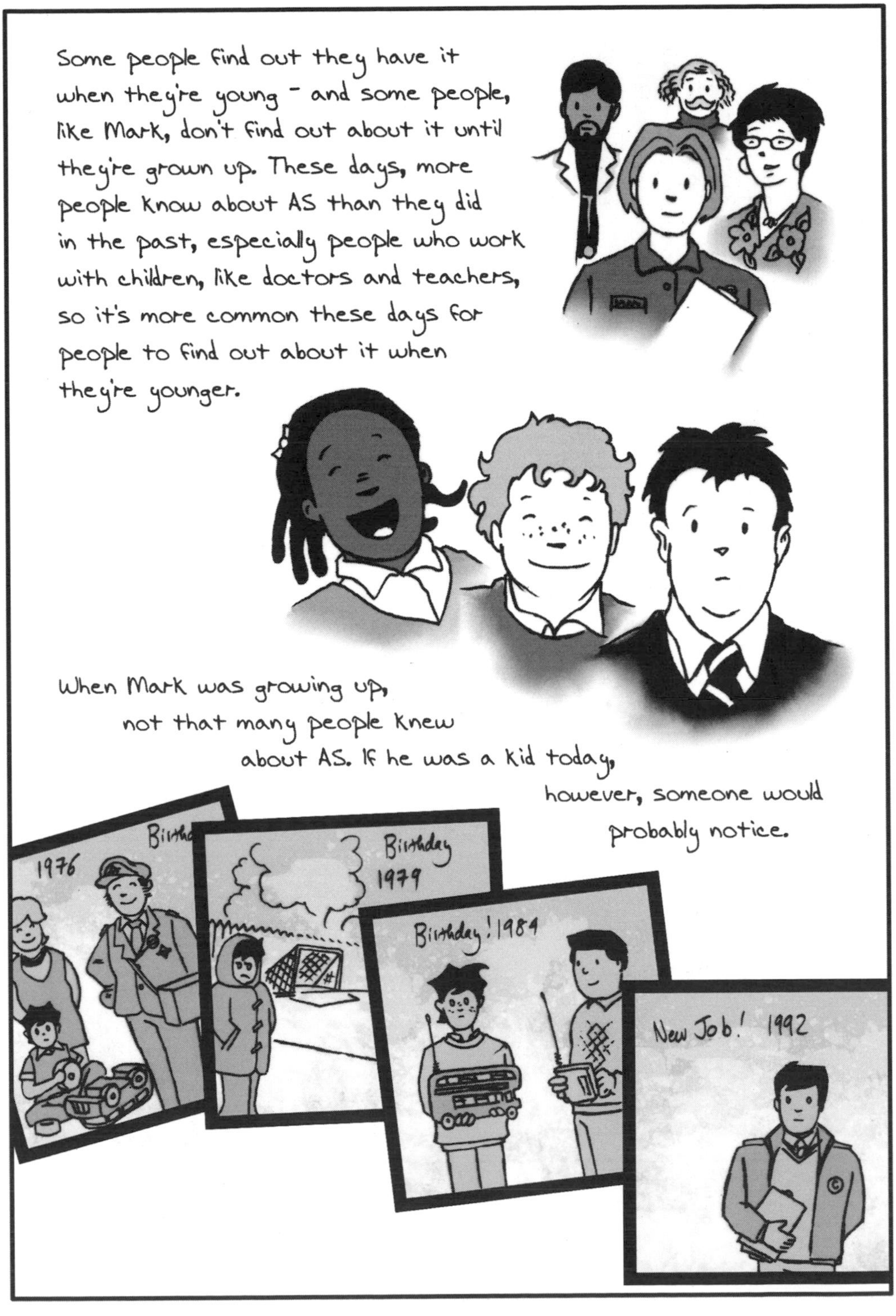
Some people find out they have it when they're young - and some people, like Mark, don't find out about it until they're grown up. These days, more people know about AS than they did in the past, especially people who work with children, like doctors and teachers, so it's more common these days for people to find out about it when they're younger.
When Mark was growing up, not that many people knew about AS. If he was a kid today, however, someone would probably notice.
1976
Birthday 1979
Birthday! 1984
New Job! 1992

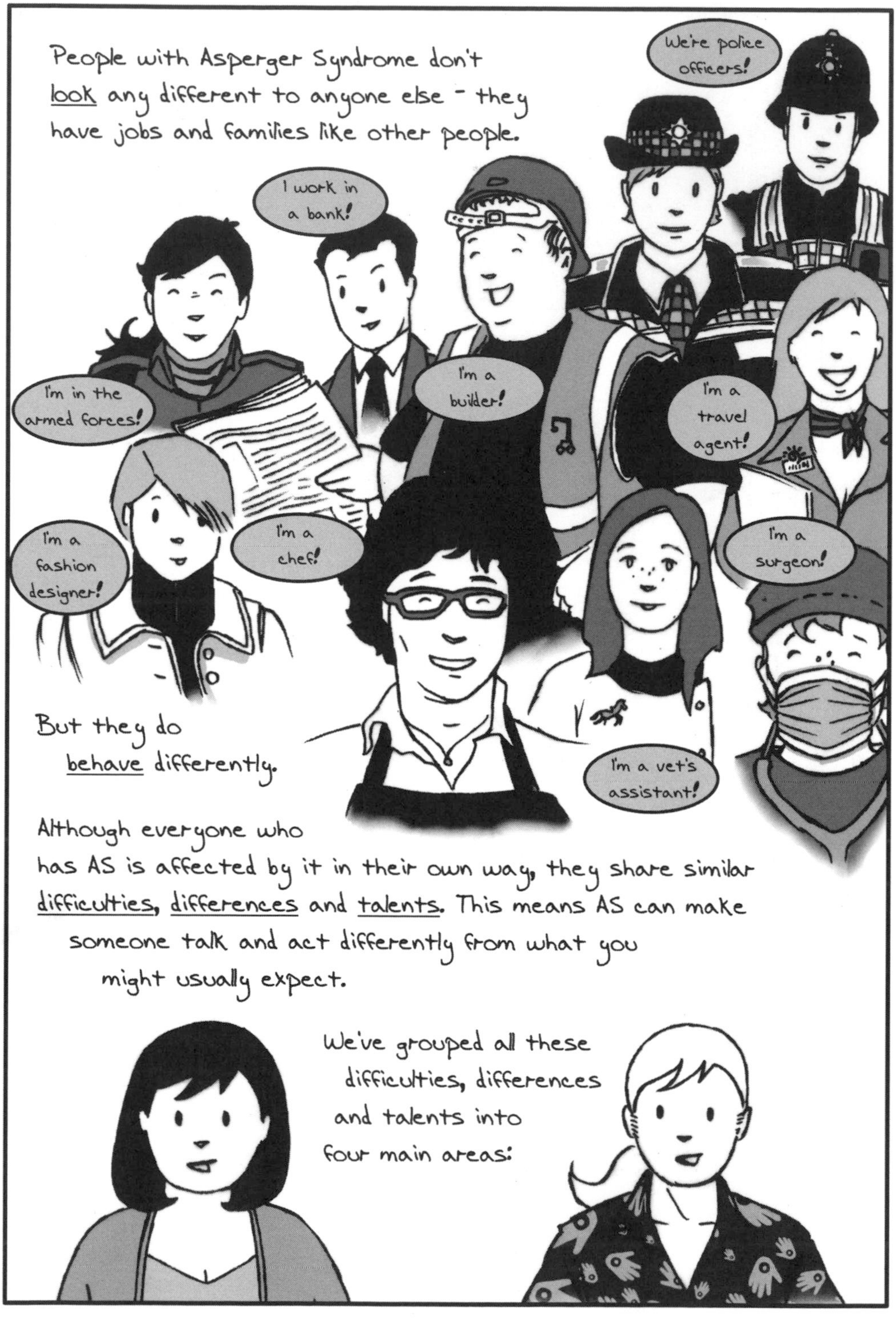
People with Asperger Syndrome don't look any different to anyone else – they have jobs and families like other people.
We're police officers!
I work in a bank!
I'm in the armed forces!
I'm a builder!
I'm a travel agent!
I'm a fashion designer!
I'm a chef!
I'm a surgeon!
I'm a vet's assistant!
But they do behave differently.
Although everyone who has AS is affected by it in their own way, they share similar difficulties, differences and talents. This means AS can make someone talk and act differently from what you might usually expect.
We've grouped all these difficulties, differences and talents into four main areas:

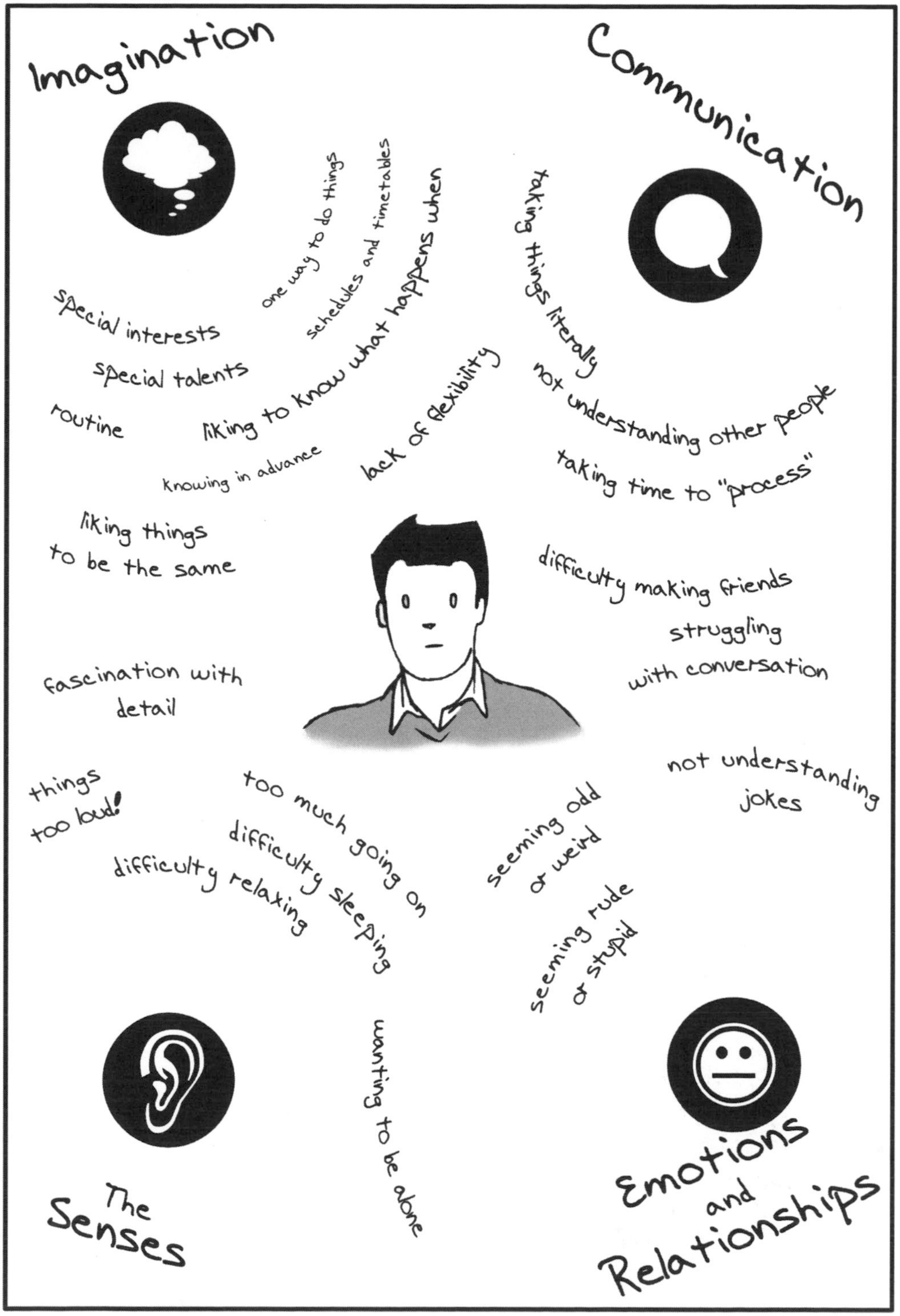
Imagination
Communication
one way to do things
schedules and timetables
liking to know what happens when
taking things literally
special interests
special talents
routine
lack of flexibility
not understanding other people
knowing in advance
taking time to "process"
liking things to be the same
difficulty making friends
struggling with conversation
fascination with detail
not understanding jokes
things too loud!
too much going on
difficulty sleeping
difficulty relaxing
seeming odd or weird
seeming rude or stupid
wanting to be alone
The Senses
Emotions and Relationships

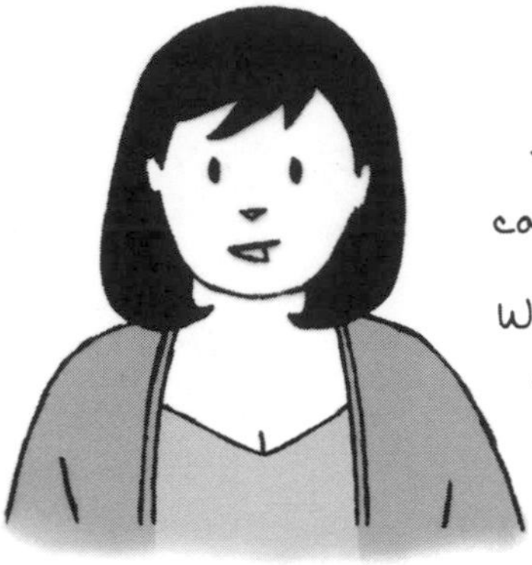

Throughout the rest of the book we'll be looking at how AS difficulties, differences and talents in each of these four main areas can affect everyday situations.

We'll also see how all these areas are connected – how difficulties with imagination, for example, are linked to difficulties with communication, or how difficulties with emotions and relationships can be linked to difficulties with the senses.

And, by listening to Sophie's story about Mark and her family, we'll see how people with AS and their families can help manage difficult situations as they understand more about Asperger Syndrome.

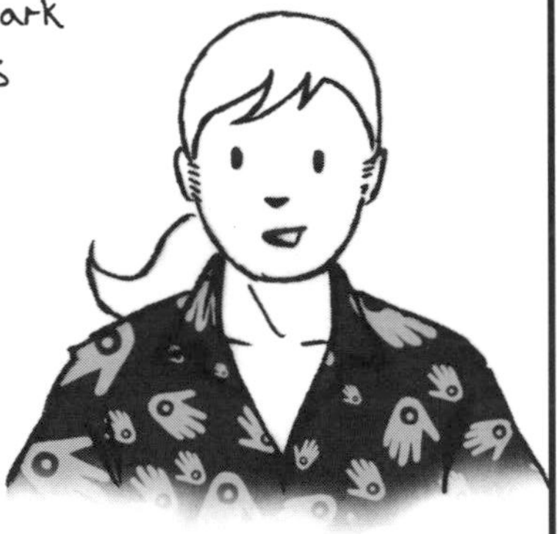

Let's look at each of these four main areas in turn, starting with:

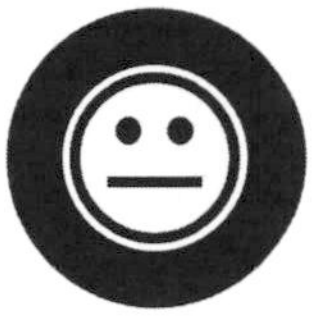

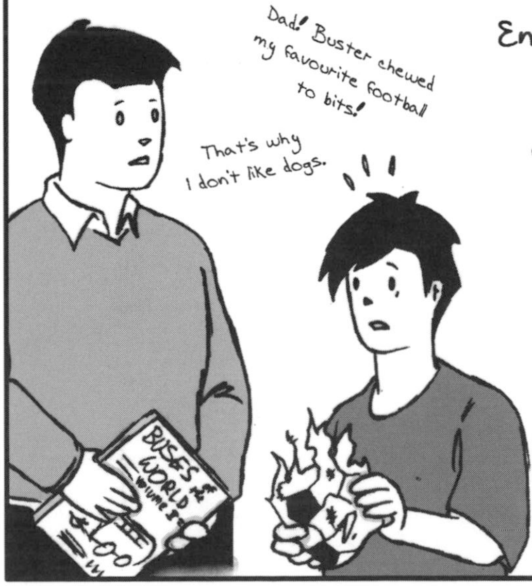
Dad! Buster chewed my favourite football to bits!
That's why I don't like dogs.

Emotions and Relationships

When we look at this area of AS, we'll see how it makes it hard for Mark to understand how other people are feeling. Sometimes people with AS have difficulty "reading" someone else's reaction to something or understanding things like facial expressions that would give them a clue about how another person feels.

Sometimes they have difficulty showing their own feelings. This can make them behave in ways that can seem odd or strange to people who don't know them very well.

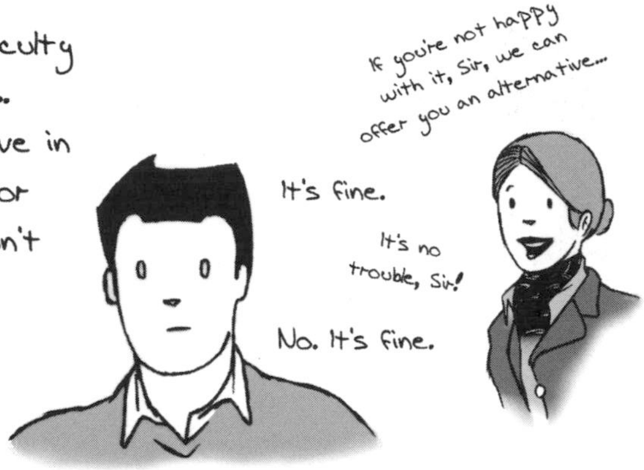
If you're not happy with it, Sir, we can offer you an alternative...
It's fine.
It's no trouble, Sir!
No. It's fine.

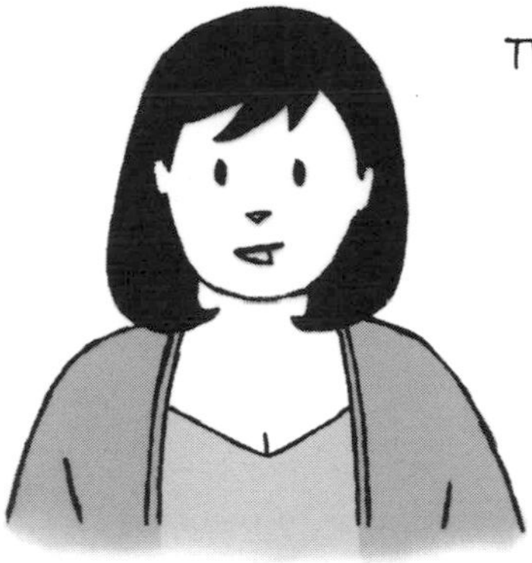

They can end up seeming like they don't care about people, and can sometimes make people they care about very upset. We'll see how this part of Mark's AS affects Sophie and the rest of the family.

Communication

Many people with AS are very good at talking – as long as it's something they like talking about. But they may not be very good at actually holding a conversation. Sometimes, when they talk, they may sound awkward, formal or rude. We'll see that Mark has difficulty sometimes understanding what people are saying to him. He sometimes needs more time to understand – or "process" – information.

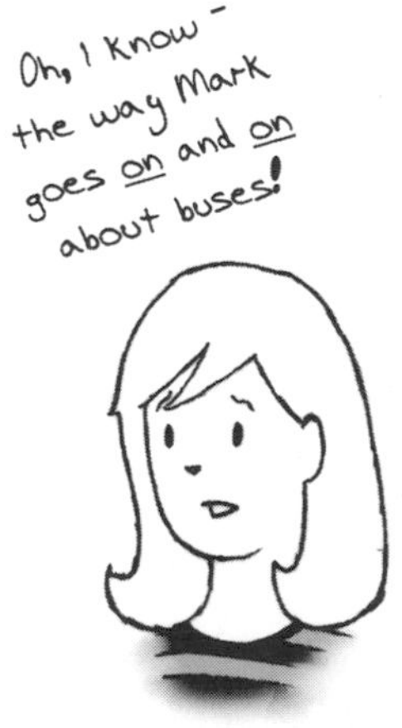
Oh, I know – the way Mark goes on and on about buses!

We'll talk more about this and about "Special Interests" in a couple of pages ...

It can be hard for people around Mark to see that he needs this extra time.

This can become a problem when there are lots of people around and lots of different conversations happening at the same time.

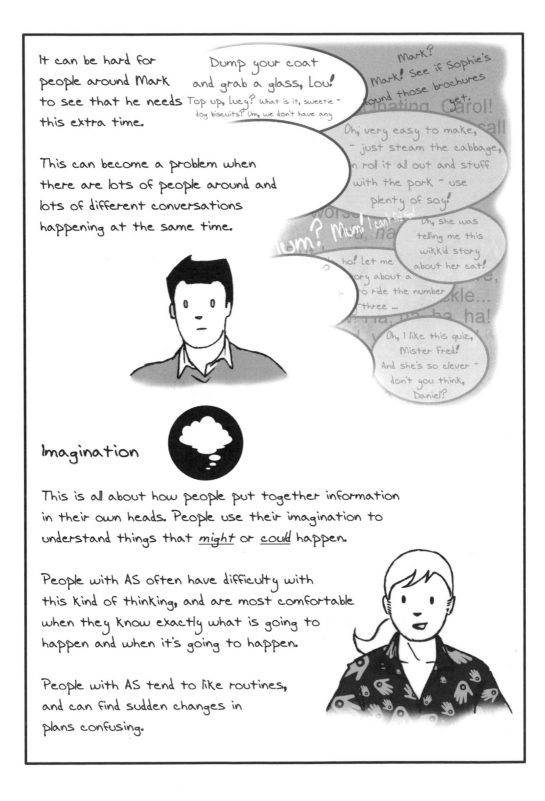

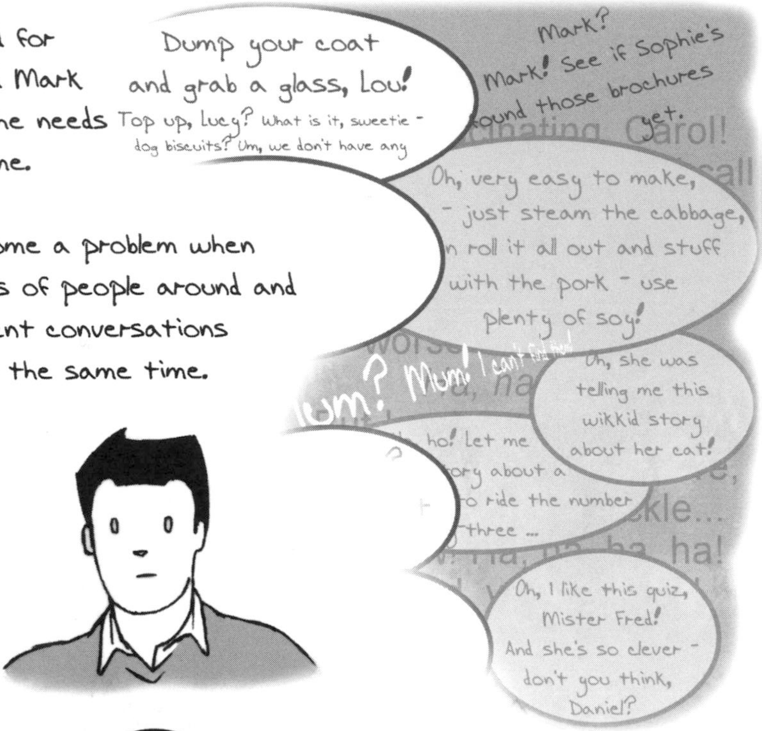
Dump your coat and grab a glass, Lou!
Top up, Lucy? What is it, sweetie - dog biscuits? Um, we don't have any
Mark? Mark! See if Sophie's found those brochures yet.
Oh, very easy to make, - just steam the cabbage, n roll it all out and stuff with the pork - use plenty of soy!
Mum? Mum!
Oh, she was telling me this wikkid story about her cat!
Oh, I like this quiz, Mister Fred! And she's so clever - don't you think, Daniel?

Imagination

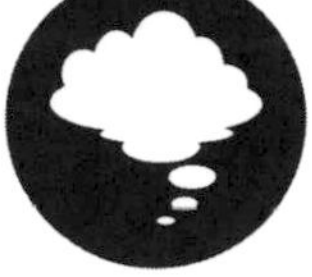

This is all about how people put together information in their own heads. People use their imagination to understand things that <u>might</u> or <u>could</u> happen.

People with AS often have difficulty with this kind of thinking, and are most comfortable when they know exactly what is going to happen and when it's going to happen.

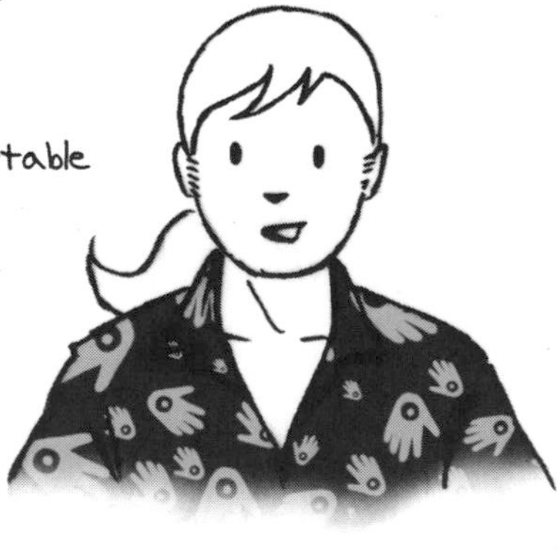

People with AS tend to like routines, and can find sudden changes in plans confusing.

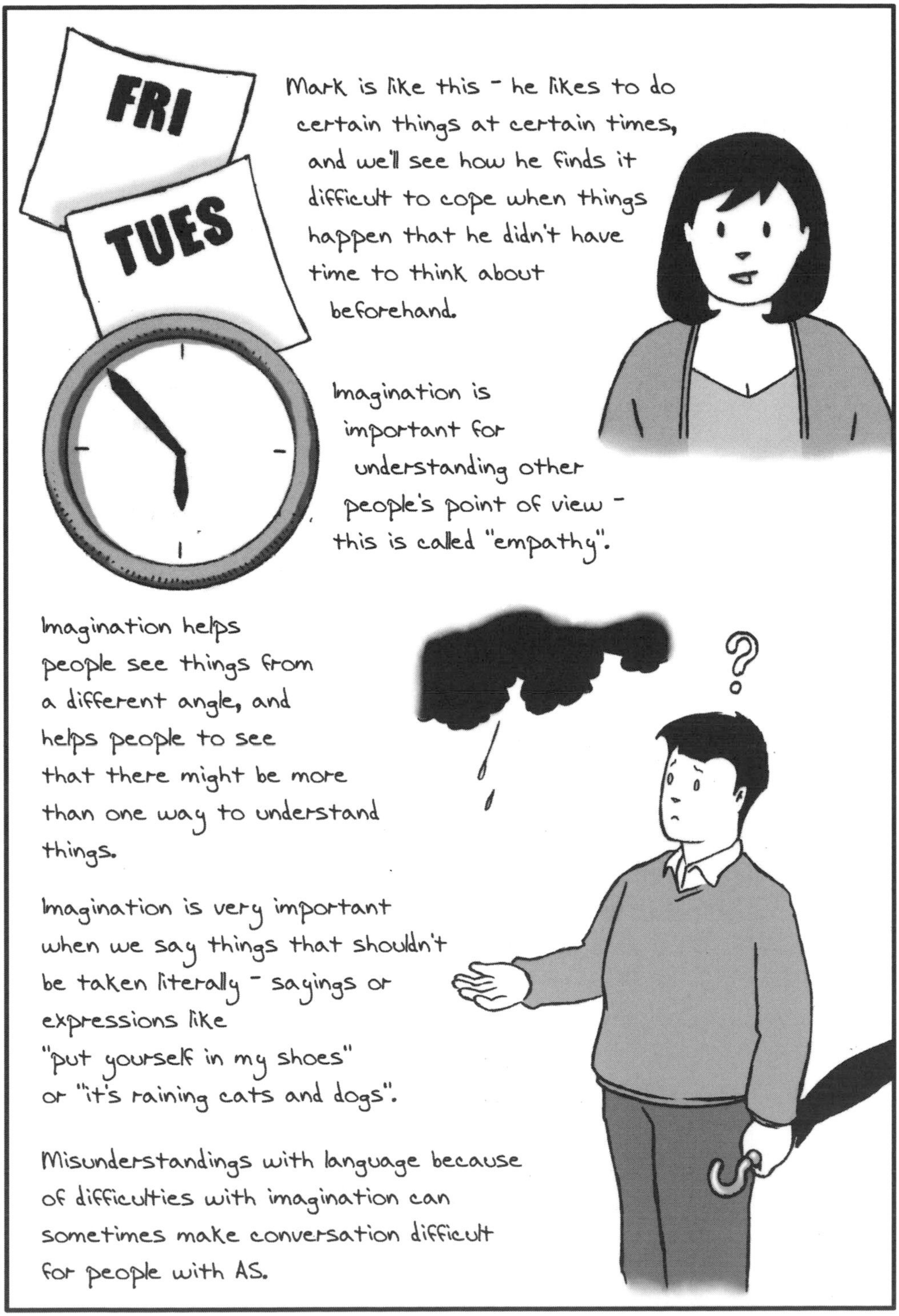
FRI
TUES
Mark is like this - he likes to do certain things at certain times, and we'll see how he finds it difficult to cope when things happen that he didn't have time to think about beforehand.
Imagination is important for understanding other people's point of view - this is called "empathy".
Imagination helps people see things from a different angle, and helps people to see that there might be more than one way to understand things.
?
Imagination is very important when we say things that shouldn't be taken literally - sayings or expressions like "put yourself in my shoes" or "it's raining cats and dogs".
Misunderstandings with language because of difficulties with imagination can sometimes make conversation difficult for people with AS.

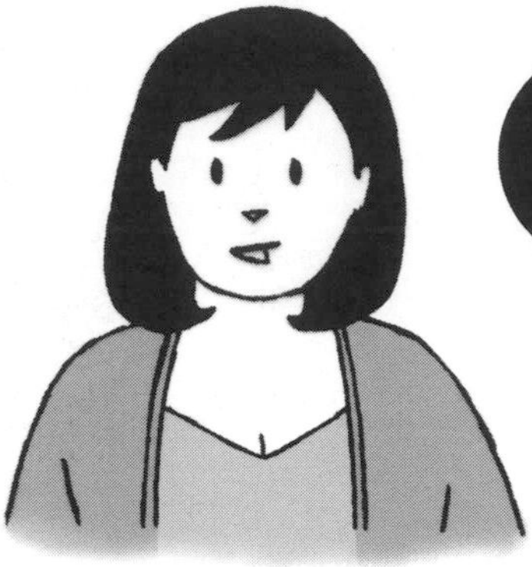

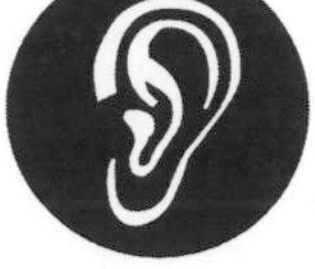

The Senses

Hearing, sight, taste, touch and smell - these are our senses. They are how we find out about the world. How we react to what we hear, what we see, what we taste, feel or smell is very important to us.

Think about how people have favourite colours or favourite foods, for example.

But people with AS can find it hard to cope with some sorts of noises, some kinds of light or certain smells.

They can find lots of different noises together really confusing, or very bright light uncomfortable, or may find particular smells or textures very unpleasant. Some people with AS even find that their sense of balance, or sense of space - their sense of what's around them - is different.

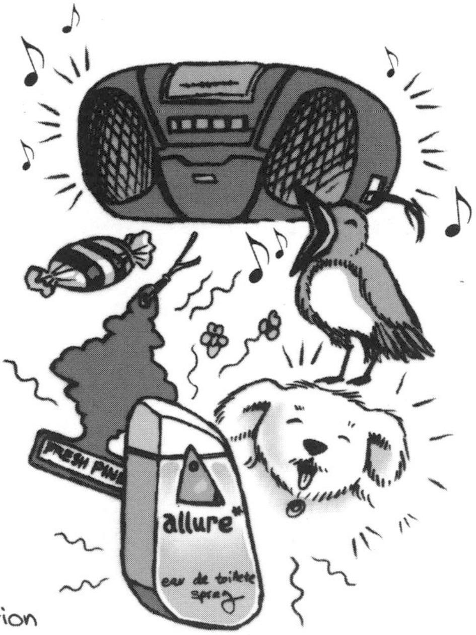
FRESH PINE
allure
eau de toilette spray

All this can sometimes make people with AS seem fussy, spoiled or clumsy to other people.

We'll see how Mark's reaction to various kinds of sense information affects how he feels and what he does.

Special Interests

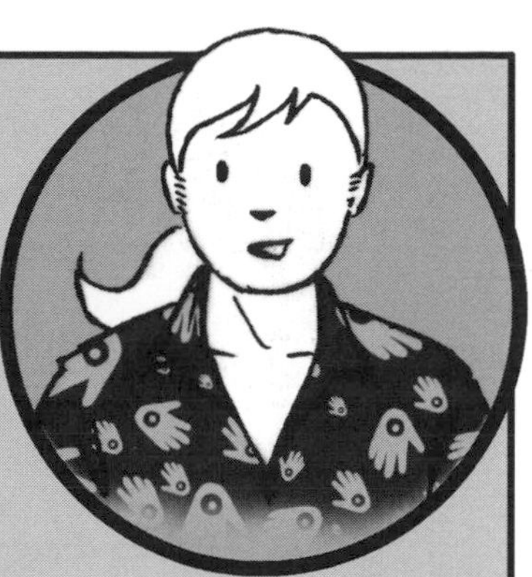

Most people with AS have what are called "Special Interests". It's something that they really like and know a lot about. Often, people with AS can be so focused on their special interest that they ignore other things that are going on around them.

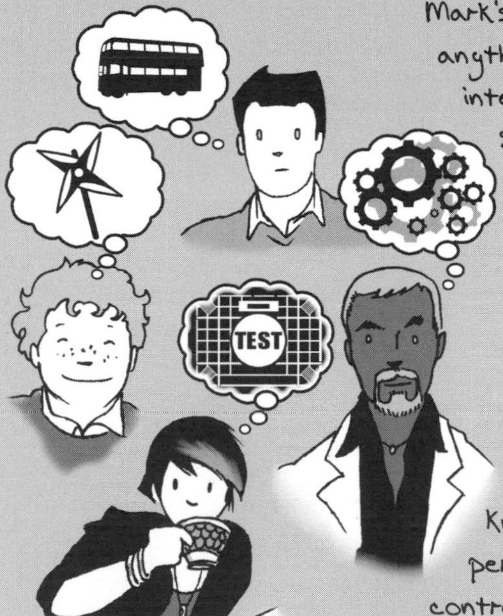
TEST

Mark's special interest is buses, but anything can become a special interest to someone with AS. Sometimes a person's special interest will change from one thing to another. Having a special interest to focus on can make people with AS feel relaxed.

Special interests are usually things that are safe and stay the same – they're predictable. Knowing a lot about a topic gives a person with AS the feeling of being in control of things. This can be important to them when the world around them seems very unpredictable and out of their control.

We're all interested in things, but people with AS may not understand that other people are not as interested as they are in their special interest. People with AS can sometimes talk about their special interest too much for other people. They may find the person with AS boring, or think they seem obsessed.

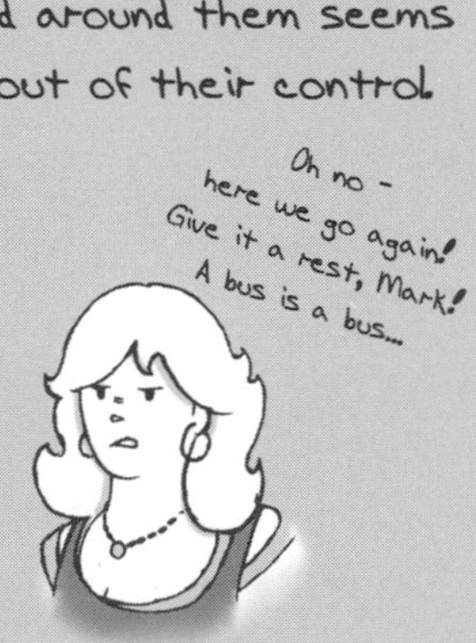
Oh no -
here we go again!
Give it a rest, Mark!
A bus is a bus...

As we follow the story of Sophie, Mark and the family, we'll see how and why it's important to understand these four main areas of Asperger Syndrome, and we'll see why it's important to understand about <u>Special Interests</u>.

We'll see that it's important to understand <u>stress,</u> and how this can affect people with Asperger Syndrome and those around them.

Stress is the feeling you can get when you are not sure what to do or what is happening. It's also the feeling you get when you think things are "too much" for you to handle. We all feel stressed at times, but some people feel it more often. When people with AS get stressed, it can make their difficulties, differences and talents become more extreme.

Think about stress as water being poured into a glass. With each thing that happens to make you stressed – something going wrong, someone making you upset – a bit of water is poured into the glass.

In the end, there's no more room in the glass and the water spills out everywhere. When stress builds up inside us, it can "spill out" as us being angry or upset.

We'll be looking at ways in which stress affects Mark and the rest of the family and some ideas for dealing with stress.

And what do you do when you find out someone in your family has AS?

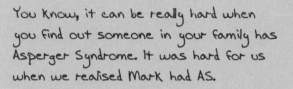

You know, it can be really hard when you find out someone in your family has Asperger Syndrome. It was hard for us when we realised Mark had AS.

You might feel frightened or embarrassed – I know I did.

You may have lots of questions, like:

How will we cope?
What can we do?
Who can we ask for help?

Finding out about Asperger Syndrome and understanding it is a really important first step. Books like this one, family support groups and AS organisations, information from doctors, the library and the internet can all be helpful

But although it can be difficult, sometimes the best way to understand AS is for you and your family to talk about it – like we had to after a Parents' Evening at Sophie's school ...

Understanding Asperger Syndrome and how
it can affect your parent is important.
The more you understand, the easier you'll
find it to cope with the everyday things
that happen for you and your family.

In the next chapter, everyone gets very
upset because of the way things happen
at the Parents' Evening at Sophie's school.

But, as we'll explain, with a bit of understanding
everyone can start to figure out how to
make things work better.

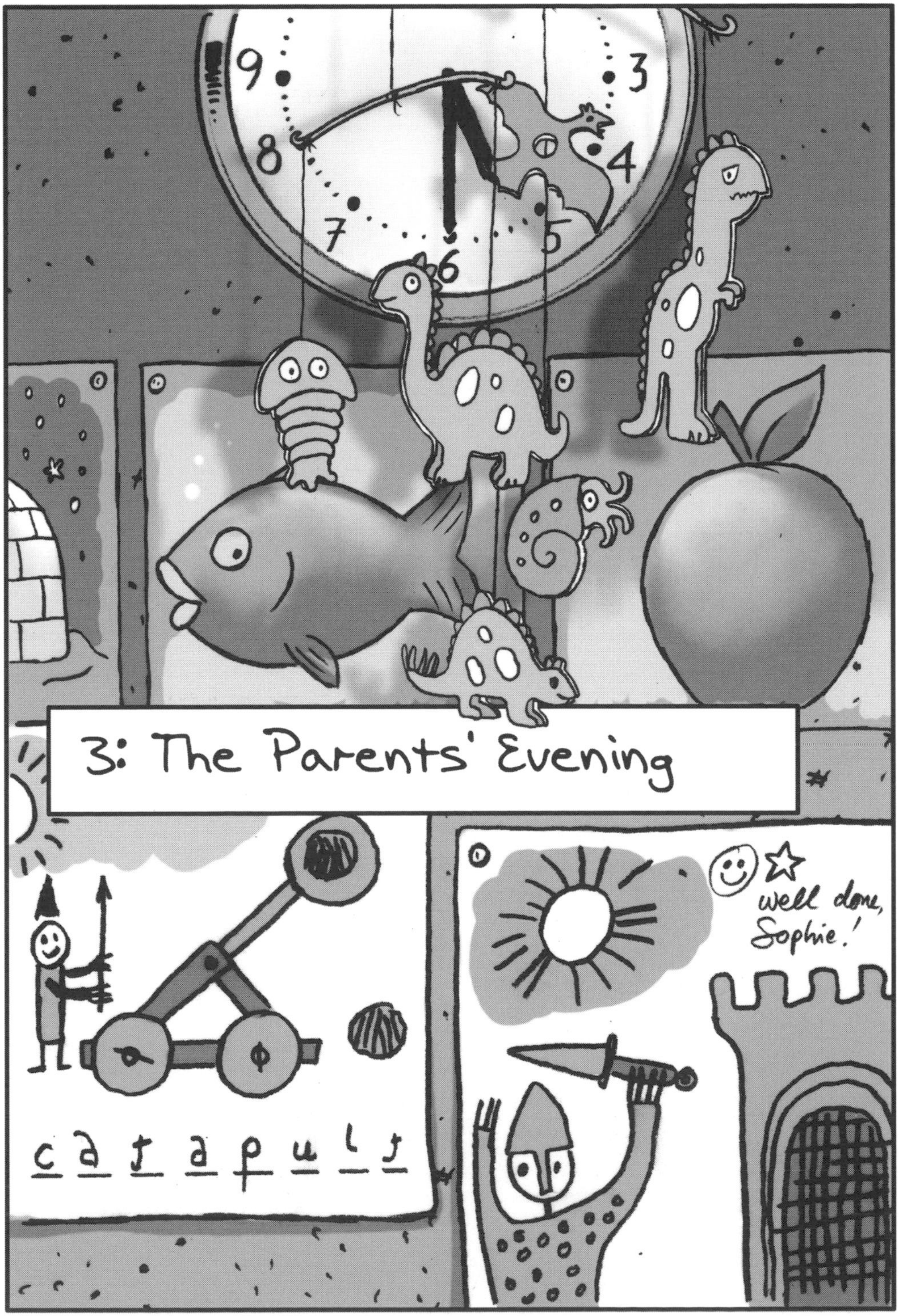
3: The Parents' Evening
catapult
well done, Sophie!

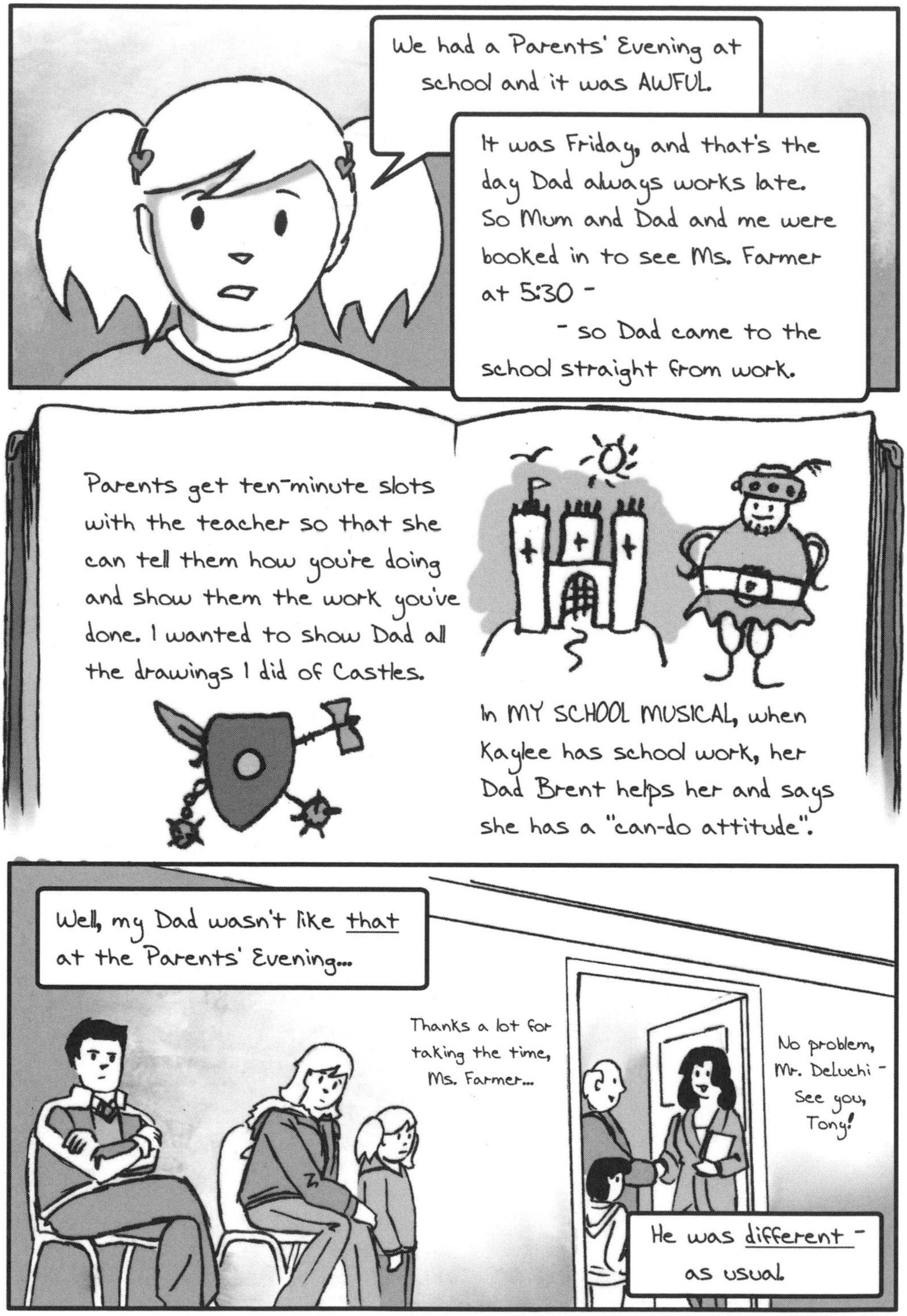
We had a Parents' Evening at school and it was AWFUL.
It was Friday, and that's the day Dad always works late. So Mum and Dad and me were booked in to see Ms. Farmer at 5:30 -
- so Dad came to the school straight from work.
Parents get ten-minute slots with the teacher so that she can tell them how you're doing and show them the work you've done. I wanted to show Dad all the drawings I did of Castles.
In MY SCHOOL MUSICAL, when Kaylee has school work, her Dad Brent helps her and says she has a "can-do attitude".
Well, my Dad wasn't like that at the Parents' Evening...
Thanks a lot for taking the time, Ms. Farmer...
No problem, Mr. Deluchi - See you, Tony!
He was different - as usual.

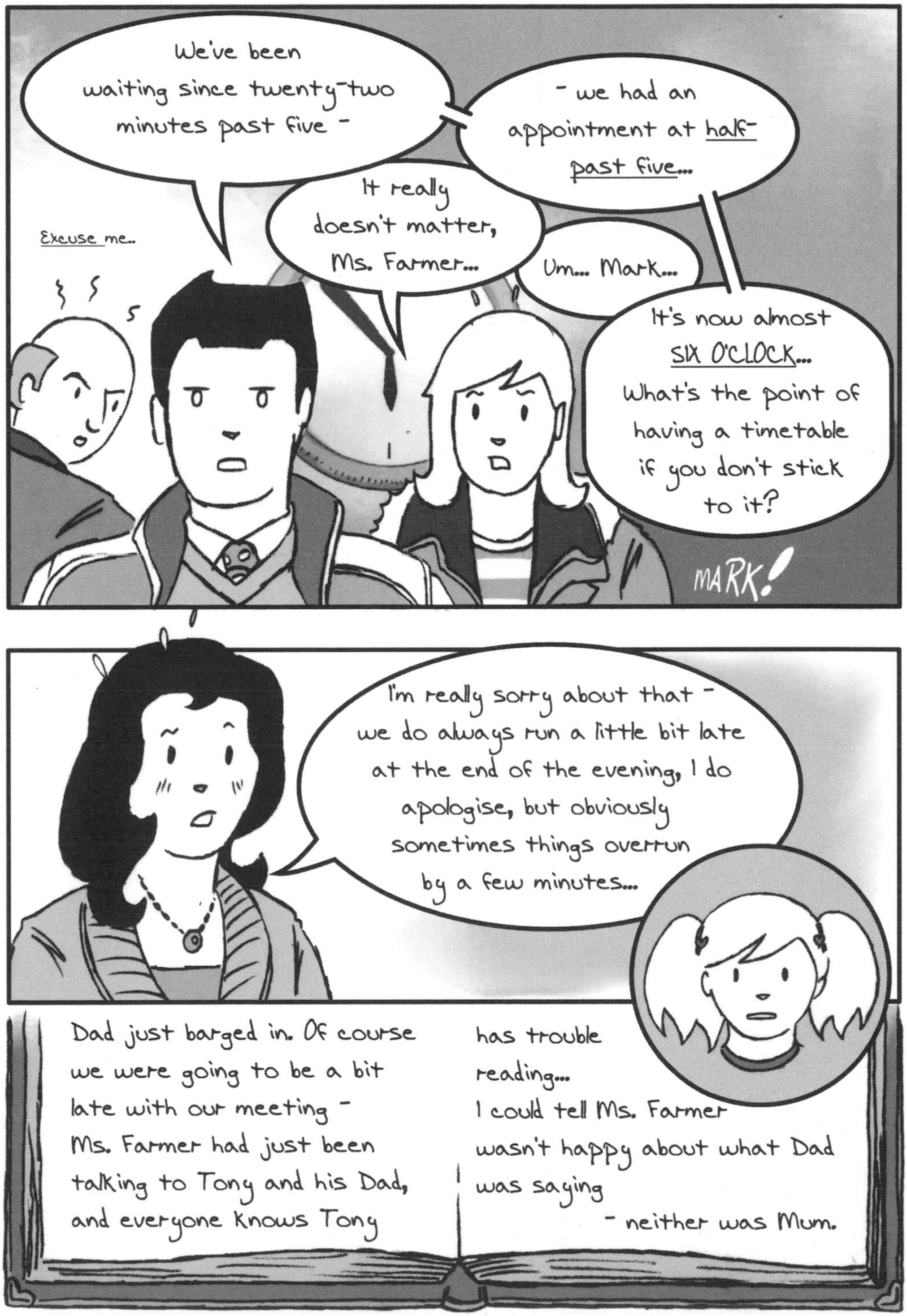
We've been waiting since twenty-two minutes past five -
- we had an appointment at half-past five...
Excuse me..
It really doesn't matter, Ms. Farmer...
Um... Mark...
It's now almost SIX O'CLOCK... What's the point of having a timetable if you don't stick to it?
MARK!
I'm really sorry about that - we do always run a little bit late at the end of the evening, I do apologise, but obviously sometimes things overrun by a few minutes...
Dad just barged in. Of course we were going to be a bit late with our meeting - Ms. Farmer had just been talking to Tony and his Dad, and everyone knows Tony has trouble reading...
I could tell Ms. Farmer wasn't happy about what Dad was saying
- neither was Mum.

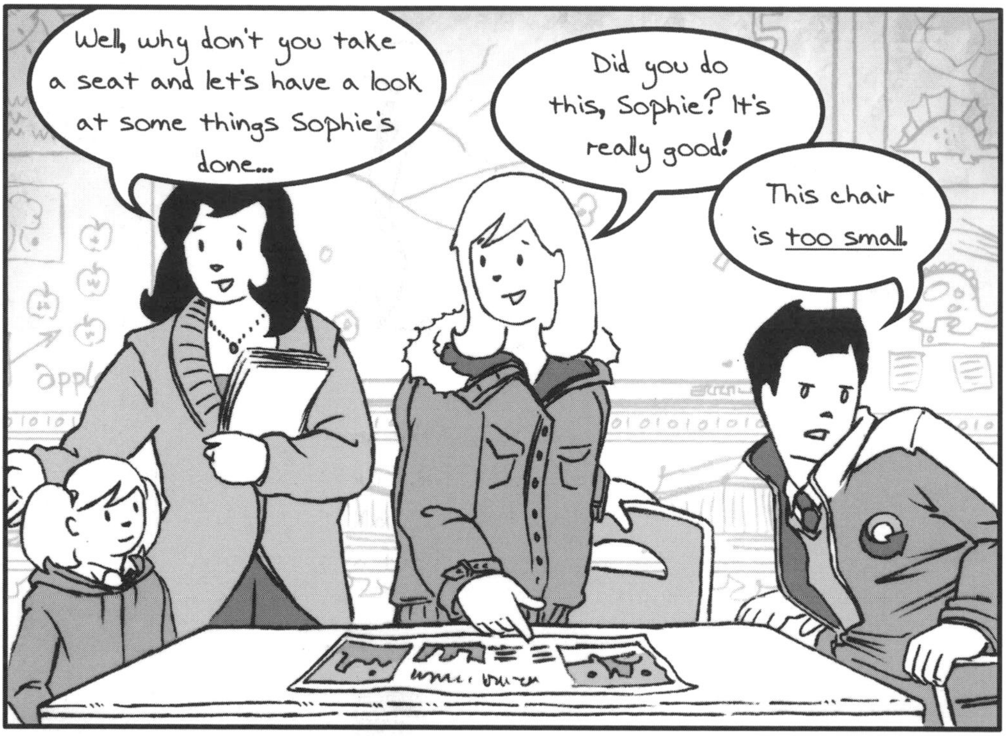
Well, why don't you take a seat and let's have a look at some things Sophie's done...
Did you do this, Sophie? It's really good!
This chair is too small.

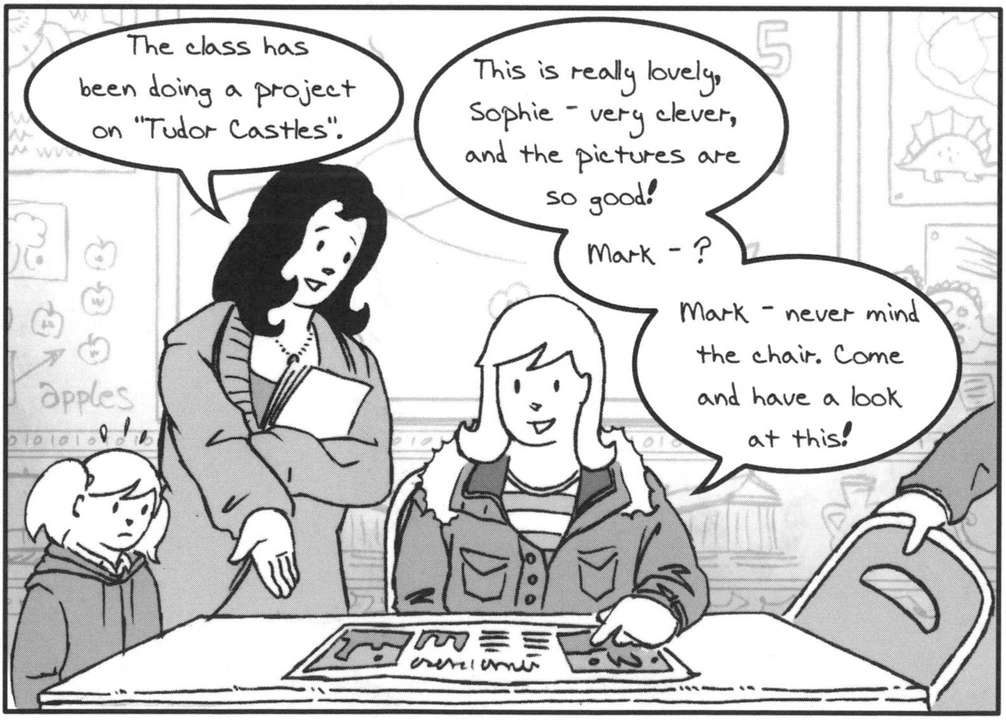
The class has been doing a project on "Tudor Castles".
This is really lovely, Sophie - very clever, and the pictures are so good!
Mark - ?
Mark - never mind the chair. Come and have a look at this!

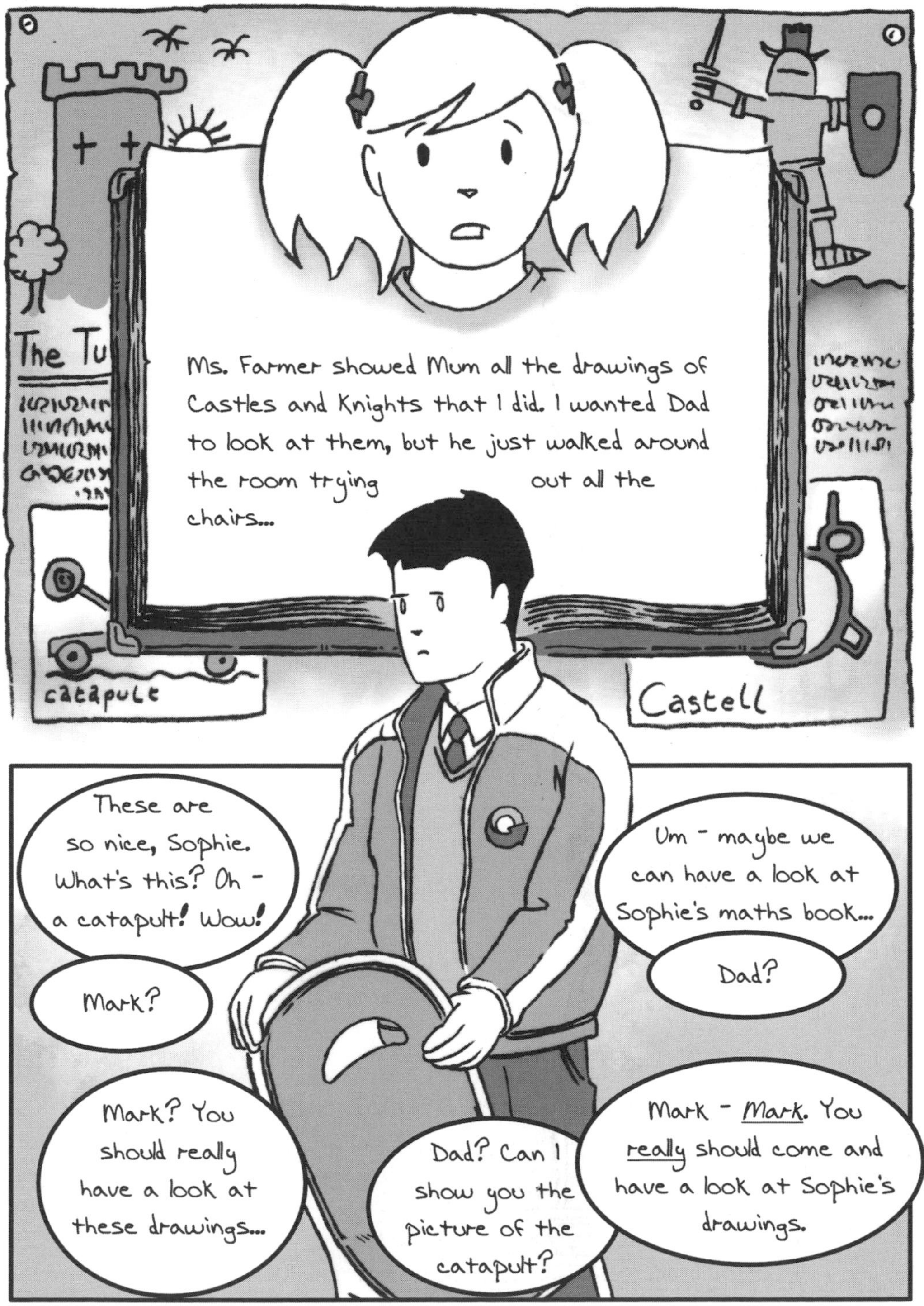
The Tu
Ms. Farmer showed Mum all the drawings of Castles and Knights that I did. I wanted Dad to look at them, but he just walked around the room trying out all the chairs...
catapult
Castell
These are so nice, Sophie. What's this? Oh - a catapult! Wow!
Mark?
Um - maybe we can have a look at Sophie's maths book...
Dad?
Mark? You should really have a look at these drawings...
Dad? Can I show you the picture of the catapult?
Mark - Mark. You really should come and have a look at Sophie's drawings.

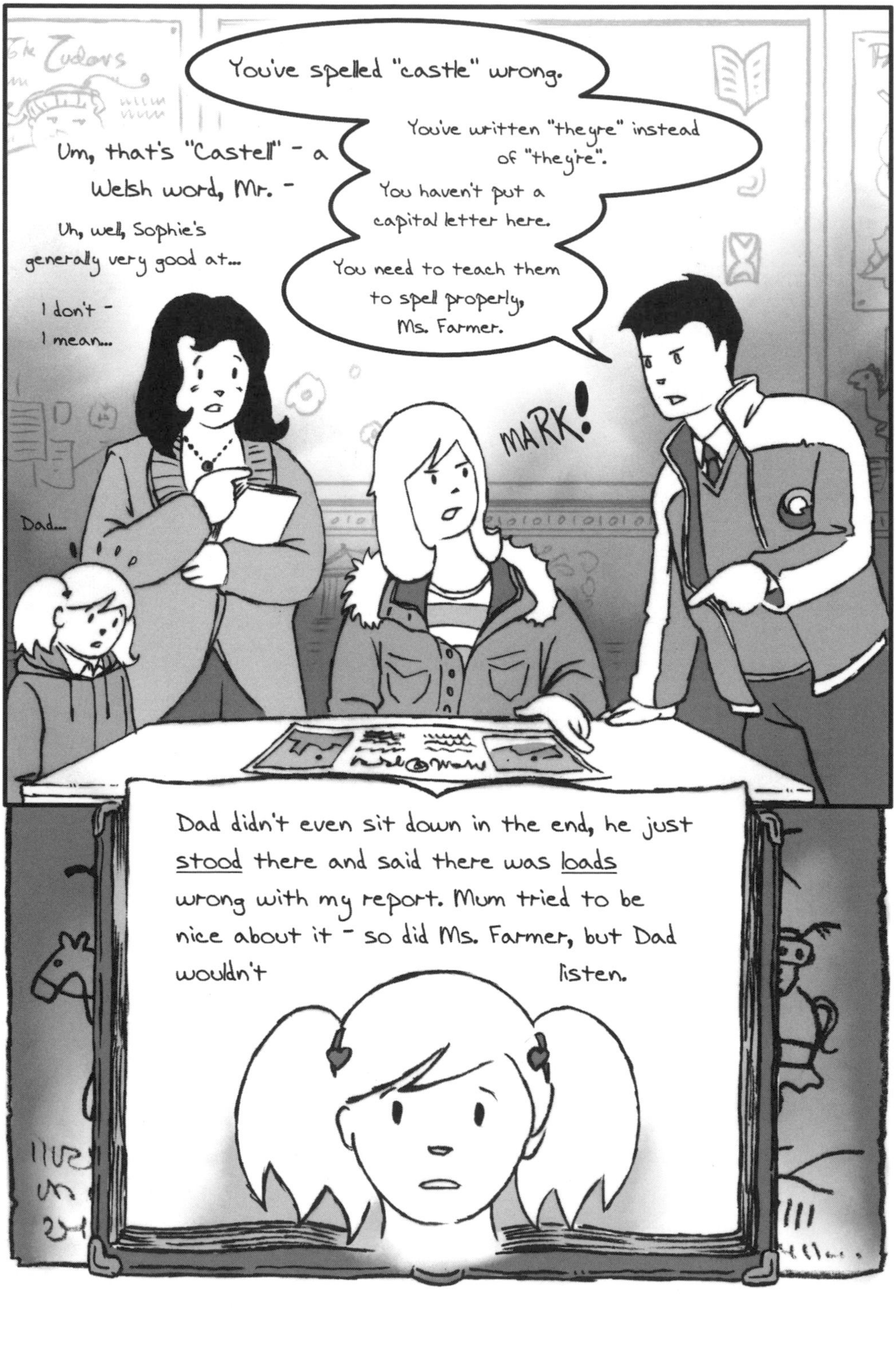
You've spelled "castle" wrong.
Um, that's "Castell" - a Welsh word, Mr. -
You've written "theyre" instead of "the'yre".
You haven't put a capital letter here.
Uh, well, Sophie's generally very good at...
I don't - I mean...
You need to teach them to spell properly, Ms. Farmer.
MARK!
Dad...
Dad didn't even sit down in the end, he just stood there and said there was loads wrong with my report. Mum tried to be nice about it - so did Ms. Farmer, but Dad wouldn't listen.

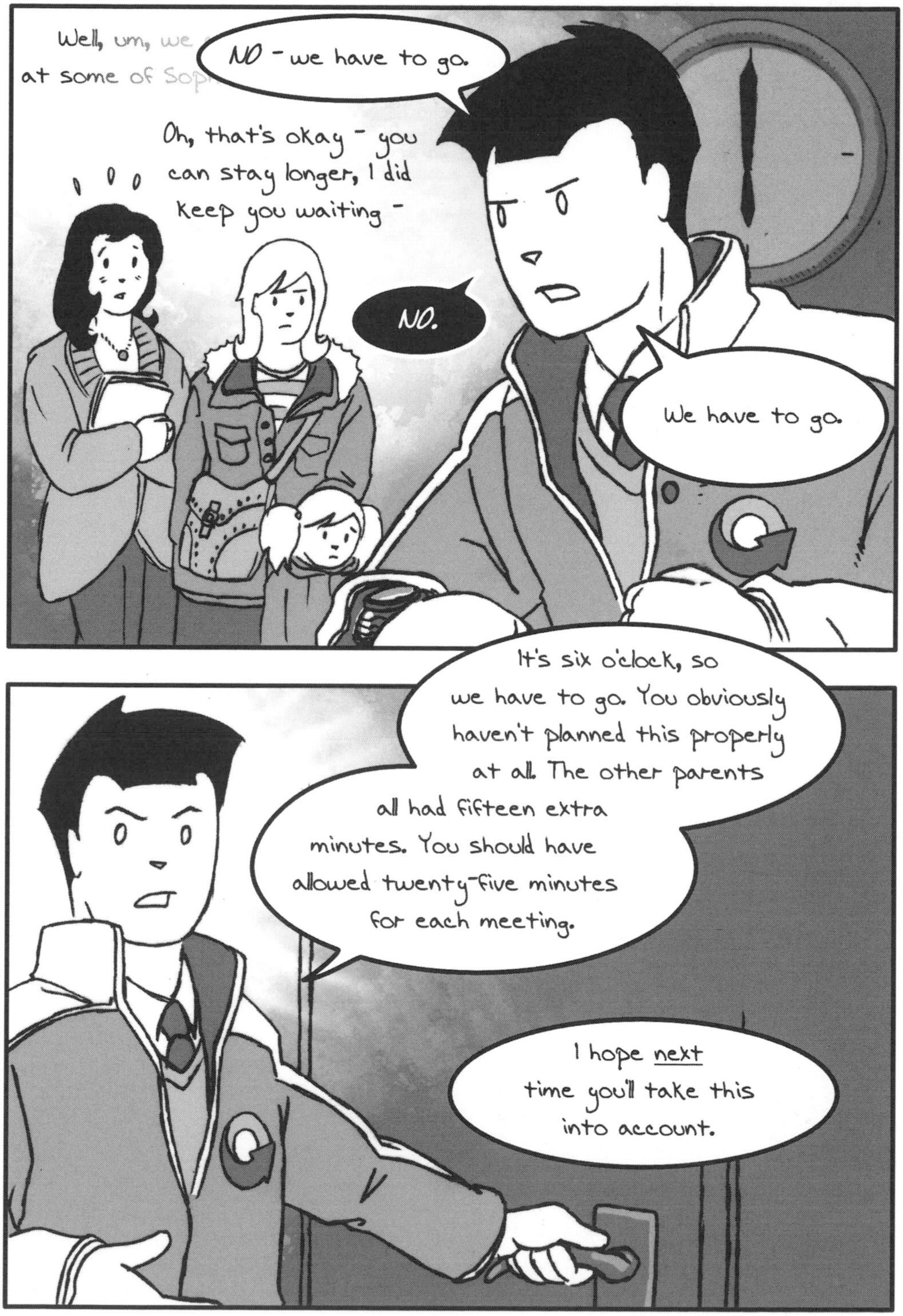
Well, um, we
at some of
NO - we have to go.
Oh, that's okay - you can stay longer, I did keep you waiting -
NO.
We have to go.
It's six o'clock, so we have to go. You obviously haven't planned this properly at all. The other parents all had fifteen extra minutes. You should have allowed twenty-five minutes for each meeting.
I hope next time you'll take this into account.

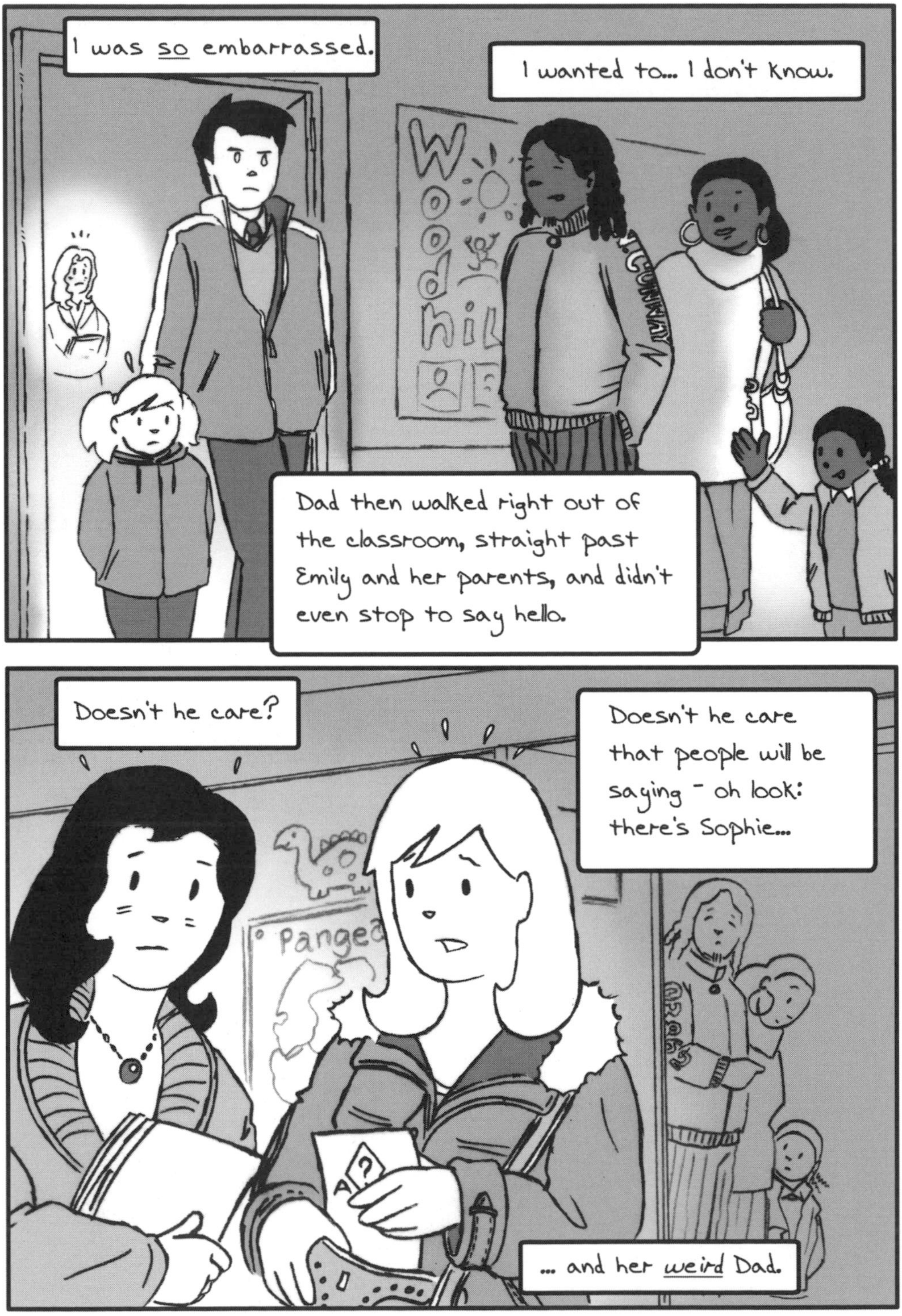
I was so embarrassed.
I wanted to... I don't know.
Dad then walked right out of the classroom, straight past Emily and her parents, and didn't even stop to say hello.
Doesn't he care?
Doesn't he care that people will be saying - oh look: there's Sophie...
... and her weird Dad.

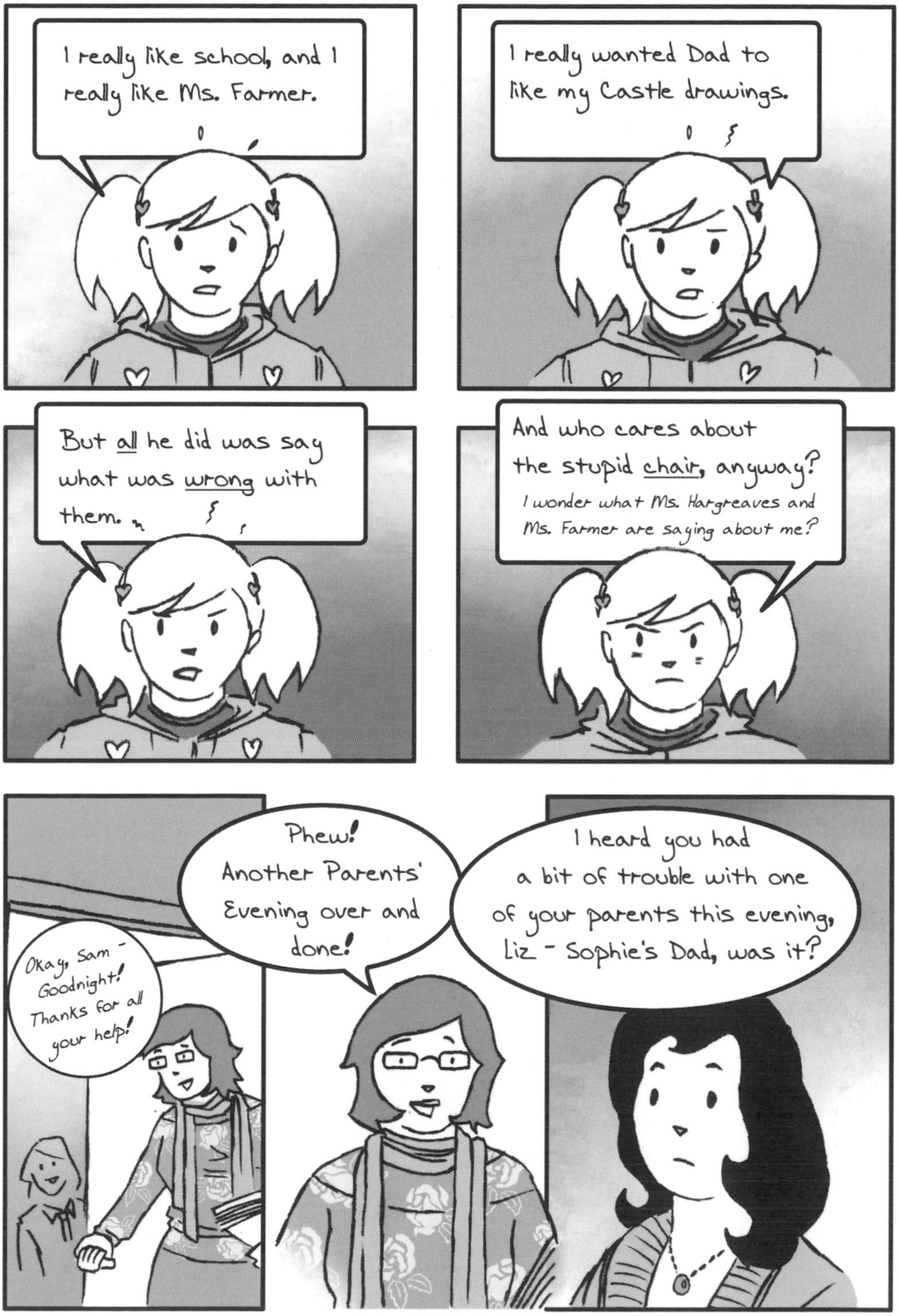
I really like school, and I really like Ms. Farmer.
I really wanted Dad to like my Castle drawings.
But all he did was say what was wrong with them.
And who cares about the stupid chair, anyway?
I wonder what Ms. Hargreaves and Ms. Farmer are saying about me?
Okay, Sam - Goodnight! Thanks for all your help!
Phew! Another Parents' Evening over and done!
I heard you had a bit of trouble with one of your parents this evening, Liz - Sophie's Dad, was it?

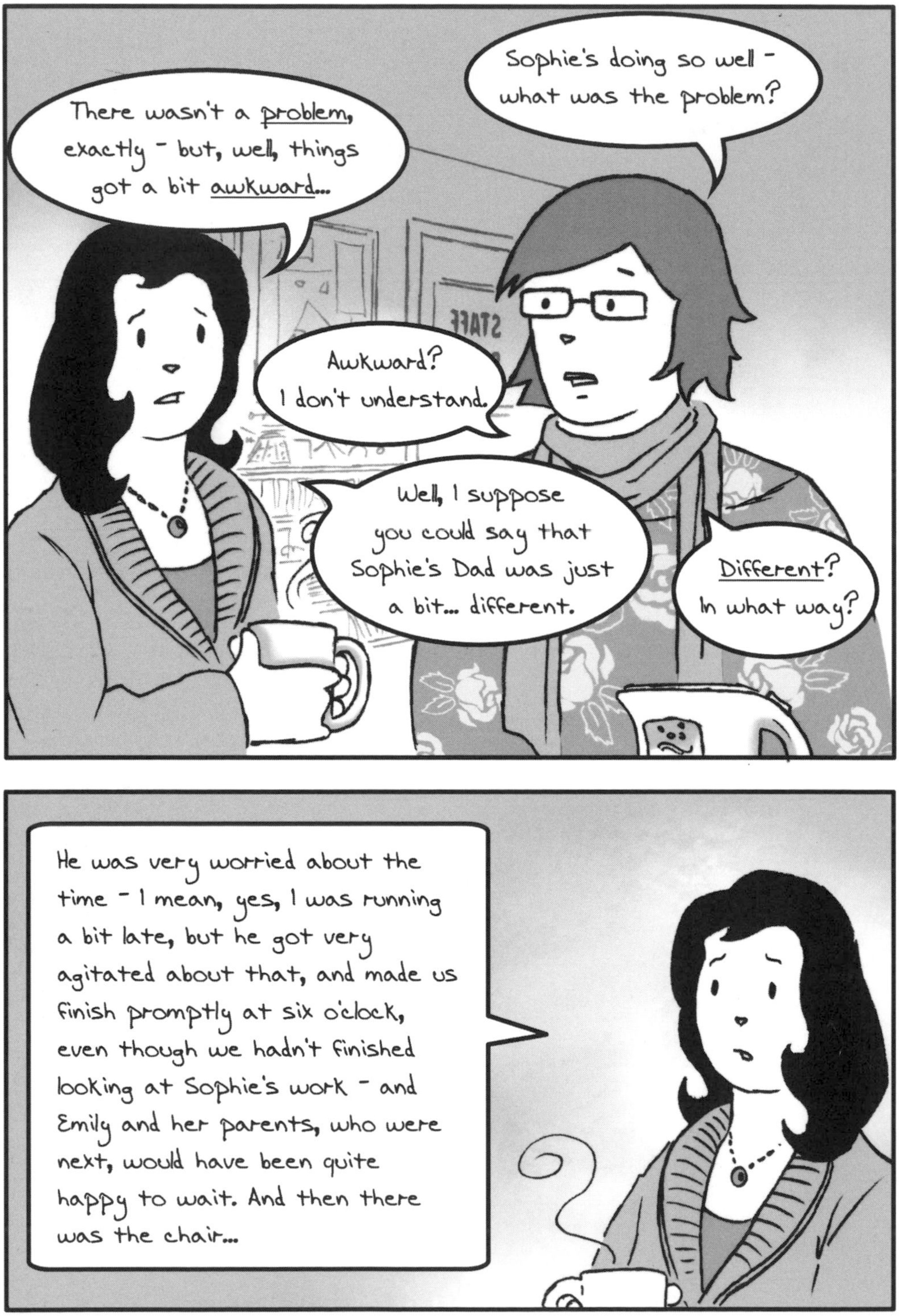
Sophie's doing so well - what was the problem?
There wasn't a problem, exactly - but, well, things got a bit awkward...
Awkward? I don't understand.
Well, I suppose you could say that Sophie's Dad was just a bit... different.
Different? In what way?
He was very worried about the time - I mean, yes, I was running a bit late, but he got very agitated about that, and made us finish promptly at six o'clock, even though we hadn't finished looking at Sophie's work - and Emily and her parents, who were next, would have been quite happy to wait. And then there was the chair...

Sophie's Mum gave me this leaflet after the meeting...
Oh!
"Asperger Syndrome" I see...
I admit, during the meeting I got quite angry about it all...
But once I read the leaflet, and Sophie's Mum explained about it, I was embarrassed that I hadn't understood!
STAFF ROOM
Don't worry, Liz - now that we know, we can maybe help Sophie -
- and her Dad!
I'm sure we can think of ways to make these meetings go more smoothly -
- for everyone!
That's a great idea, Jane! I know I'll be happy to help Sophie and her family.

Mark - listen to me. The way you treated Sophie and her teacher this evening was just plain rude.
The teacher was late. She should plan her meetings better. What's the use of -
Just forget the time thing for the moment, Mark -
- I'm talking about Sophie.
Sophie?
What's this got to do with Sophie?

You were very rude to Sophie, Mark - you did nothing but criticise her drawings..
I was only trying to help, she needs -
What she needs is encouragement Mark - not criticism. She's nine - you can't talk to her like you did.

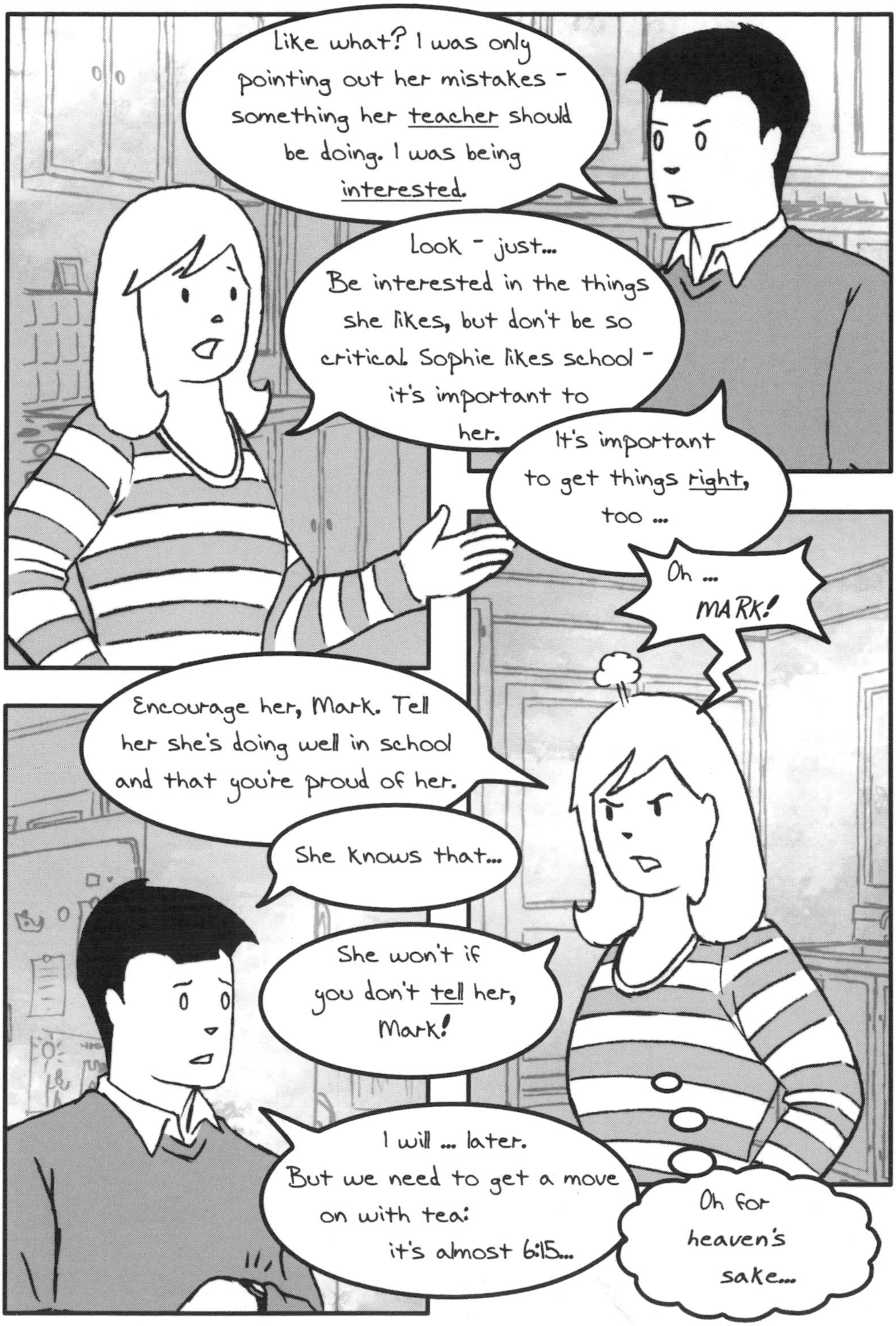
Like what? I was only pointing out her mistakes - something her teacher should be doing. I was being interested.
Look - just... Be interested in the things she likes, but don't be so critical. Sophie likes school - it's important to her.
It's important to get things right, too ...
Oh ... MARK!
Encourage her, Mark. Tell her she's doing well in school and that you're proud of her.
She knows that...
She won't if you don't tell her, Mark!
I will ... later. But we need to get a move on with tea: it's almost 6:15...
Oh for heaven's sake...

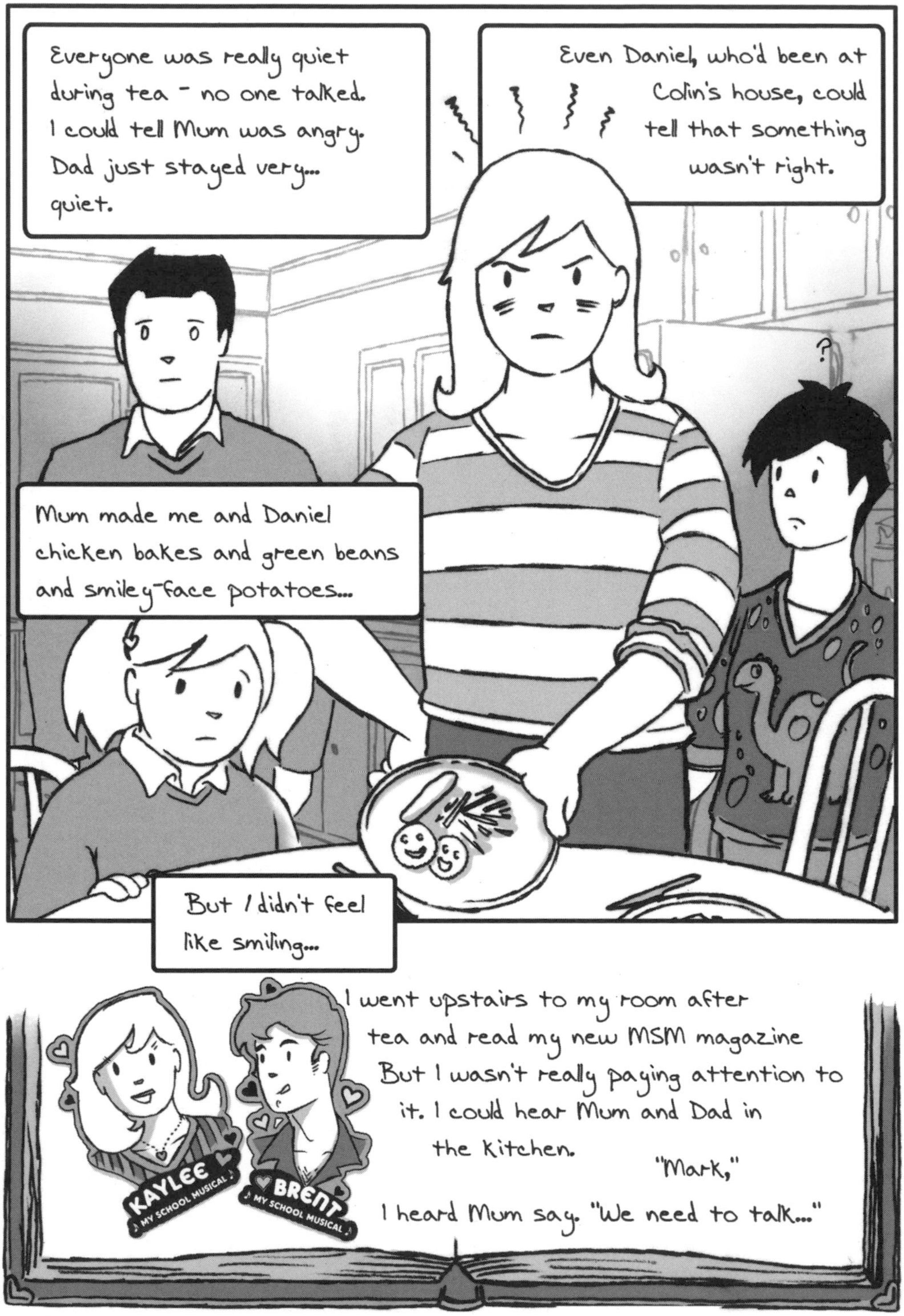
Everyone was really quiet during tea - no one talked. I could tell Mum was angry. Dad just stayed very... quiet.
Even Daniel, who'd been at Colin's house, could tell that something wasn't right.
?
Mum made me and Daniel chicken bakes and green beans and smiley-face potatoes...
But I didn't feel like smiling...
KAYLEE
MY SCHOOL MUSICAL
BRENT
MY SCHOOL MUSICAL
I went upstairs to my room after tea and read my new MSM magazine But I wasn't really paying attention to it. I could hear Mum and Dad in the kitchen.
"Mark,"
I heard Mum say. "We need to talk..."

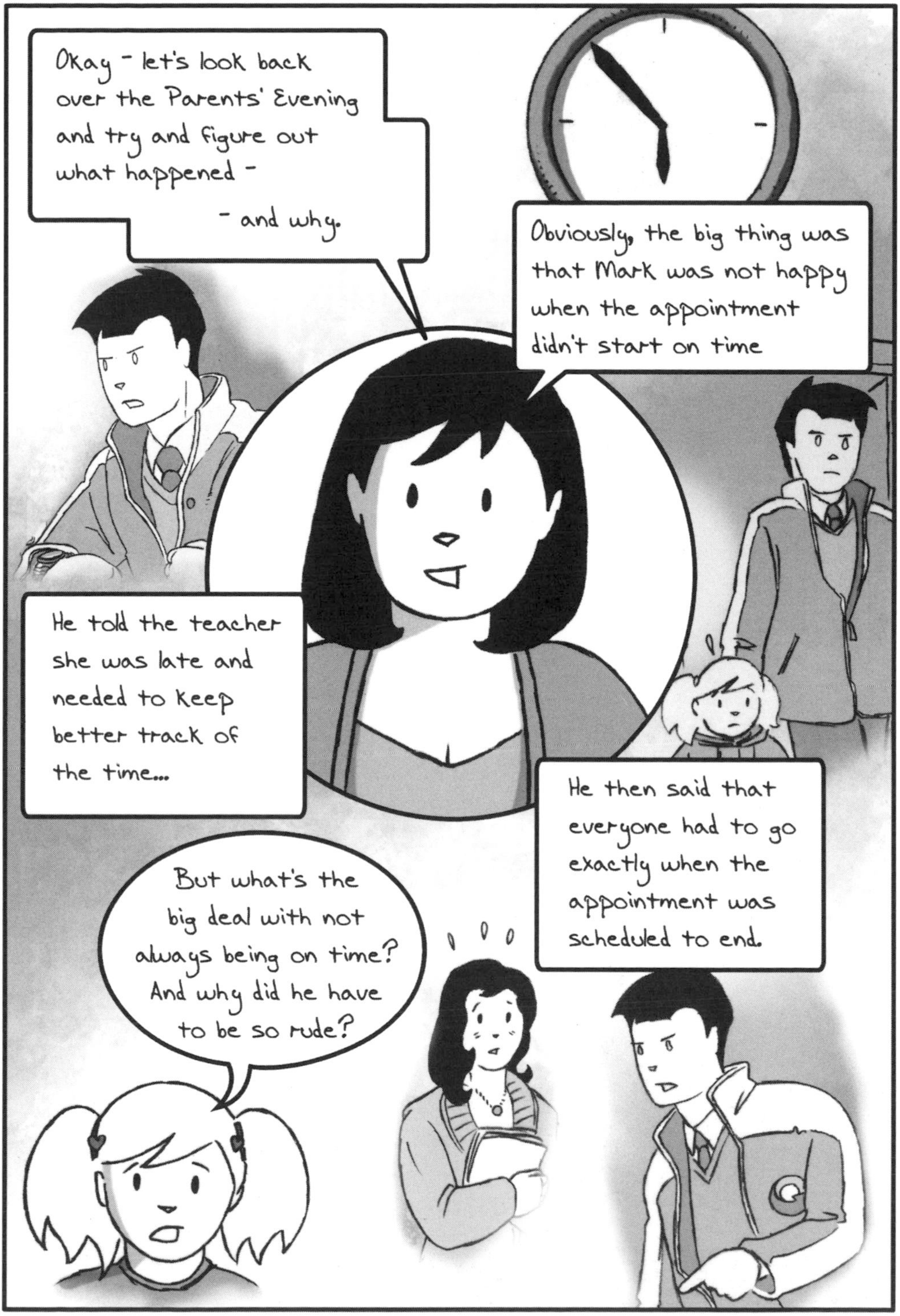
Okay - let's look back over the Parents' Evening and try and figure out what happened -
- and why.
Obviously, the big thing was that Mark was not happy when the appointment didn't start on time
He told the teacher she was late and needed to keep better track of the time...
He then said that everyone had to go exactly when the appointment was scheduled to end.
But what's the big deal with not always being on time? And why did he have to be so rude?

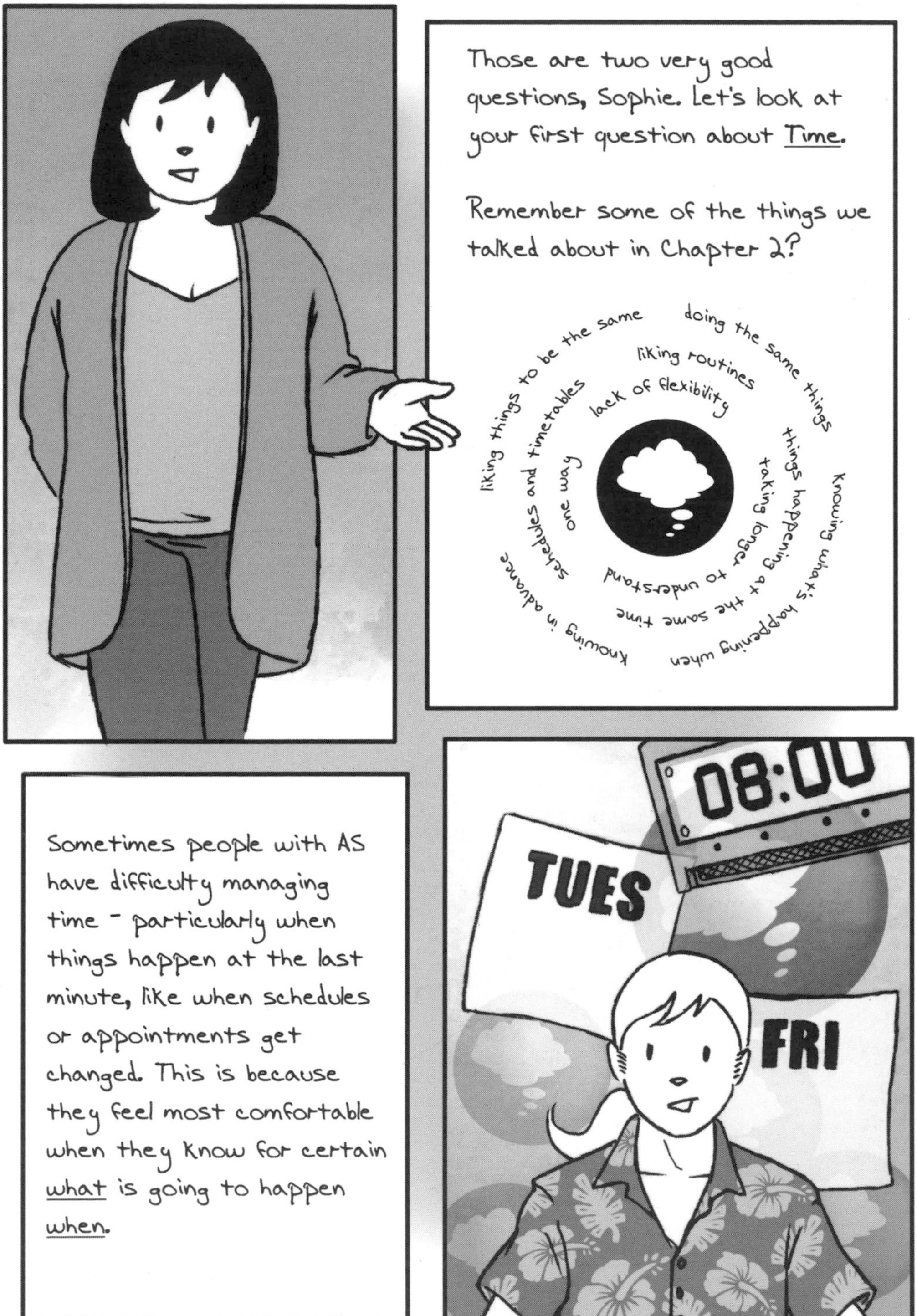
Those are two very good questions, Sophie. Let's look at your first question about Time.
Remember some of the things we talked about in Chapter 2?
liking things to be the same
doing the same things
knowing what's happening when
knowing in advance
schedules and timetables
liking routines
things happening at the same time
taking longer to understand
one way
lack of flexibility
Sometimes people with AS have difficulty managing time - particularly when things happen at the last minute, like when schedules or appointments get changed. This is because they feel most comfortable when they know for certain what is going to happen when.
08:00
TUES
FRI

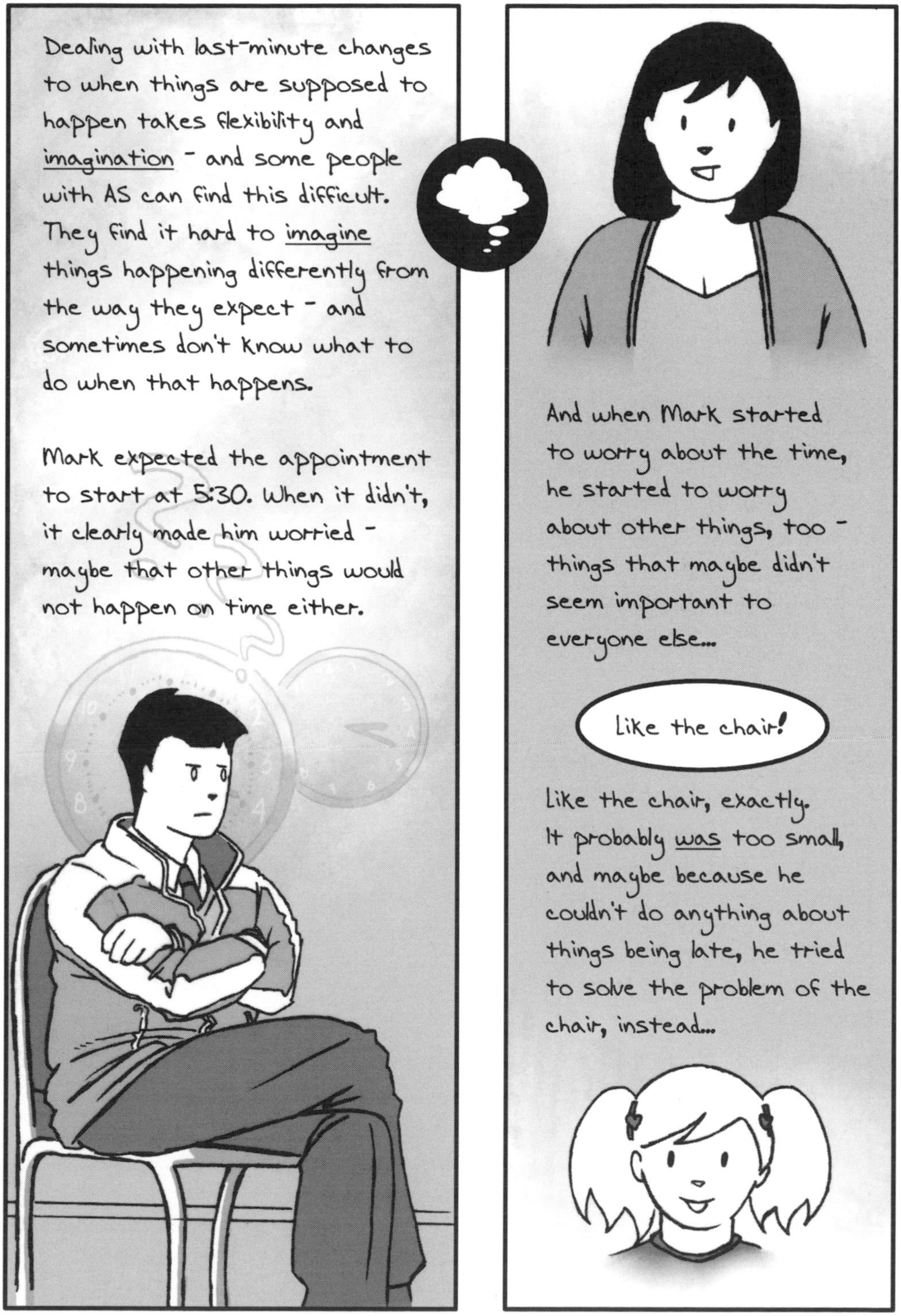
Dealing with last-minute changes to when things are supposed to happen takes flexibility and imagination - and some people with AS can find this difficult. They find it hard to imagine things happening differently from the way they expect - and sometimes don't know what to do when that happens.
Mark expected the appointment to start at 5:30. When it didn't, it clearly made him worried - maybe that other things would not happen on time either.
And when Mark started to worry about the time, he started to worry about other things, too - things that maybe didn't seem important to everyone else...
Like the chair!
Like the chair, exactly. It probably was too small, and maybe because he couldn't do anything about things being late, he tried to solve the problem of the chair, instead...

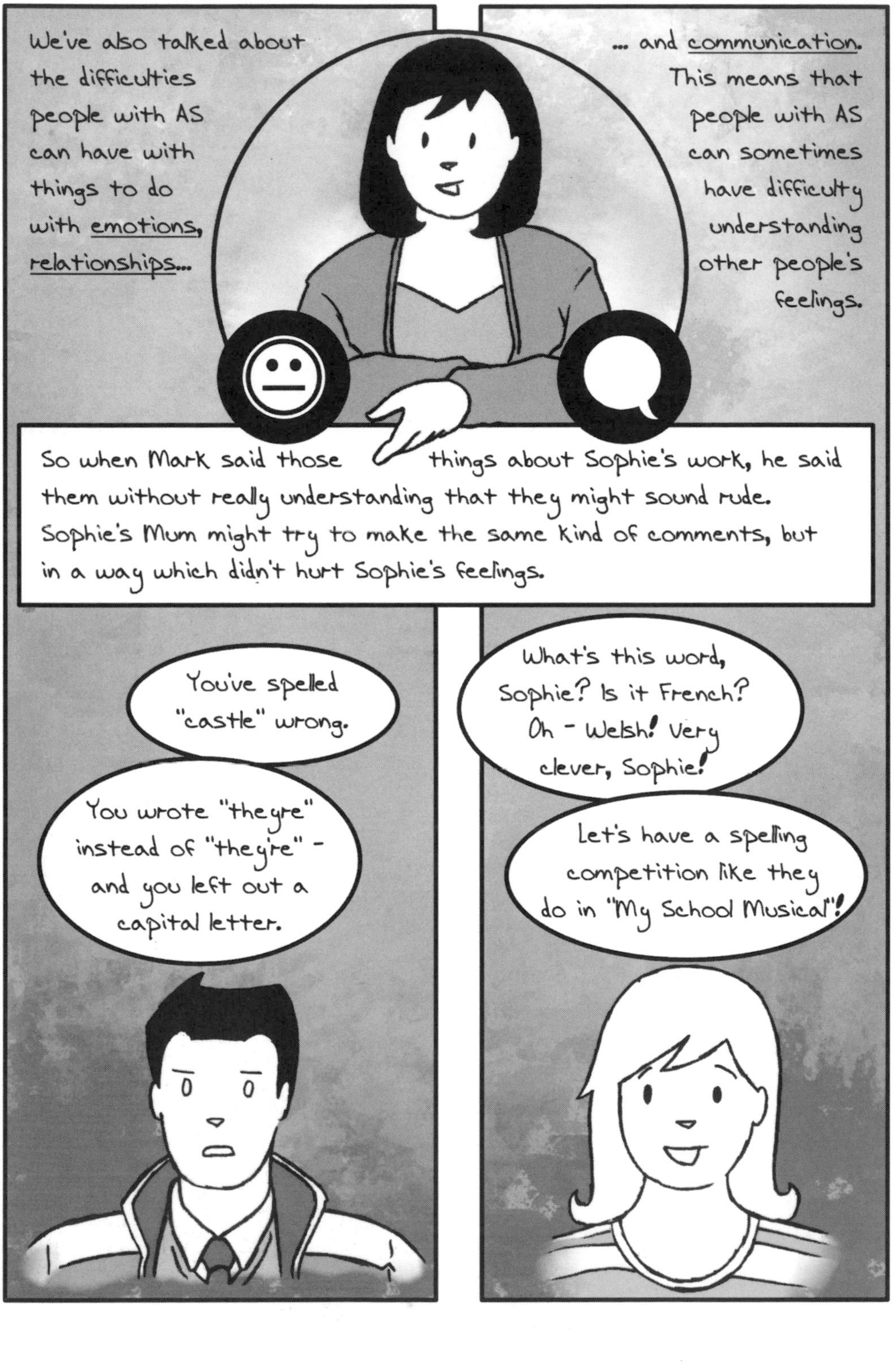
We've also talked about the difficulties people with AS can have with things to do with emotions, relationships...
... and communication. This means that people with AS can sometimes have difficulty understanding other people's feelings.
So when Mark said those things about Sophie's work, he said them without really understanding that they might sound rude. Sophie's Mum might try to make the same kind of comments, but in a way which didn't hurt Sophie's feelings.
You've spelled "castle" wrong.
You wrote "theyre" instead of "they're" - and you left out a capital letter.
What's this word, Sophie? Is it French? Oh - Welsh! Very clever, Sophie!
Let's have a spelling competition like they do in "My School Musical"!

So Mark certainly didn't <u>mean</u> to be rude, and he didn't <u>mean</u> to hurt Sophie's feelings, but because he finds it difficult to understand other people's feelings, he didn't understand that the <u>way</u> he said those things would sound rude.

He also didn't <u>mean</u> to make Sophie and Ms. Farmer feel unhappy and embarrassed.

By the end of the day, the whole family was feeling bad...

...everything was late we di... ...ne for supper... ...what's the use... ...if y... ...it...

I don't know what we're going to do about... ...he behave... ...complete... ...way was... ...How can he... ...like that? H... ...to

Why did Dad say all those mean things about my project? It must... ...will M... ...P... ...ves... ...thin...

Why is everyone in such a bad mood?

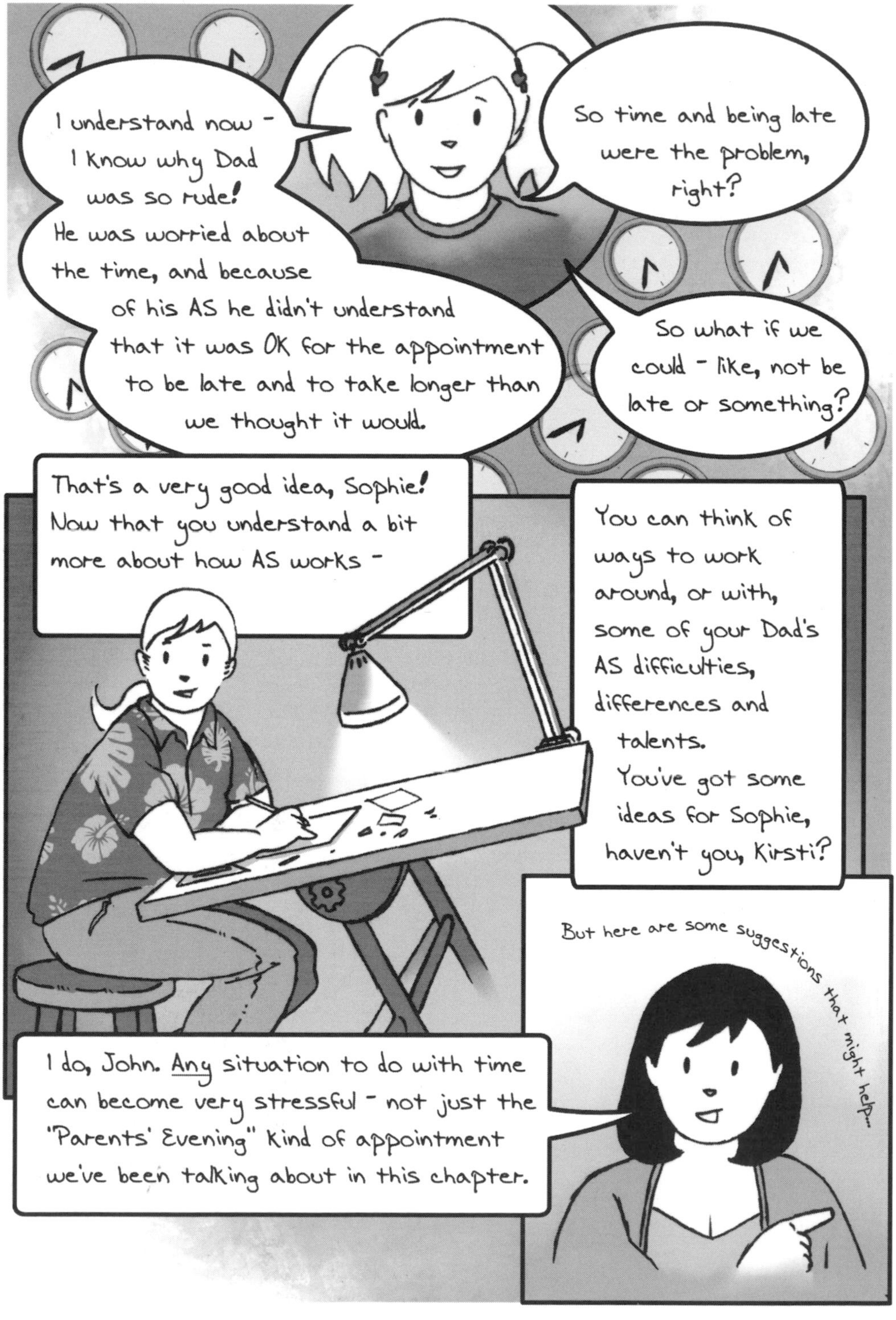
I understand now - I know why Dad was so rude! He was worried about the time, and because of his AS he didn't understand that it was OK for the appointment to be late and to take longer than we thought it would.
So time and being late were the problem, right?
So what if we could - like, not be late or something?
That's a very good idea, Sophie! Now that you understand a bit more about how AS works -
You can think of ways to work around, or with, some of your Dad's AS difficulties, differences and talents. You've got some ideas for Sophie, haven't you, Kirsti?
I do, John. Any situation to do with time can become very stressful - not just the "Parents' Evening" kind of appointment we've been talking about in this chapter.
But here are some suggestions that might help...

1. If there's a choice of times for an appointment, try picking an early one – there are less likely to be delays.

2. Make sure everyone understands in advance if scheduled events might end up being shorter or longer.

3. Avoid sudden or last-minute changes in plans if possible. Perhaps have a "Plan B" and reschedule the appointment in advance if it looks like a last-minute change is going to be unavoidable.

4. Talk about feelings often. Explain clearly what makes people feel angry, sad, hurt or embarrassed – and why these feelings are important.

1. Perhaps Mark could have arranged to leave work early so that they could have a slot near the start of the Parents' Evening.

2. Maybe explain to Ms. Farmer before the day of the meeting that Mark likes to keep to time. She could then reassure him beforehand that it's okay for the appointment to last more than ten minutes.

3. Mark, Vicky and Sophie could talk to Sophie's teachers. They might be able to help find a different time to meet.

4. Sophie and Vicky can help Mark by telling him clearly if he's making people feel uncomfortable, angry or hurt – but they must remember he might be feeling angry or confused himself.

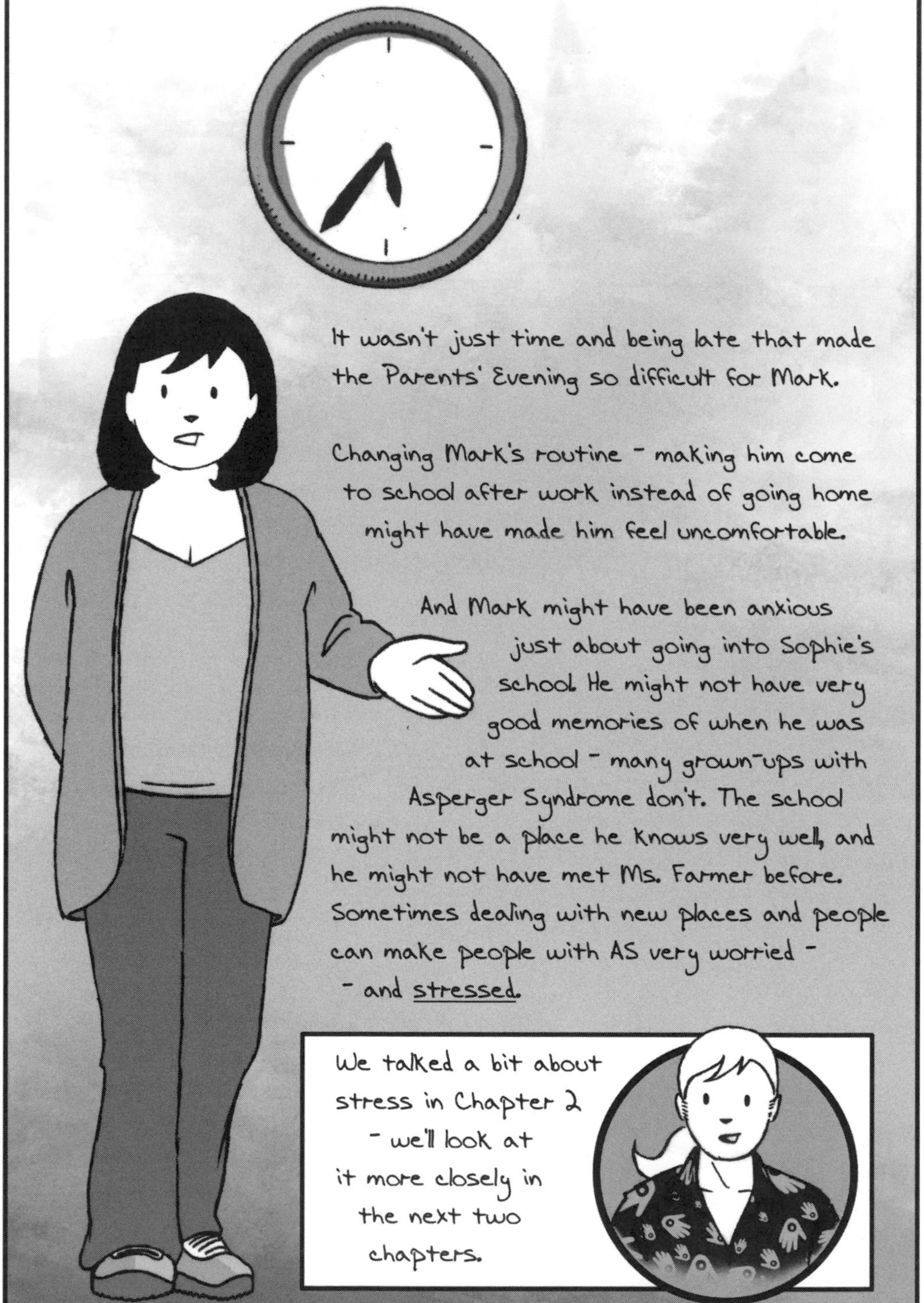
It wasn't just time and being late that made the Parents' Evening so difficult for Mark.
Changing Mark's routine – making him come to school after work instead of going home might have made him feel uncomfortable.
And Mark might have been anxious just about going into Sophie's school. He might not have very good memories of when he was at school – many grown-ups with Asperger Syndrome don't. The school might not be a place he knows very well, and he might not have met Ms. Farmer before. Sometimes dealing with new places and people can make people with AS very worried – – and stressed.
We talked a bit about stress in Chapter 2 – we'll look at it more closely in the next two chapters.

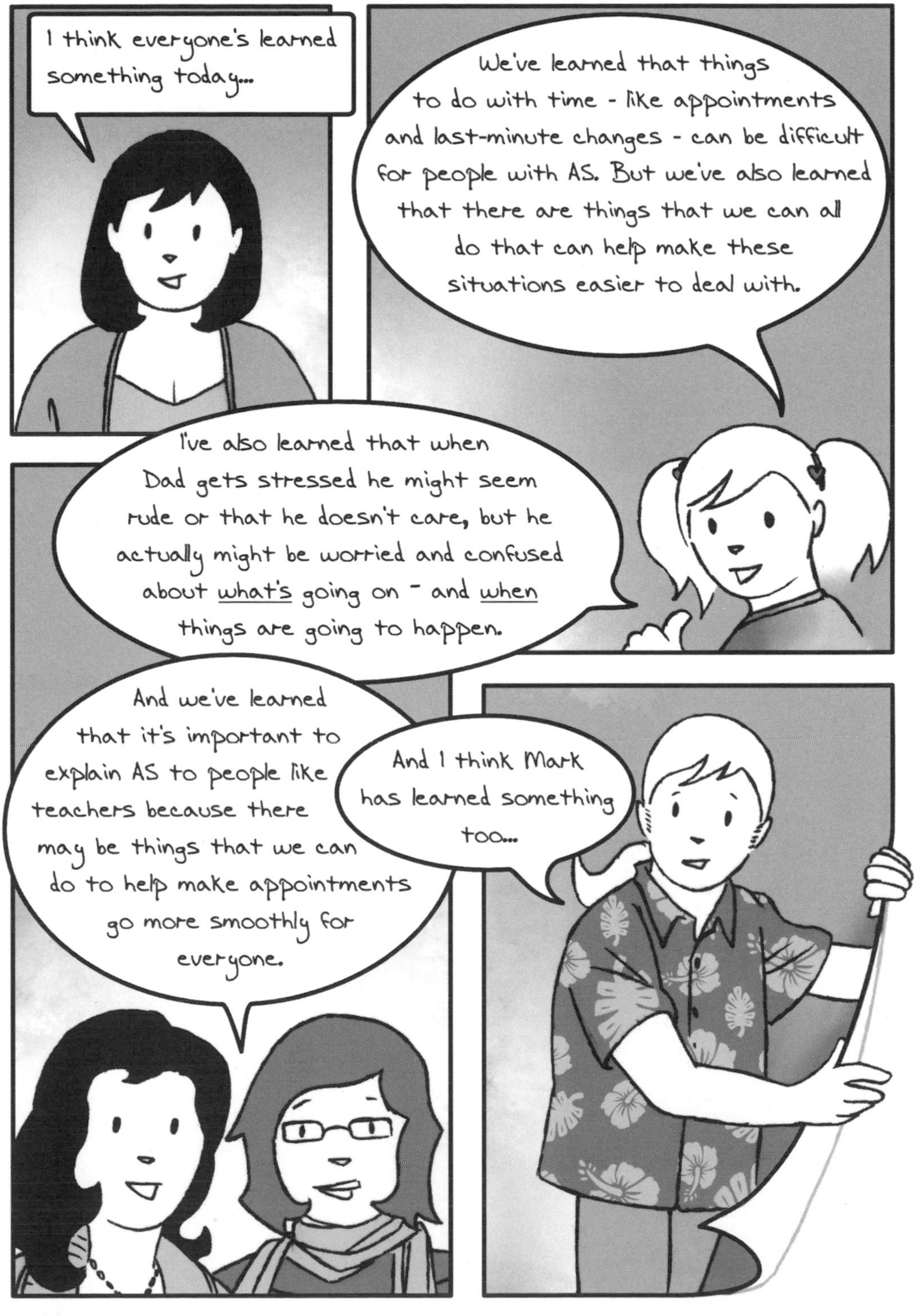
I think everyone's learned something today...
We've learned that things to do with time - like appointments and last-minute changes - can be difficult for people with AS. But we've also learned that there are things that we can all do that can help make these situations easier to deal with.
I've also learned that when Dad gets stressed he might seem rude or that he doesn't care, but he actually might be worried and confused about what's going on - and when things are going to happen.
And we've learned that it's important to explain AS to people like teachers because there may be things that we can do to help make appointments go more smoothly for everyone.
And I think Mark has learned something too...

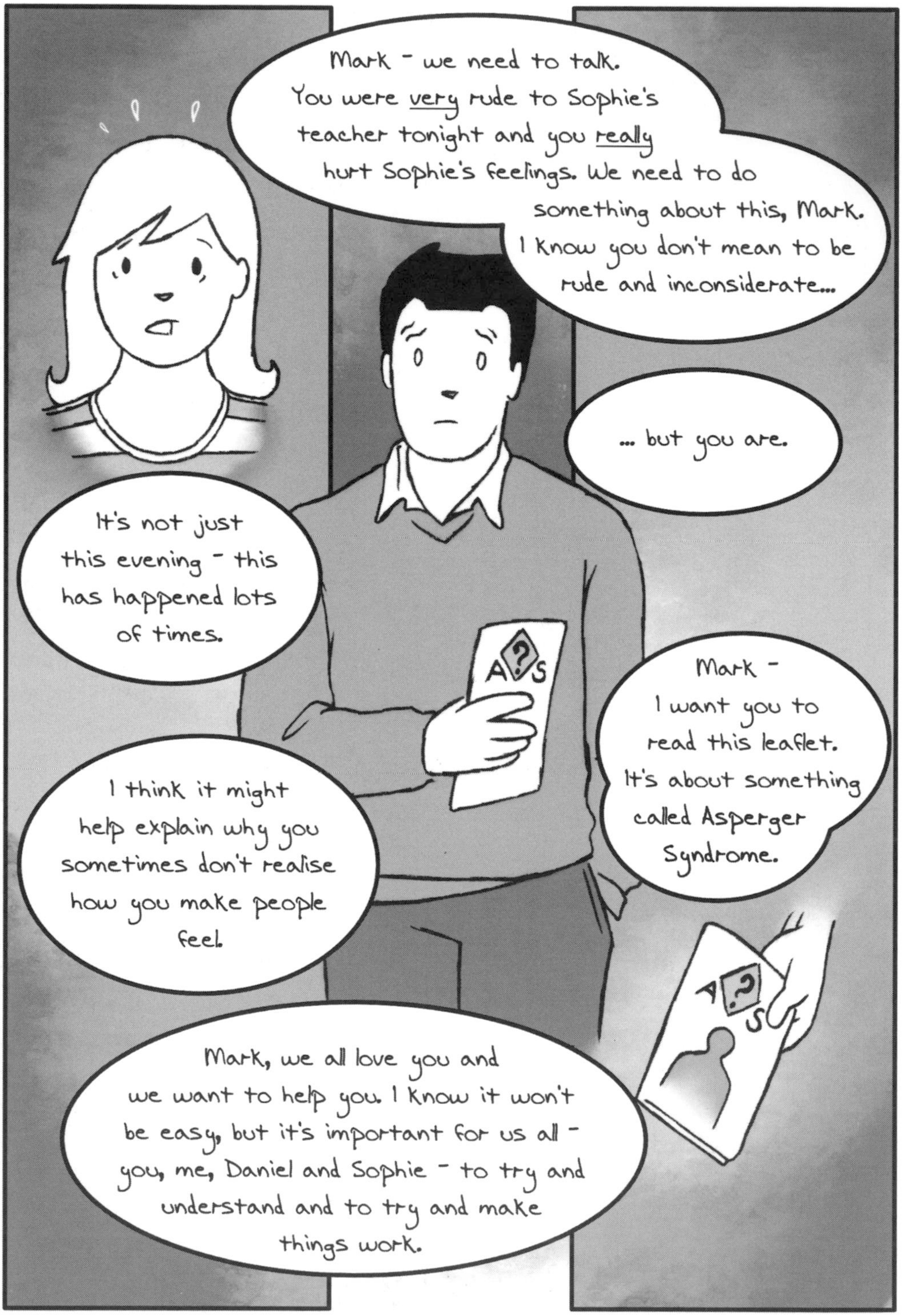
Mark - we need to talk. You were very rude to Sophie's teacher tonight and you really hurt Sophie's feelings. We need to do something about this, Mark. I know you don't mean to be rude and inconsiderate...
... but you are.
It's not just this evening - this has happened lots of times.
Mark - I want you to read this leaflet. It's about something called Asperger Syndrome.
I think it might help explain why you sometimes don't realise how you make people feel.
Mark, we all love you and we want to help you. I know it won't be easy, but it's important for us all - you, me, Daniel and Sophie - to try and understand and to try and make things work.

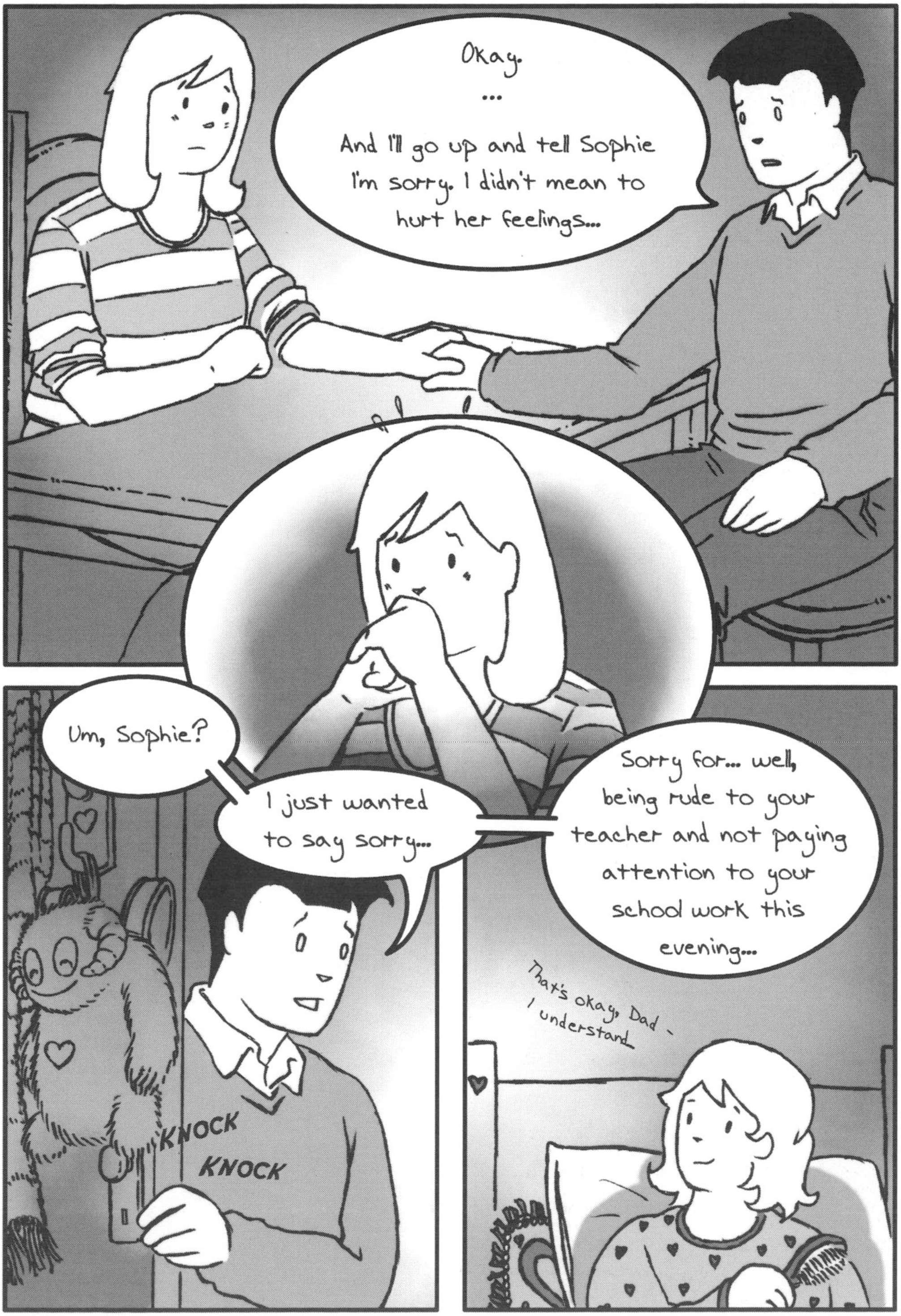
Okay.
...
And I'll go up and tell Sophie I'm sorry. I didn't mean to hurt her feelings...
Um, Sophie?
I just wanted to say sorry...
KNOCK
KNOCK
Sorry for... well, being rude to your teacher and not paying attention to your school work this evening...
That's okay, Dad - I understand.

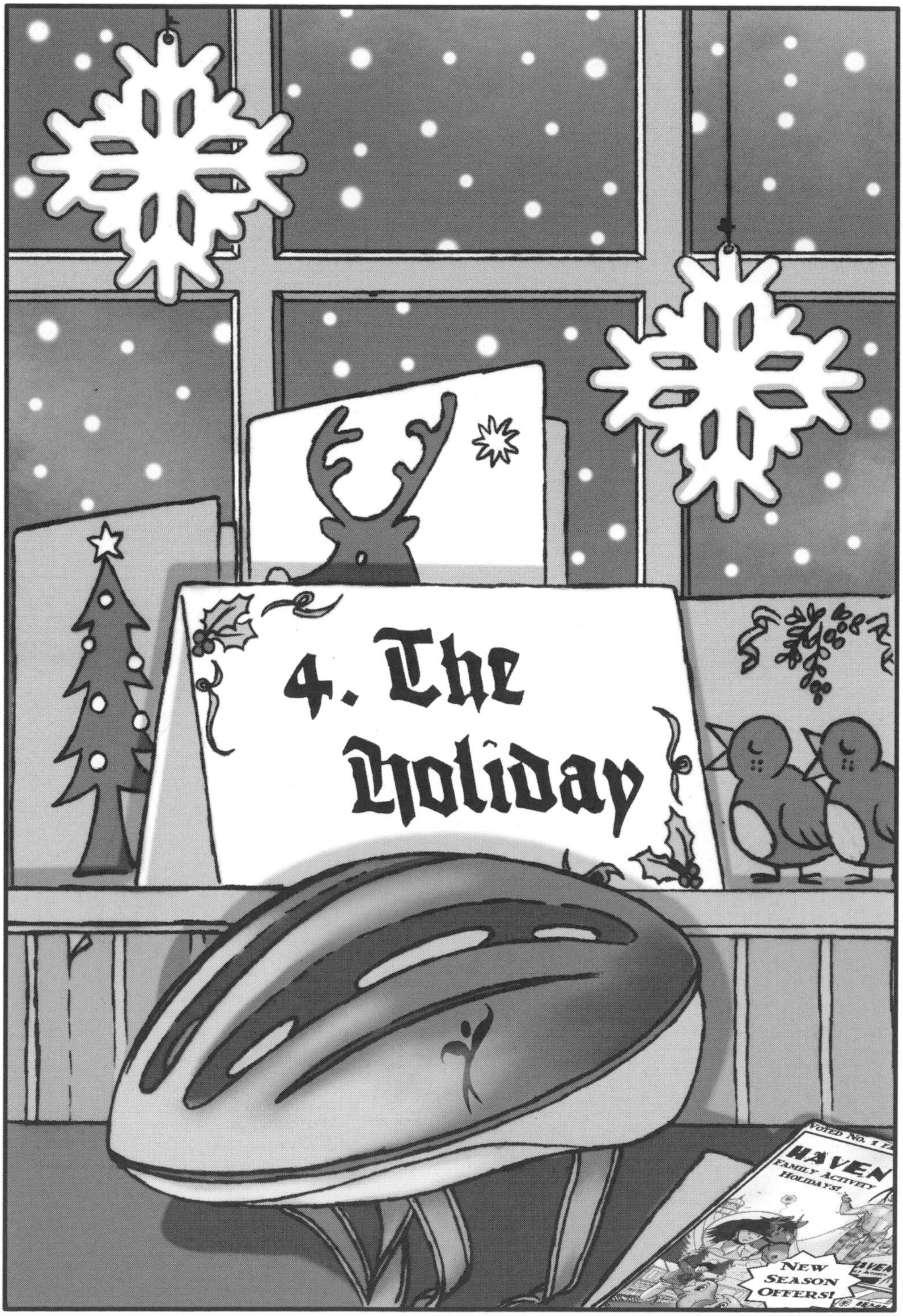
4. The Holiday
FAMILY ACTIVITY HOLIDAYS!
NEW SEASON OFFERS!

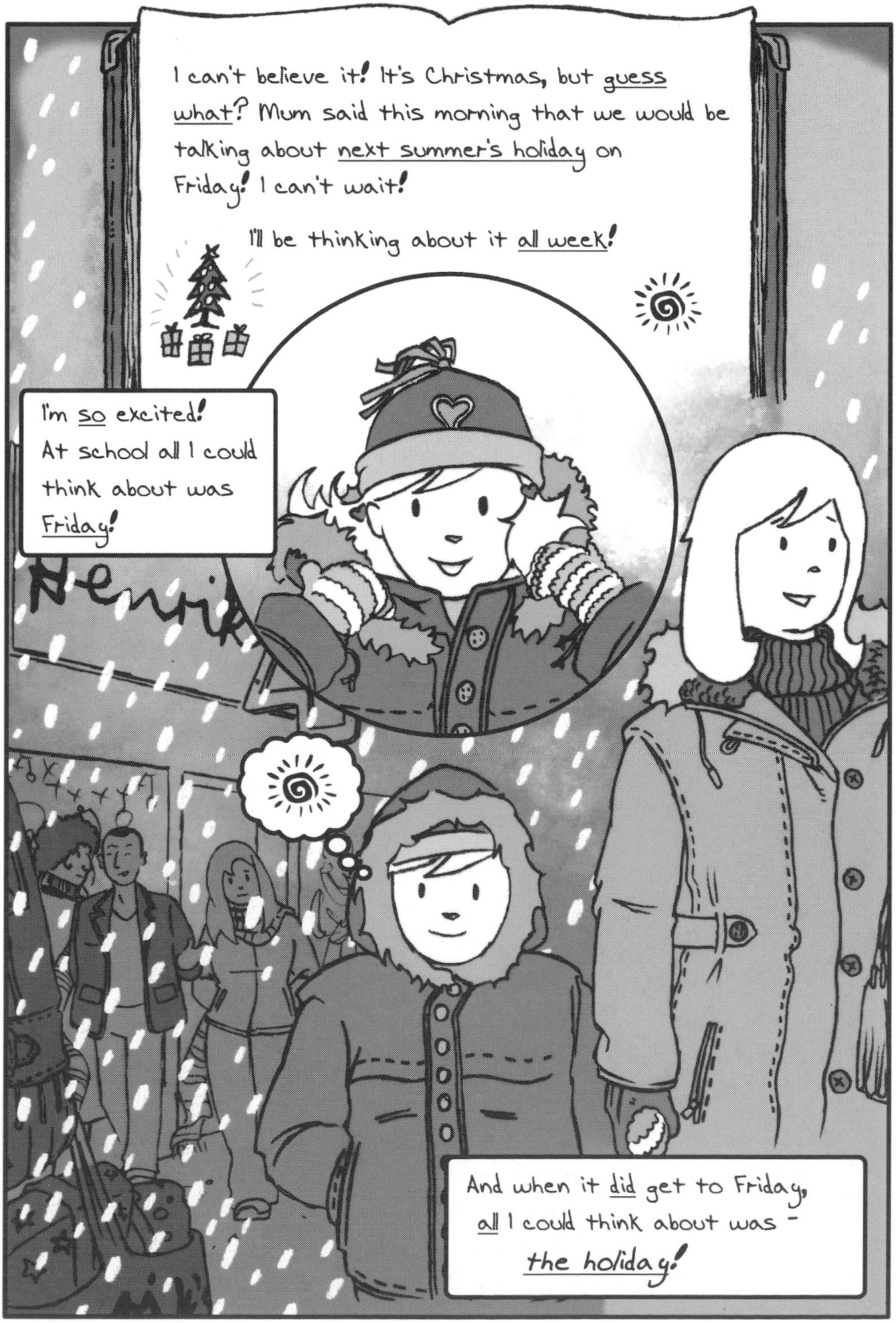
I can't believe it! It's Christmas, but guess what? Mum said this morning that we would be talking about next summer's holiday on Friday! I can't wait!
I'll be thinking about it all week!
I'm so excited! At school all I could think about was Friday!
And when it did get to Friday, all I could think about was - the holiday!

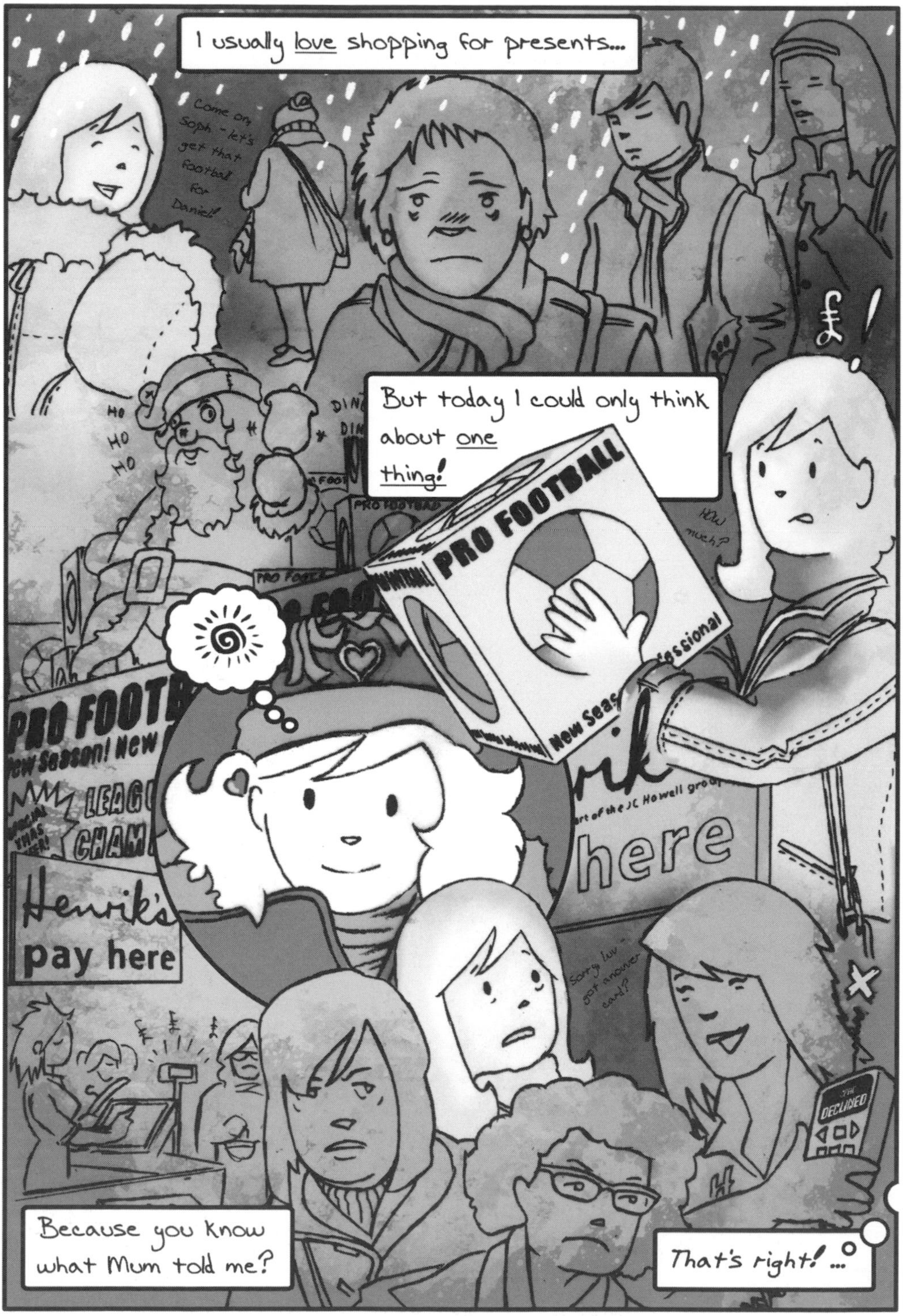
I usually love shopping for presents...
Come on Soph - let's get that football for Daniel!
HO HO HO
But today I could only think about one thing!
PRO FOOTBALL
How much?
£!
Henrik's
pay here
here
Sorry luv - got another card?
Because you know what Mum told me?
That's right! ...

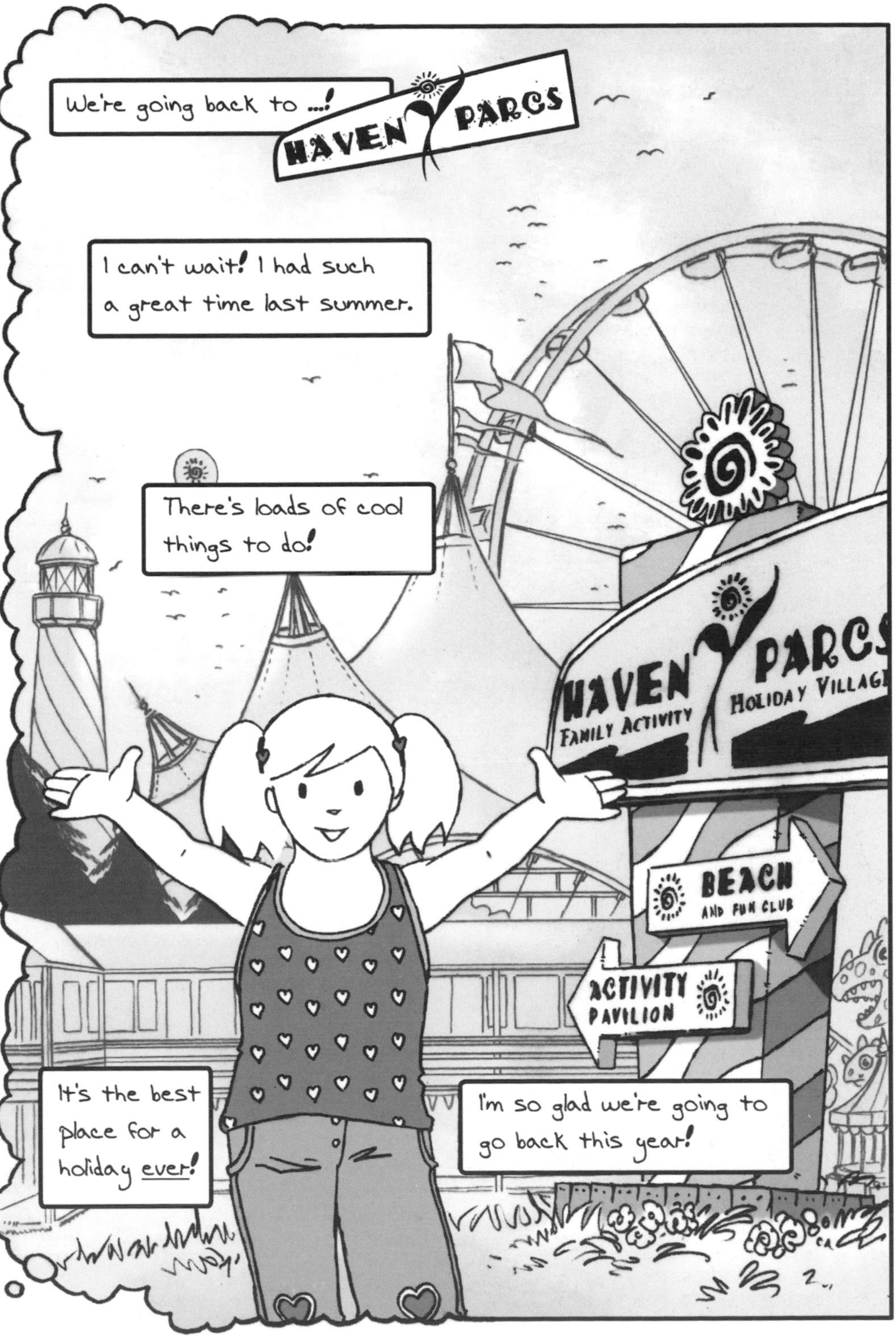
We're going back to ...!
HAVEN PARCS
I can't wait! I had such a great time last summer.
There's loads of cool things to do!
HAVEN PARCS
FAMILY ACTIVITY
HOLIDAY VILLAG
BEACH
AND FUN CLUB
ACTIVITY PAVILION
It's the best place for a holiday ever!
I'm so glad we're going to go back this year!

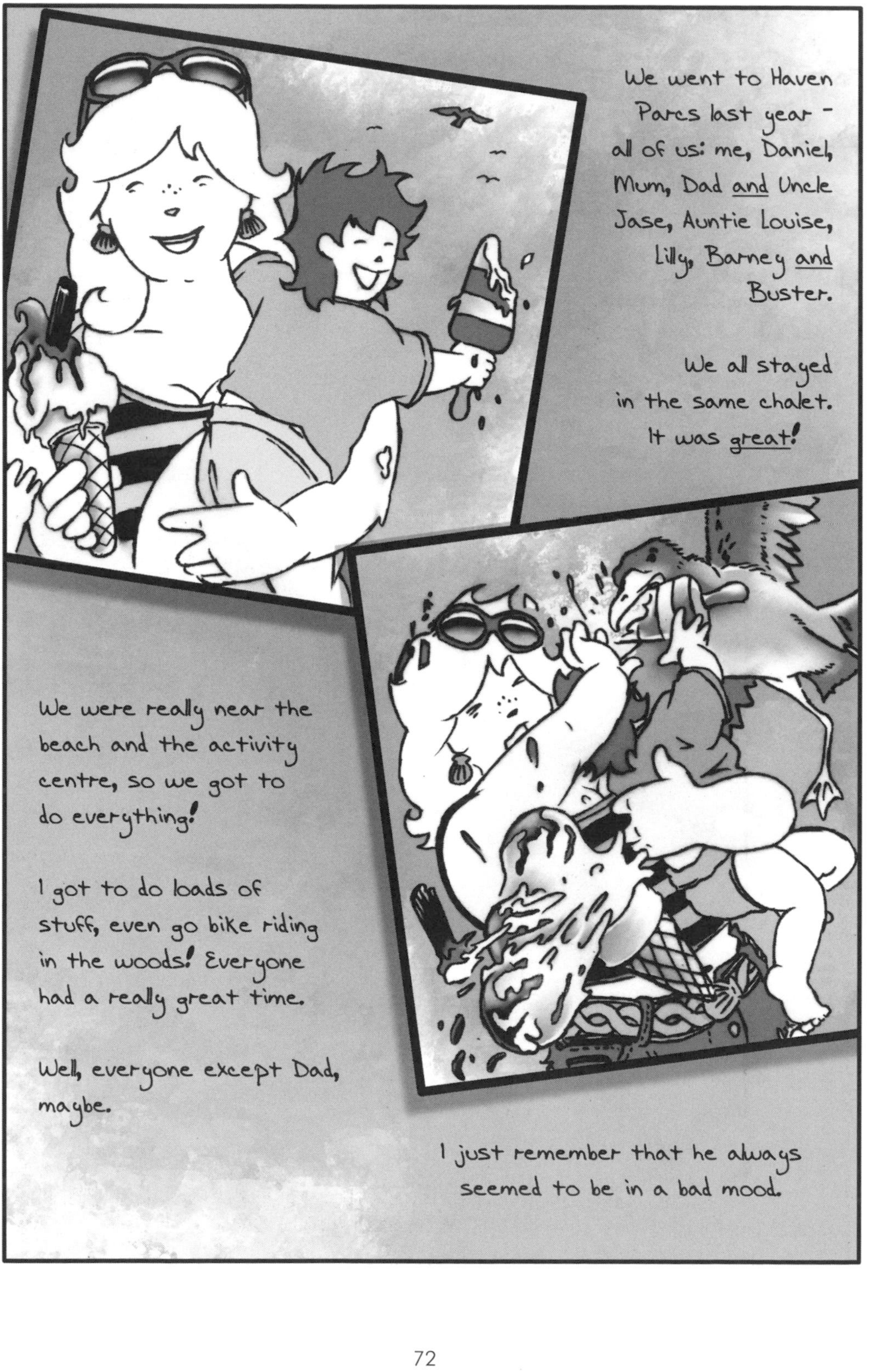
We went to Haven Parcs last year - all of us: me, Daniel, Mum, Dad and Uncle Jase, Auntie Louise, Lilly, Barney and Buster.
We all stayed in the same chalet. It was great!
We were really near the beach and the activity centre, so we got to do everything!
I got to do loads of stuff, even go bike riding in the woods! Everyone had a really great time.
Well, everyone except Dad, maybe.
I just remember that he always seemed to be in a bad mood.

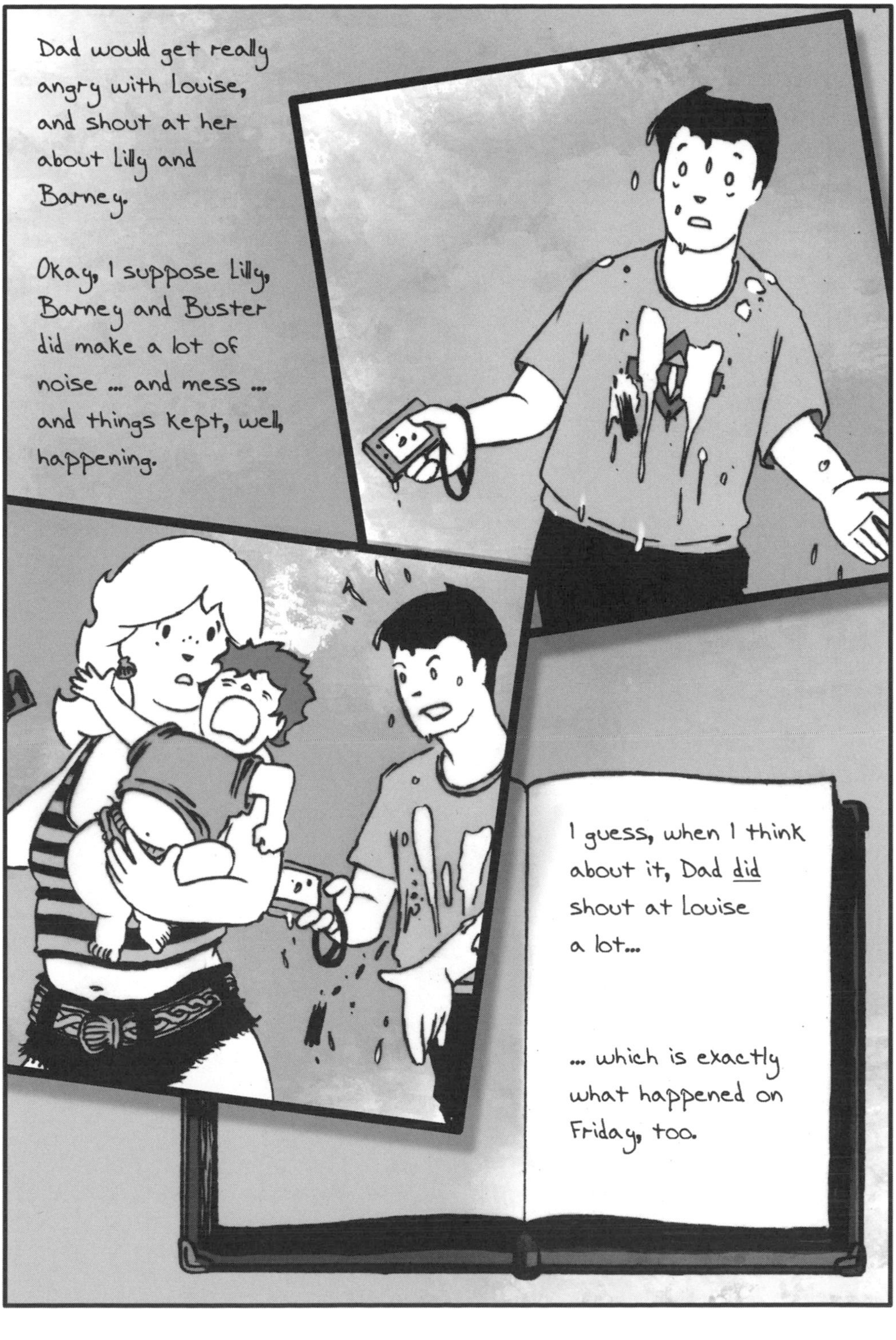
Dad would get really angry with Louise, and shout at her about Lilly and Barney.
Okay, I suppose Lilly, Barney and Buster did make a lot of noise ... and mess ... and things kept, well, happening.
I guess, when I think about it, Dad did shout at Louise a lot...
... which is exactly what happened on Friday, too.

BANG!
We're back! Phew! Town was - Hey, Lucy! What are you doing here?
You forgot that salsa CD at work - thought I'd drop it off. Grab a glass - there's a bottle of Rioja in the kitchen!
Hi, Mum! C'mon, c'mon - what happened next?
Oh, yeh - well, then Frank, the one who is allergic to cats - he said -
- a vowel to start
vowel... a consonant...
consonant... another
consonant please, Carol.
Roger. Okay everyone,
your time starts... now.
tick-tock-tick-tock-tick
deedle, doodle,
diddly-dee.
BONG!
CRUNCH CRUNCH
So then Malcolm coughed up this HUGE hairball...
Uh, hi. He's, um, watching telly ... Uh, okay ... Um, Vicky?
Hiya, Mark. Where's your Dad?
Eew! Gross!
What are you doing out here in the kitchen? Come into the lounge.
Okay, Mum!
Psst! Quick, Soph - run and put Daniel's present under your bed!
THUMP, THUMP, THUMP, THUMP!
Sorry, Mark - what were you saying?

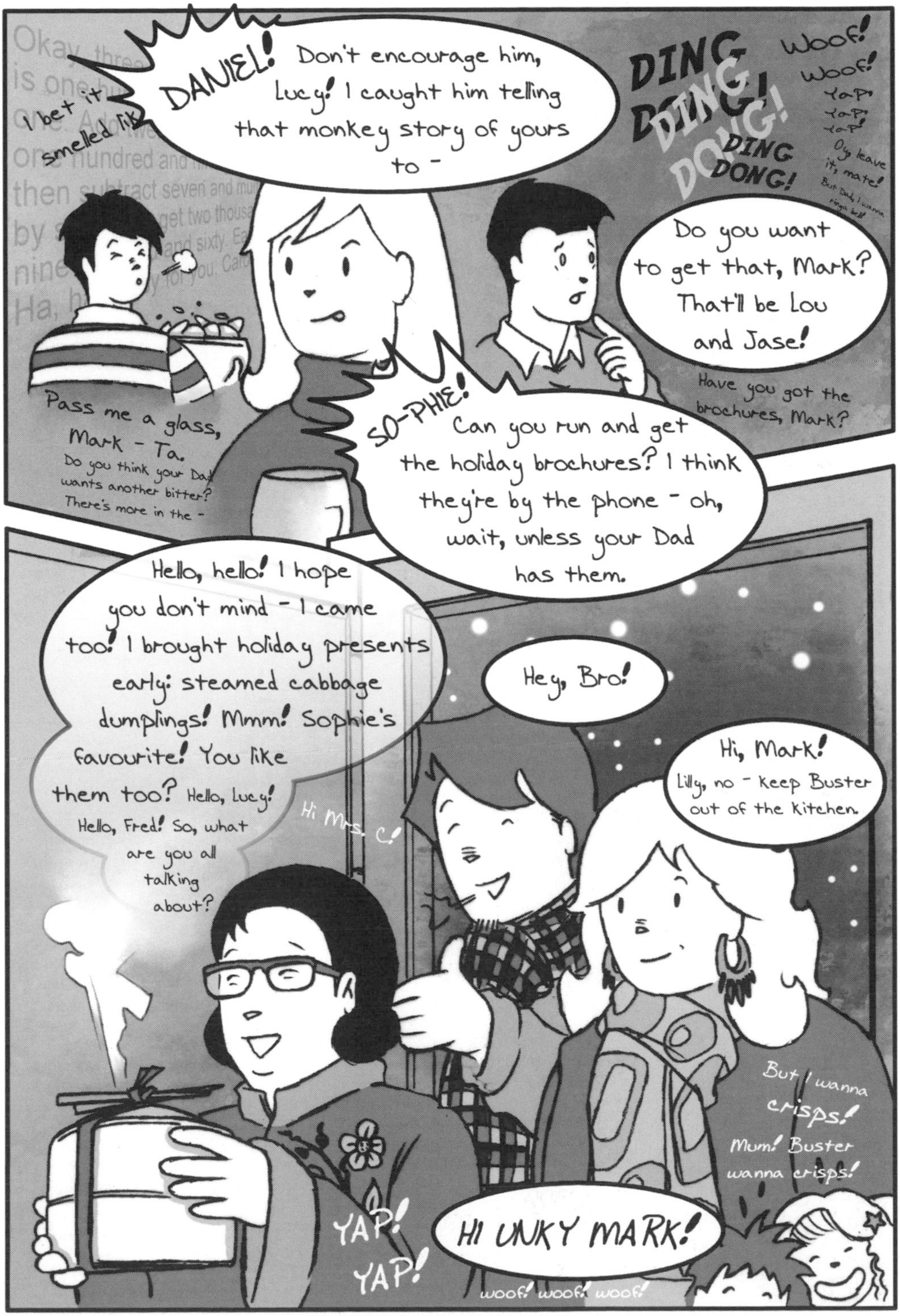
I bet it smelled lik
DANIEL! Don't encourage him, Lucy! I caught him telling that monkey story of yours to -
DING DONG! DING DONG! DING DONG!
Woof! Woof! Yap! Yap! Yap!
Oy, leave it, mate!
Do you want to get that, Mark? That'll be Lou and Jase!
Have you got the brochures, Mark?
Pass me a glass, Mark - Ta.
Do you think your Dad wants another bitter? There's more in the -
SO-PHIE! Can you run and get the holiday brochures? I think they're by the phone - oh, wait, unless your Dad has them.
Hello, hello! I hope you don't mind - I came too! I brought holiday presents early: steamed cabbage dumplings! Mmm! Sophie's favourite! You like them too? Hello, Lucy! Hello, Fred! So, what are you all talking about?
Hey, Bro!
Hi Mrs. C!
Hi, Mark! Lilly, no - keep Buster out of the kitchen.
But I wanna crisps!
Mum! Buster wanna crisps!
YAP! YAP!
HI UNKY MARK!
woof! woof! woof!

Hiya, Jason - there's tins in the fridge. See if your Dad wants another - he's in the lounge watching his quiz programme.
Dump your coat and grab a glass, Lou!
Top up, Lucy? What is it, sweetie - dog biscuits? Um, we don't have any
Mark?
Mark! See if Sophie's
those brochures
Carol!
No more glasses for me, Vicky - not for another seven months...
Oh, very easy to make, - just steam the cabbage, roll it all out and stuff with the pork - use plenty of soy!
Aunty Vicky, Aunty Vicky - Buster wants a dog biscuit!
No, I wanna give biscuit!
Mum? Mum!
Oh, she was telling me this wikkid story about her cat!
ho! Let me
three ...
Yap! Yap! Yap! Yap! Yap!
... months? Lou - you don't mean ...
Indicator went blue this morning!
Oh, I like this quiz, Mister Fred! And she's so clever - don't you think, Daniel?
No! Really?
Wait - does that mean...?
Oh, my ... Jason, Louise - CONGRATULATIONS!

Oh Louise - I can't believe it! I know you've always wanted another baby!
So whens ... see - seven months from now makes it
That's so cool! The baby can come on holiday with us!
Congrats, girl! I'll keep your pints cold for you - ha, ha!
Your grandma used to say ... baby born i...
Here, come and sit down. Get comfy!
Shall I turn the radiator up?
I'm fine, guys! Stop fussing!
Congratulations Mister Jason!
Do you know if it's a boy or girl?
Congratulations, son!
Mark - you're going to be an Uncle again!
Hey, hey! Easy Mrs. C!
Kiss!
Call it Wayne! No, David - no give it grandpa's name!
Not smelly baby sister - baby Bruvver!
A bootiful new baby sister!
Sister! Bruvver! Sister! Bruvver!
Yap! Yap! Yap! Yap! Yap! Yap! Yap! Yap! Yap! Yap! Yap! Yap!
It was about now that Dad started shouting ...

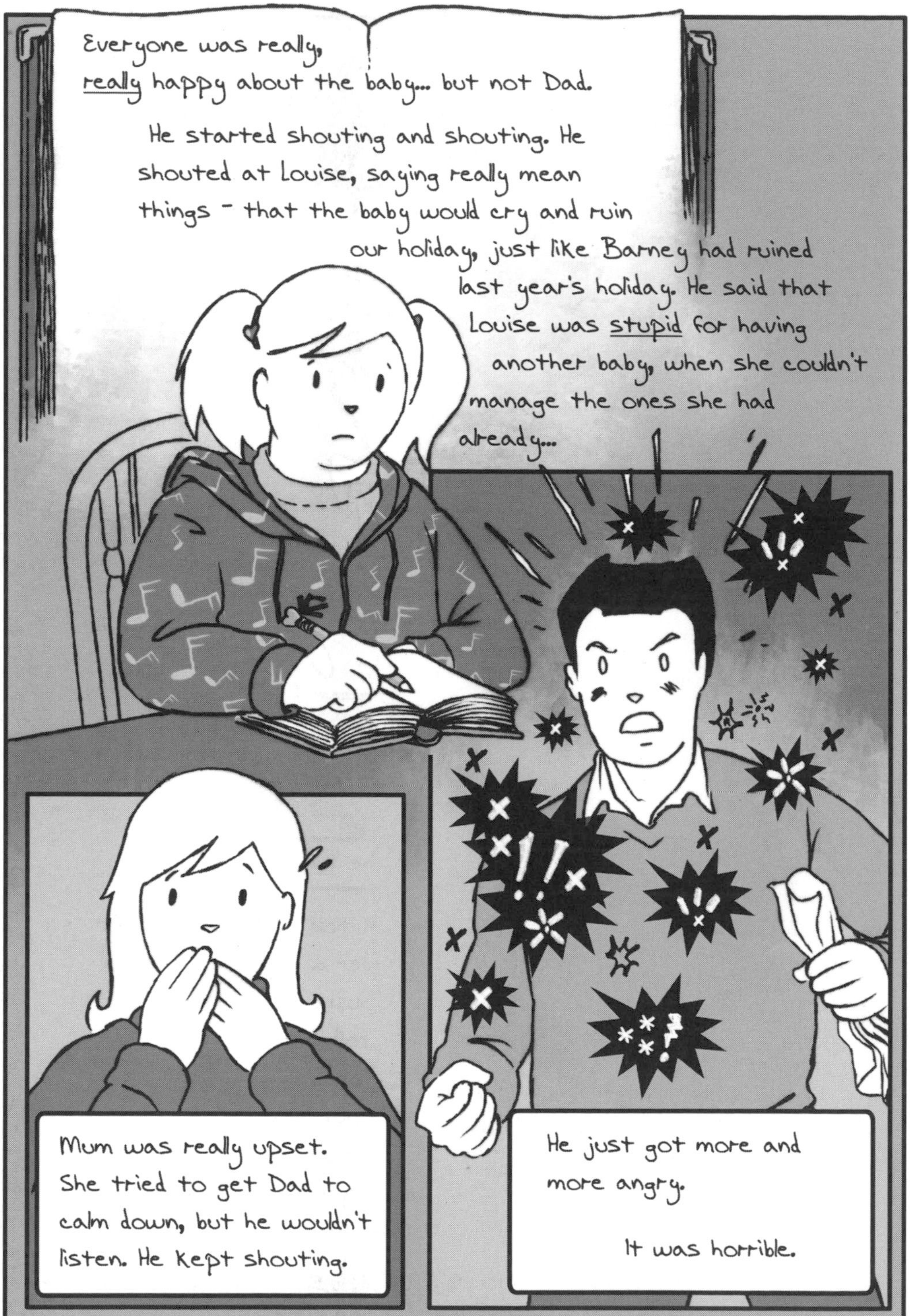
Everyone was really, really happy about the baby... but not Dad.
He started shouting and shouting. He shouted at Louise, saying really mean things – that the baby would cry and ruin our holiday, just like Barney had ruined last year's holiday. He said that Louise was stupid for having another baby, when she couldn't manage the ones she had already...
Mum was really upset. She tried to get Dad to calm down, but he wouldn't listen. He kept shouting.
He just got more and more angry.
It was horrible.

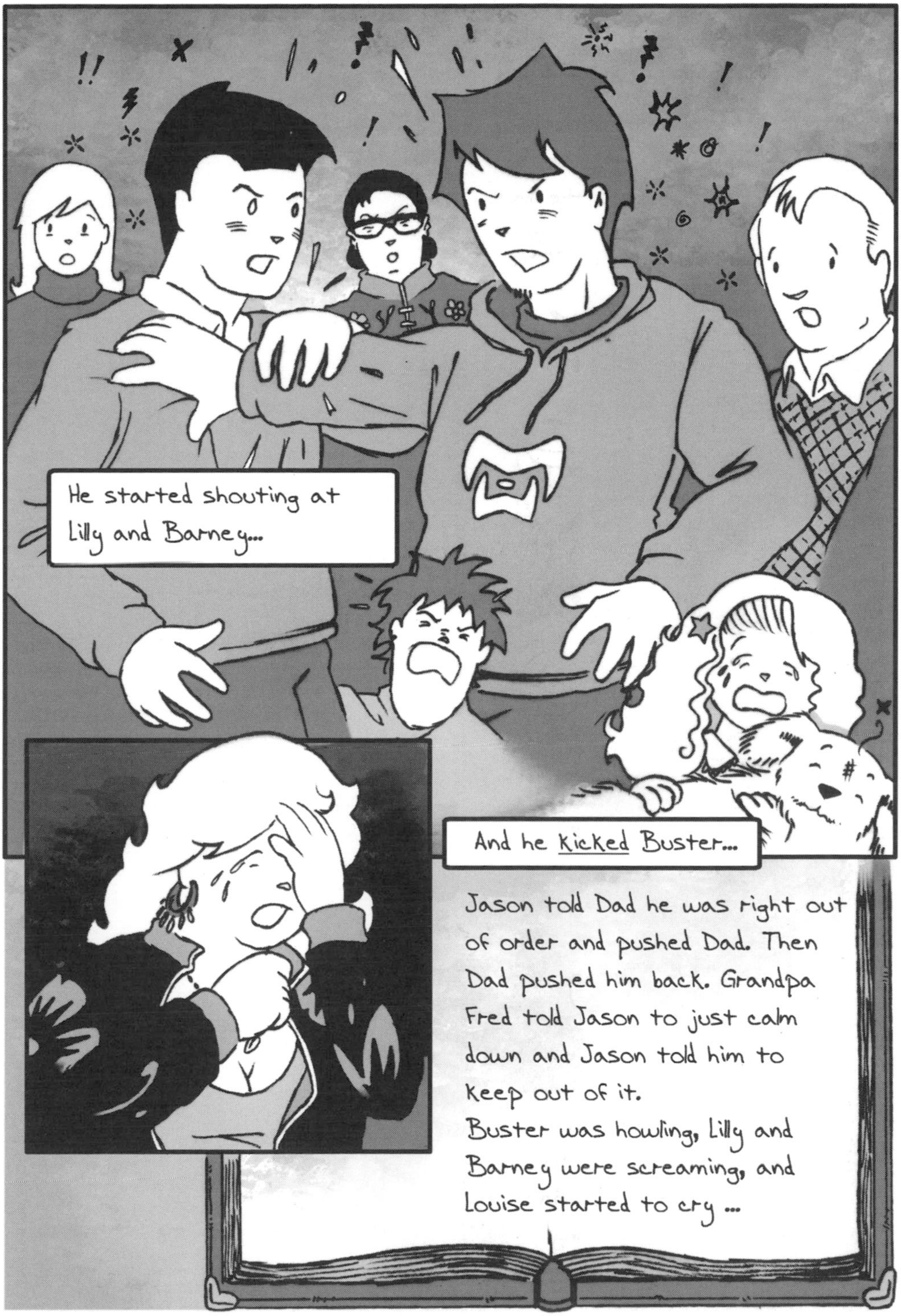
He started shouting at Lilly and Barney...
And he Kicked Buster...
Jason told Dad he was right out of order and pushed Dad. Then Dad pushed him back. Grandpa Fred told Jason to just calm down and Jason told him to keep out of it.
Buster was howling, Lilly and Barney were screaming, and Louise started to cry ...

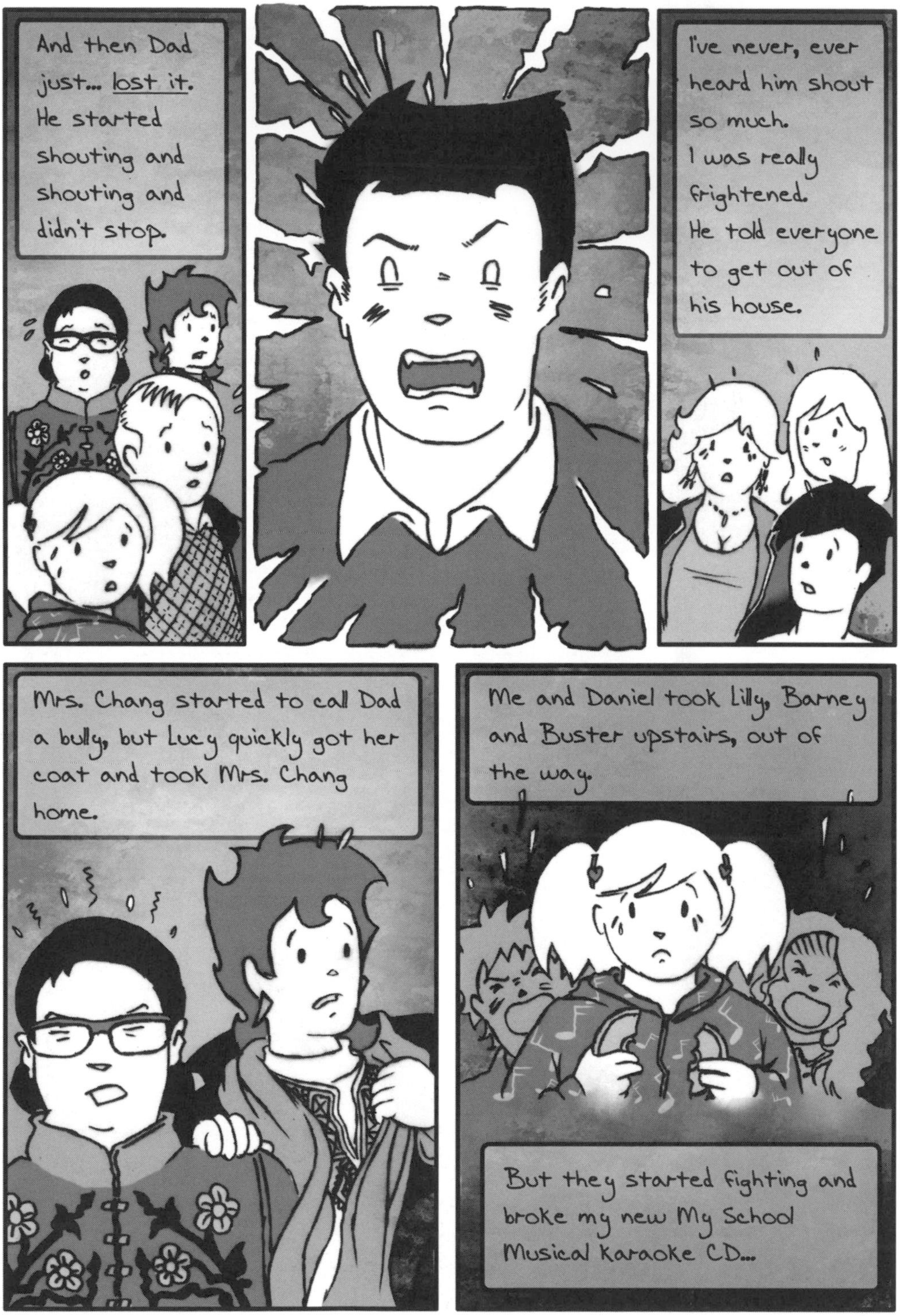
And then Dad just... lost it. He started shouting and shouting and didn't stop.
I've never, ever heard him shout so much. I was really frightened. He told everyone to get out of his house.
Mrs. Chang started to call Dad a bully, but Lucy quickly got her coat and took Mrs. Chang home.
Me and Daniel took Lilly, Barney and Buster upstairs, out of the way.
But they started fighting and broke my new My School Musical Karaoke CD...

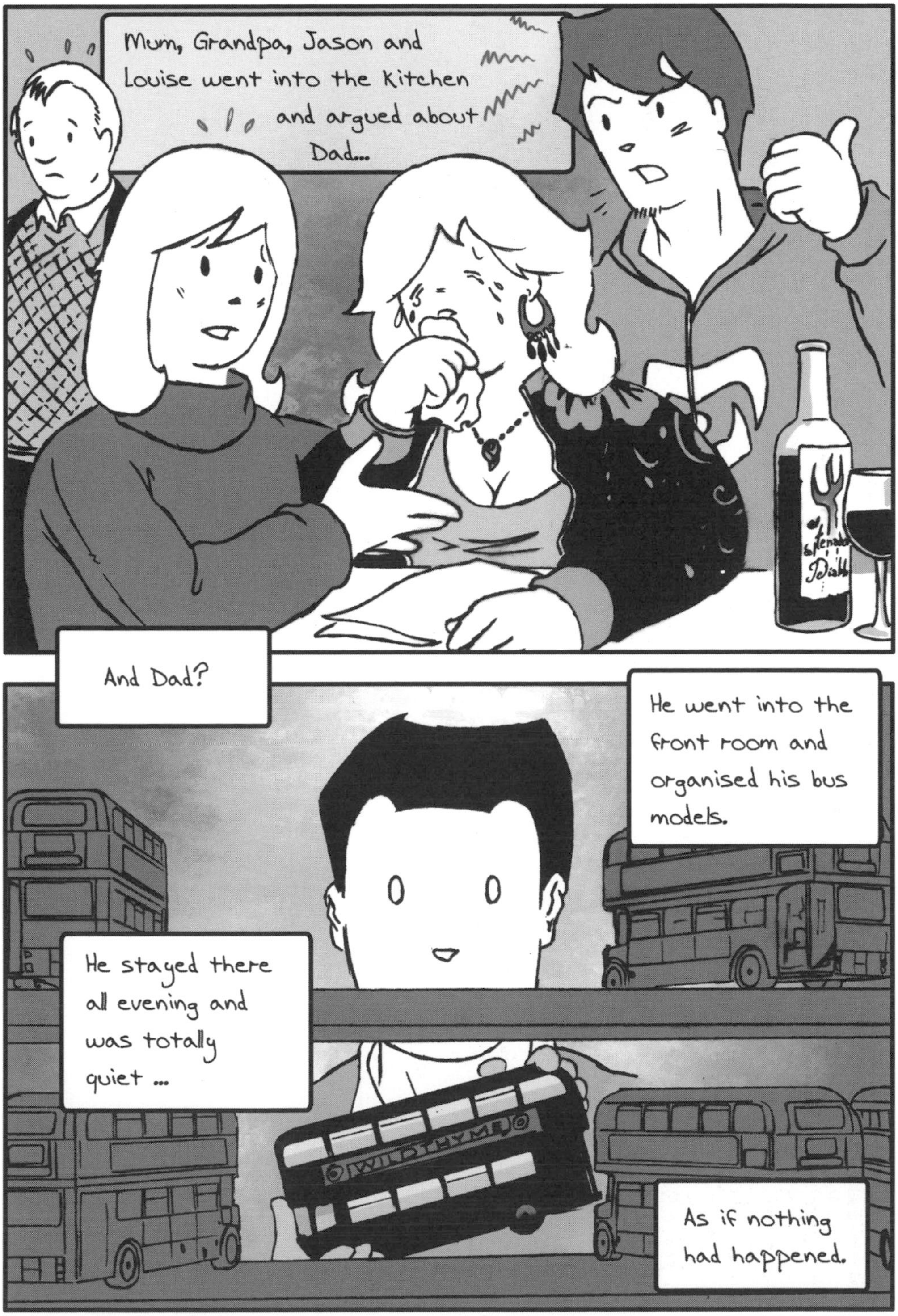
Mum, Grandpa, Jason and Louise went into the kitchen and argued about Dad...
And Dad?
He went into the front room and organised his bus models.
He stayed there all evening and was totally quiet ...
WILDTHYME
As if nothing had happened.

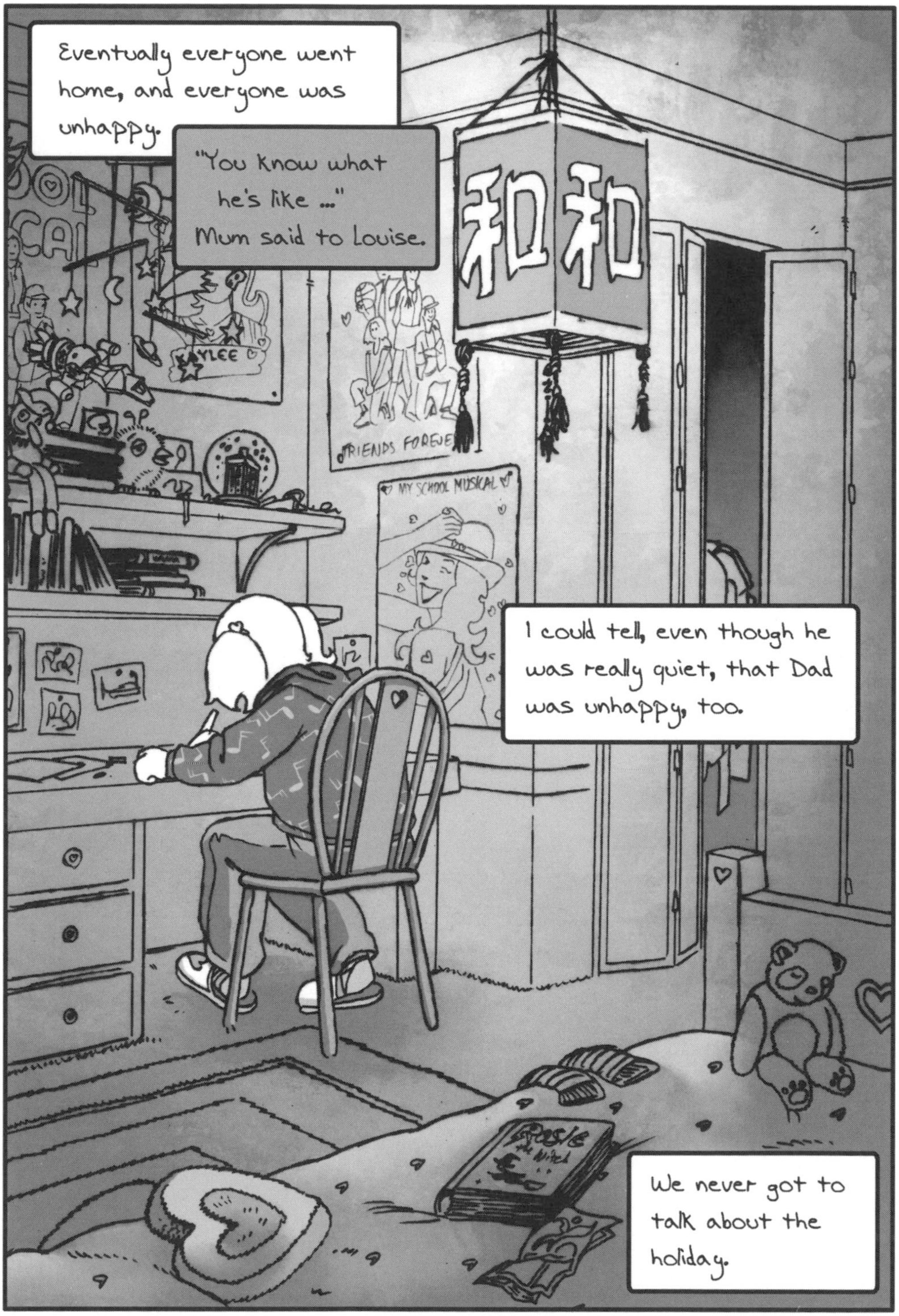
Eventually everyone went home, and everyone was unhappy.
"You know what he's like ..." Mum said to Louise.
和 和
FRIENDS FOREVER
MY SCHOOL MUSICAL
KAYLEE
I could tell, even though he was really quiet, that Dad was unhappy, too.
We never got to talk about the holiday.

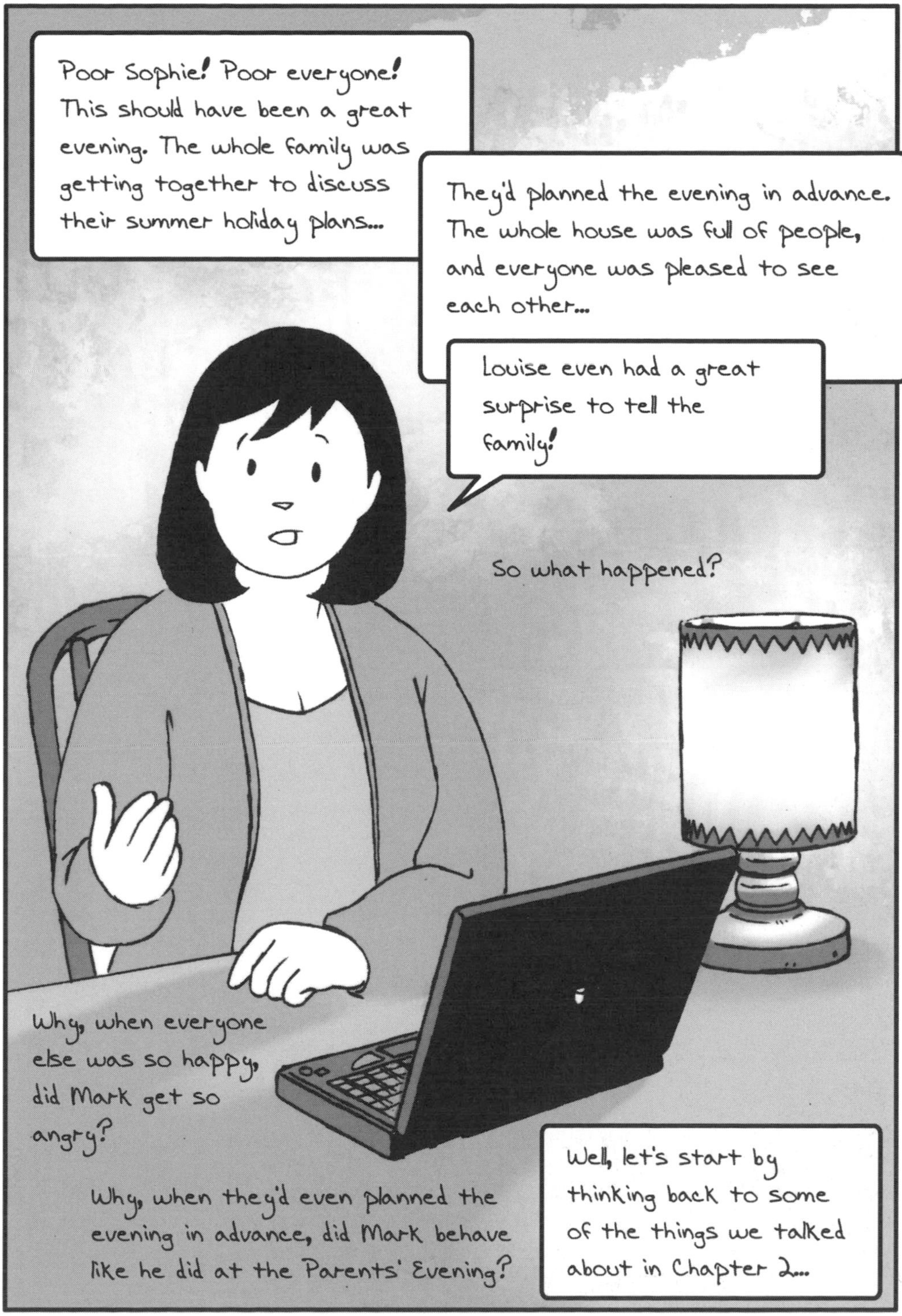
Poor Sophie! Poor everyone! This should have been a great evening. The whole family was getting together to discuss their summer holiday plans...
They'd planned the evening in advance. The whole house was full of people, and everyone was pleased to see each other...
Louise even had a great surprise to tell the family!
So what happened?
Why, when everyone else was so happy, did Mark get so angry?
Why, when they'd even planned the evening in advance, did Mark behave like he did at the Parents' Evening?
Well, let's start by thinking back to some of the things we talked about in Chapter 2...

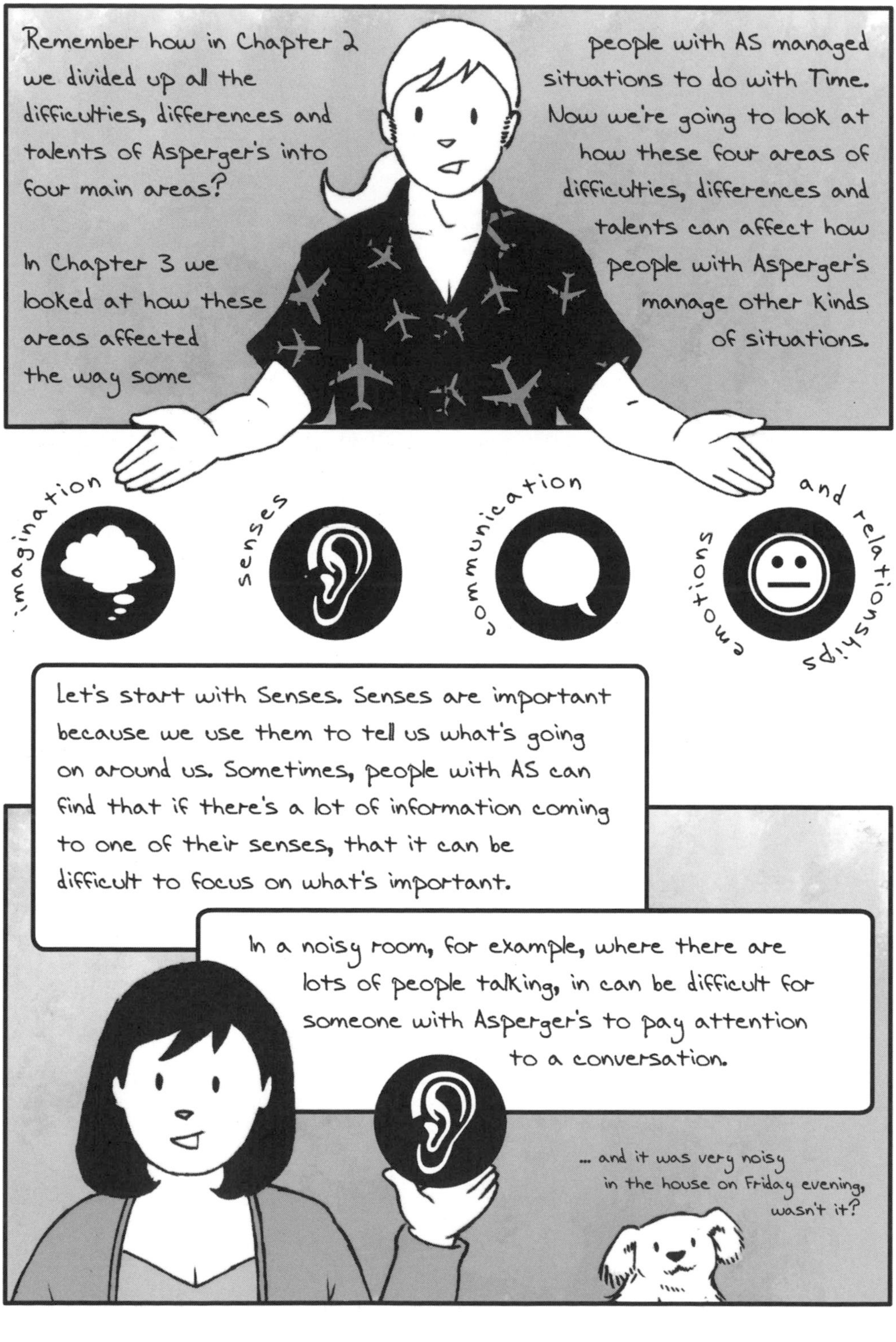
Remember how in Chapter 2 we divided up all the difficulties, differences and talents of Asperger's into four main areas?
In Chapter 3 we looked at how these areas affected the way some people with AS managed situations to do with Time.
Now we're going to look at how these four areas of difficulties, differences and talents can affect how people with Asperger's manage other kinds of situations.
imagination
senses
communication
emotions and relationships
Let's start with Senses. Senses are important because we use them to tell us what's going on around us. Sometimes, people with AS can find that if there's a lot of information coming to one of their senses, that it can be difficult to focus on what's important.
In a noisy room, for example, where there are lots of people talking, in can be difficult for someone with Asperger's to pay attention to a conversation.
... and it was very noisy in the house on Friday evening, wasn't it?

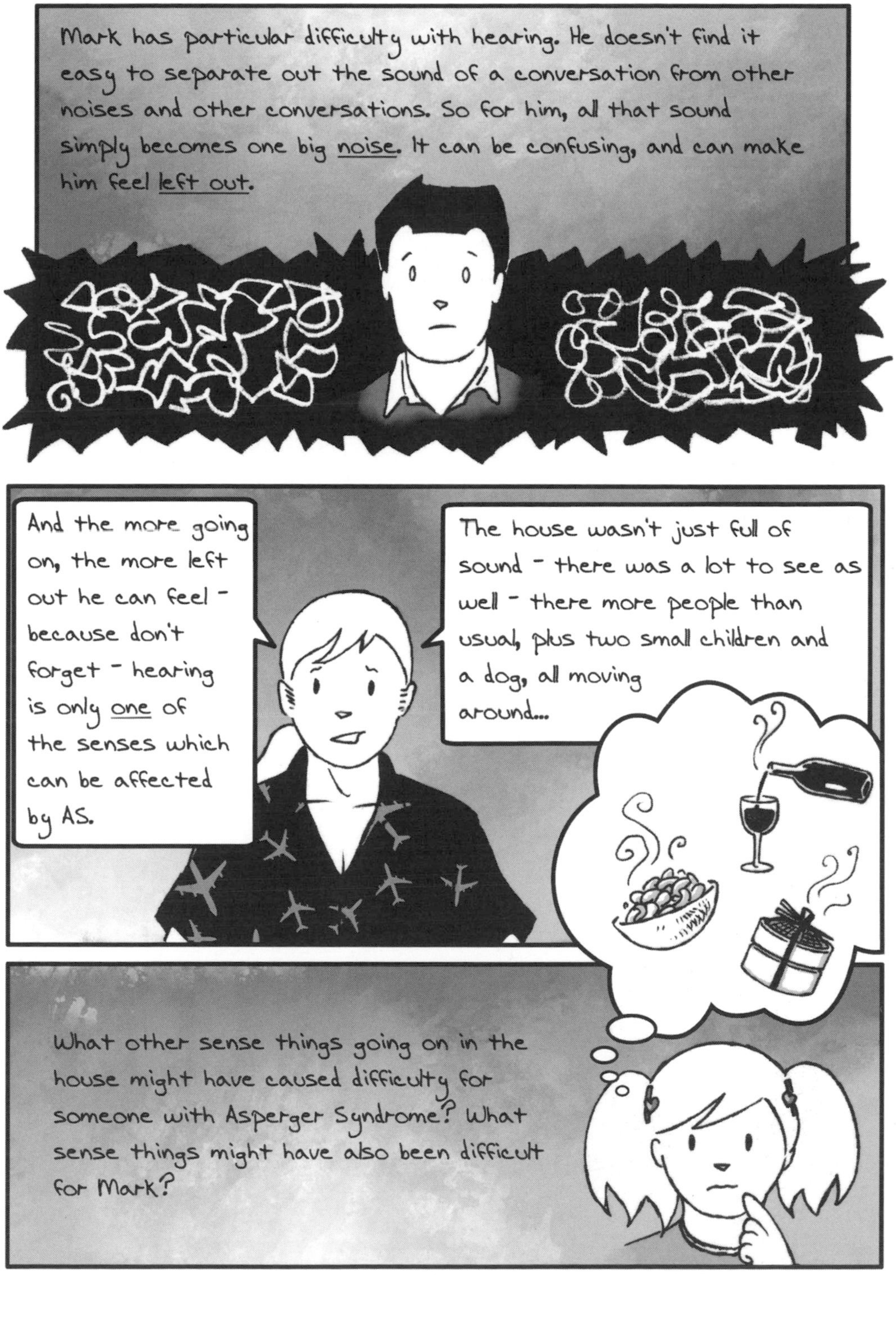
Mark has particular difficulty with hearing. He doesn't find it easy to separate out the sound of a conversation from other noises and other conversations. So for him, all that sound simply becomes one big noise. It can be confusing, and can make him feel left out.
And the more going on, the more left out he can feel - because don't forget - hearing is only one of the senses which can be affected by AS.
The house wasn't just full of sound - there was a lot to see as well - there more people than usual, plus two small children and a dog, all moving around...
What other sense things going on in the house might have caused difficulty for someone with Asperger Syndrome? What sense things might have also been difficult for Mark?

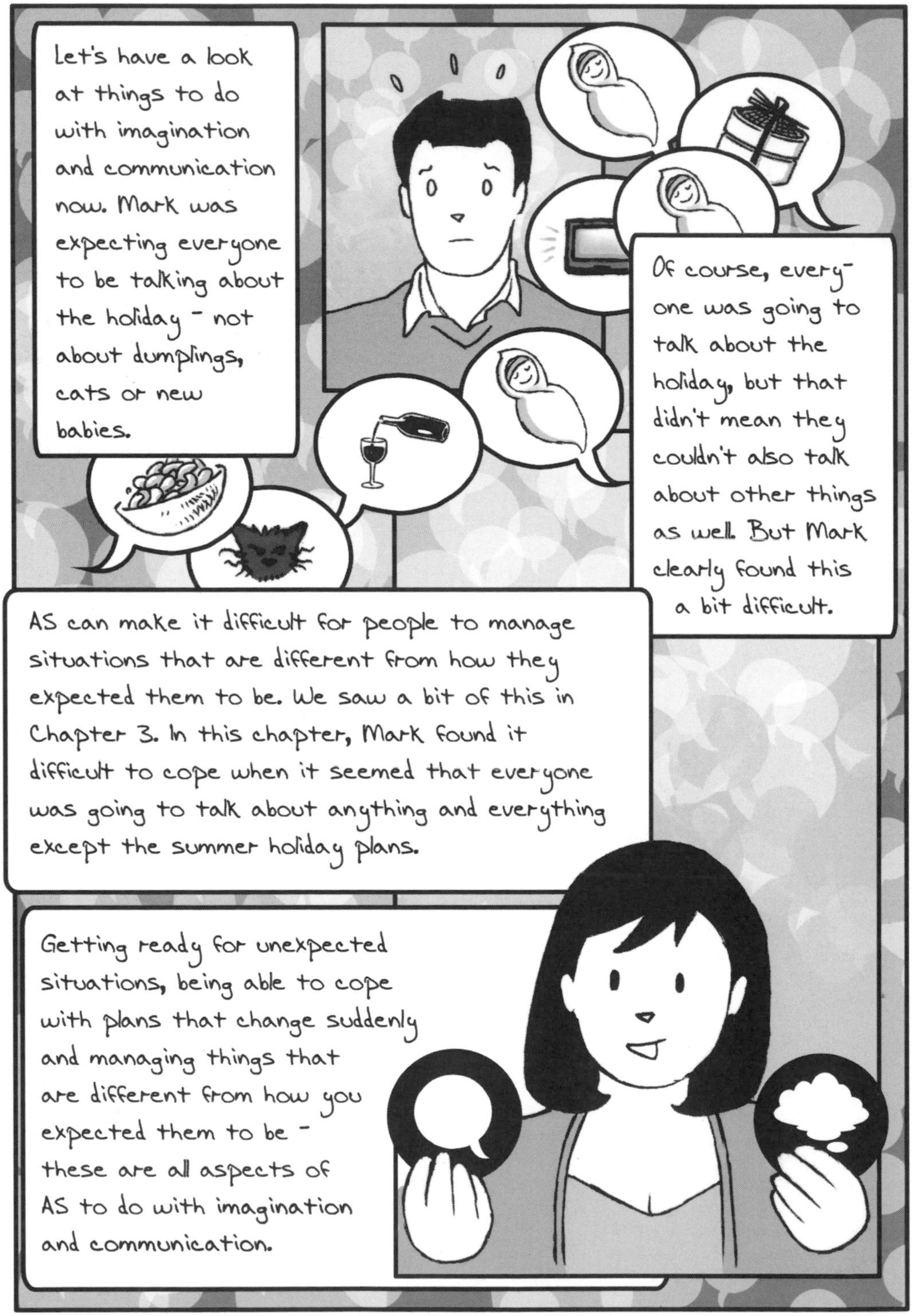
Let's have a look at things to do with imagination and communication now. Mark was expecting everyone to be talking about the holiday – not about dumplings, cats or new babies.
Of course, everyone was going to talk about the holiday, but that didn't mean they couldn't also talk about other things as well. But Mark clearly found this a bit difficult.
AS can make it difficult for people to manage situations that are different from how they expected them to be. We saw a bit of this in Chapter 3. In this chapter, Mark found it difficult to cope when it seemed that everyone was going to talk about anything and everything except the summer holiday plans.
Getting ready for unexpected situations, being able to cope with plans that change suddenly and managing things that are different from how you expected them to be – these are all aspects of AS to do with imagination and communication.

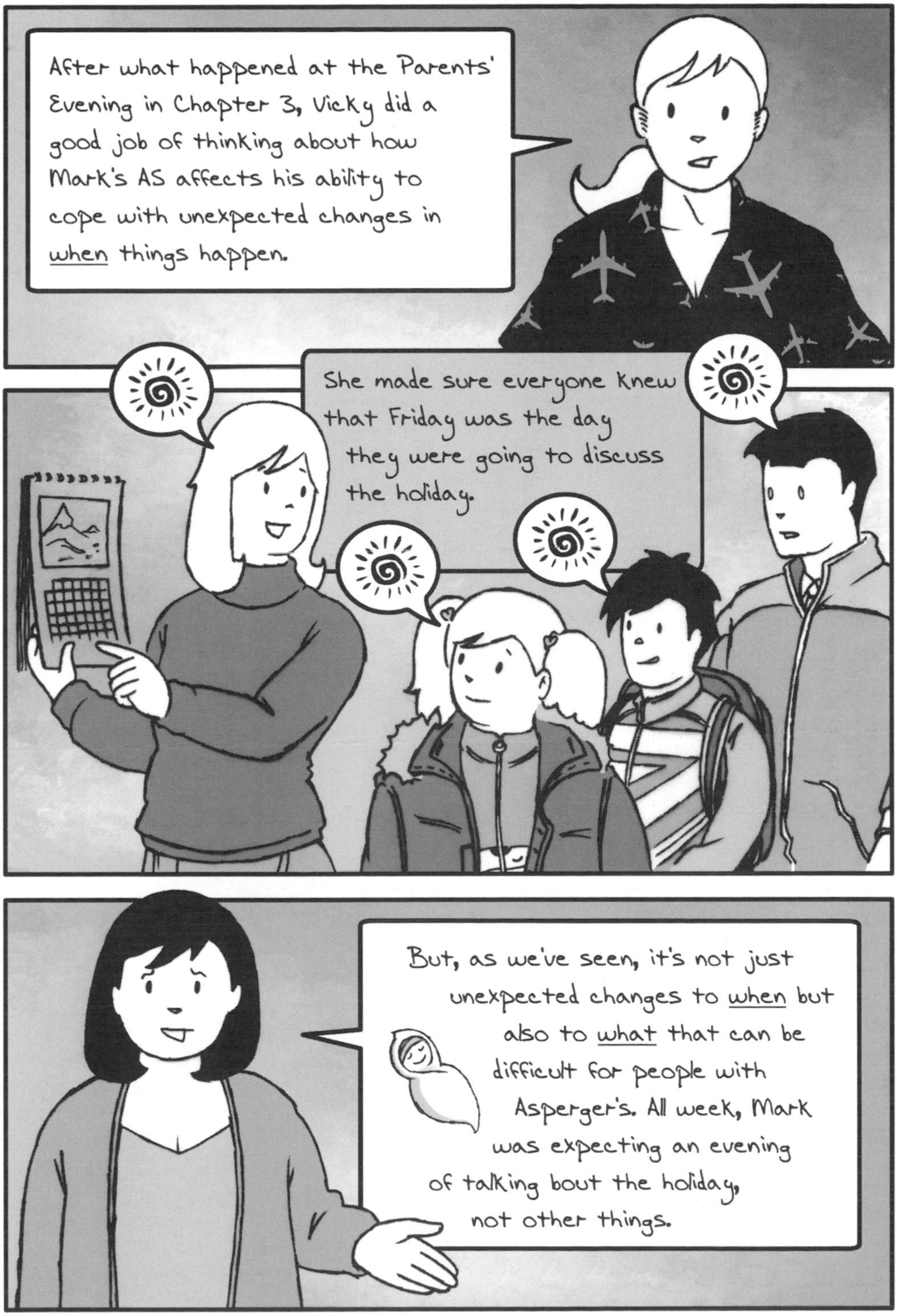
After what happened at the Parents' Evening in Chapter 3, Vicky did a good job of thinking about how Mark's AS affects his ability to cope with unexpected changes in when things happen.
She made sure everyone knew that Friday was the day they were going to discuss the holiday.
But, as we've seen, it's not just unexpected changes to when but also to what that can be difficult for people with Asperger's. All week, Mark was expecting an evening of talking bout the holiday, not other things.

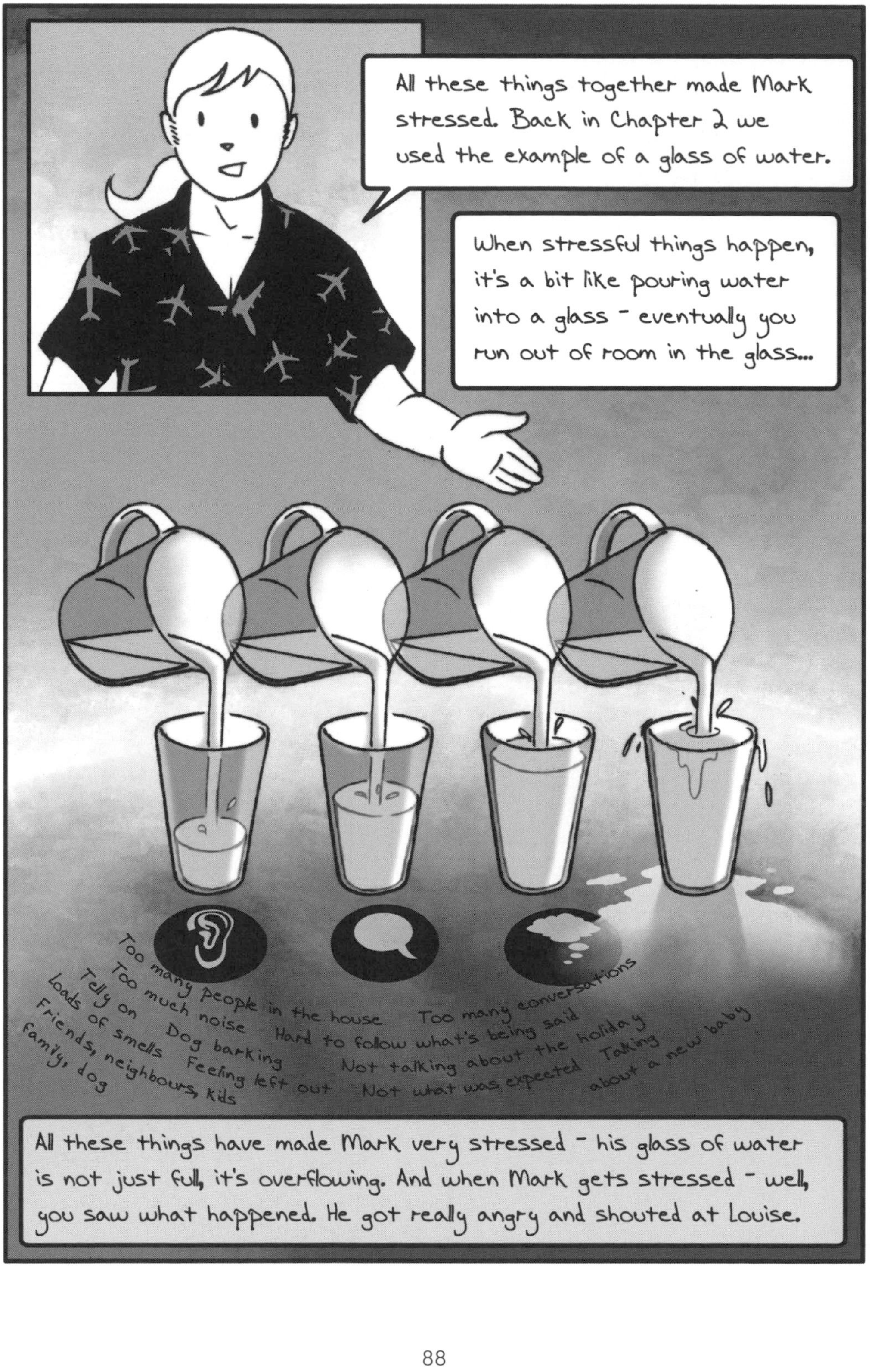
All these things together made Mark stressed. Back in Chapter 2 we used the example of a glass of water.
When stressful things happen, it's a bit like pouring water into a glass – eventually you run out of room in the glass...
Too many people in the house
Too much noise
Telly on
Loads of smells
Friends, neighbours, kids
family, dog
Dog barking
Feeling left out
Too many conversations
Hard to follow what's being said
Not talking about the holiday
Not what was expected
Talking about a new baby
All these things have made Mark very stressed – his glass of water is not just full, it's overflowing. And when Mark gets stressed – well, you saw what happened. He got really angry and shouted at Louise.

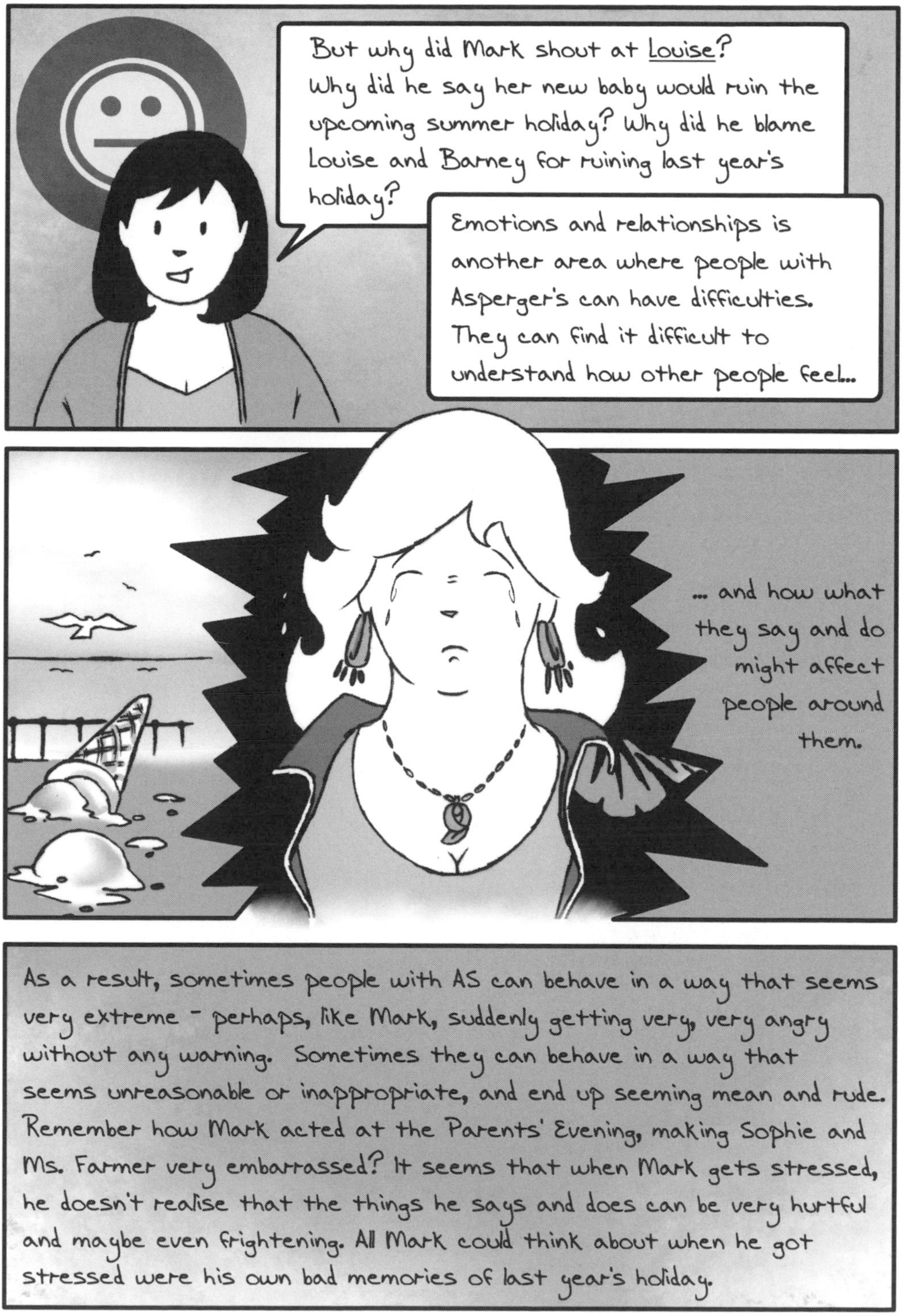
But why did Mark shout at Louise? Why did he say her new baby would ruin the upcoming summer holiday? Why did he blame Louise and Barney for ruining last year's holiday?
Emotions and relationships is another area where people with Asperger's can have difficulties. They can find it difficult to understand how other people feel...
... and how what they say and do might affect people around them.
As a result, sometimes people with AS can behave in a way that seems very extreme - perhaps, like Mark, suddenly getting very, very angry without any warning. Sometimes they can behave in a way that seems unreasonable or inappropriate, and end up seeming mean and rude. Remember how Mark acted at the Parents' Evening, making Sophie and Ms. Farmer very embarrassed? It seems that when Mark gets stressed, he doesn't realise that the things he says and does can be very hurtful and maybe even frightening. All Mark could think about when he got stressed were his own bad memories of last year's holiday.

Try and make sure that there's not too much happening at the same time. Turn off radios and televisions, for example, if it's important that people are able to hear and talk clearly. Keep the number of people down and maybe avoid cooking or serving food and drinks if there are important things that need to be discussed.

Now that we've had a look at what the problems were, let's look at some ways of making a situation like that evening work better for Mark and everyone.

A really easy way to make sure everyone in the family knows what's happening when is to use a big wall calendar. Pick one with enough space on it to write down what's happening on what days. Hang it where everyone can see it easily – in the front hall or the kitchen, perhaps.

DECEMBER

sun	mon	tue	wed	thur	fri	sat
		1	2	3	4	5	7
8	9	10	11	12	13	14
15	16	17	18	19	20	21
22	23	24	25	26	27	28
29	30	31				

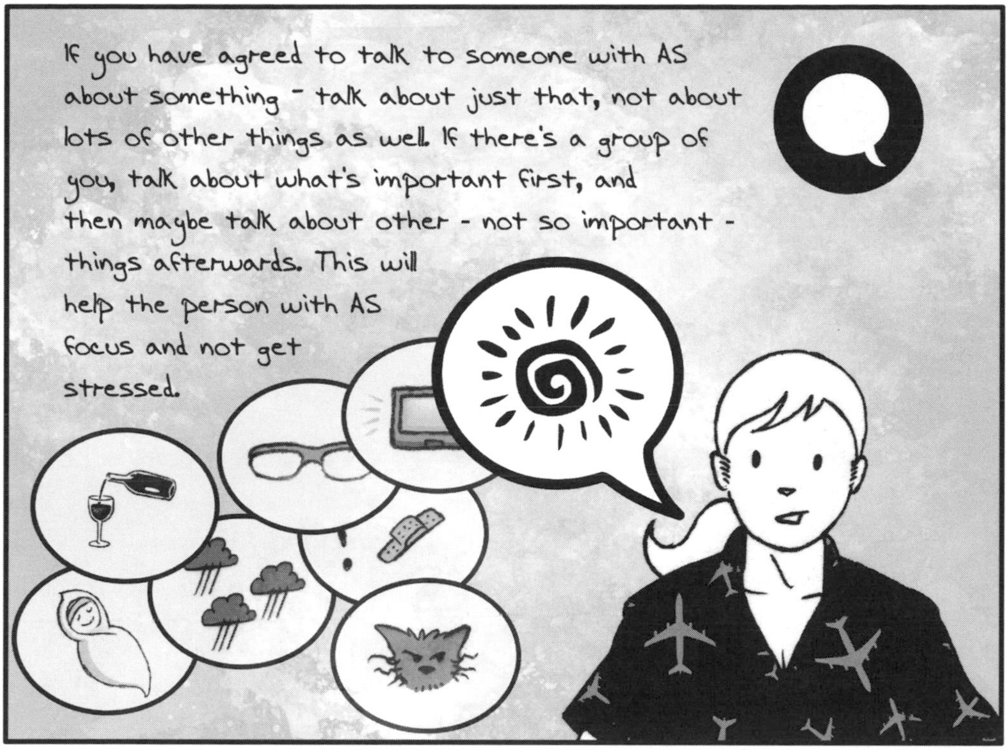
If you have agreed to talk to someone with AS about something – talk about just that, not about lots of other things as well. If there's a group of you, talk about what's important first, and then maybe talk about other - not so important - things afterwards. This will help the person with AS focus and not get stressed.

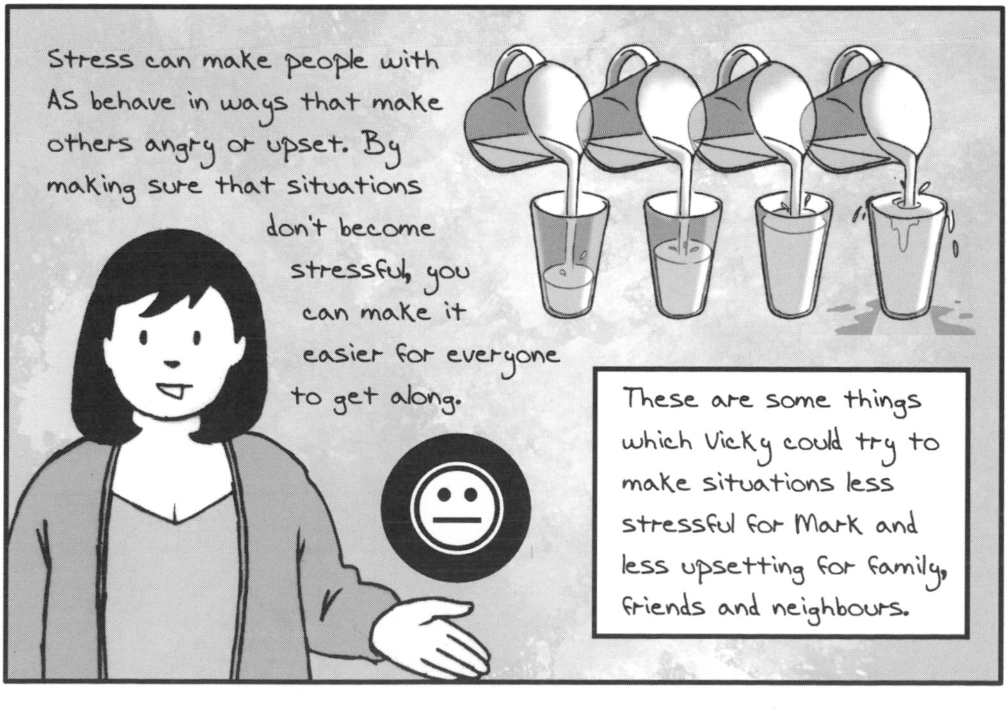
Stress can make people with AS behave in ways that make others angry or upset. By making sure that situations don't become stressful, you can make it easier for everyone to get along.
These are some things which Vicky could try to make situations less stressful for Mark and less upsetting for family, friends and neighbours.

I've been talking to Mark. He and I have decided that we need to work harder to make evenings like these better for him – and for everyone. We talked through the ideas and Mark was happy to try some of them out.
We're going to start with a big calendar on the wall in the kitchen. Mark thinks that will be really useful.
I also want to change the way we organise Friday evenings. We're a big family ...
It's not always possible to keep the house as calm and quiet as Mark would like.
I'd like to think of a way for us all to get to do the things we like to do –
– the way we like to do them. I think that's important for Sophie and Daniel.
And maybe when Mark's less stressed we can talk about the holiday ...

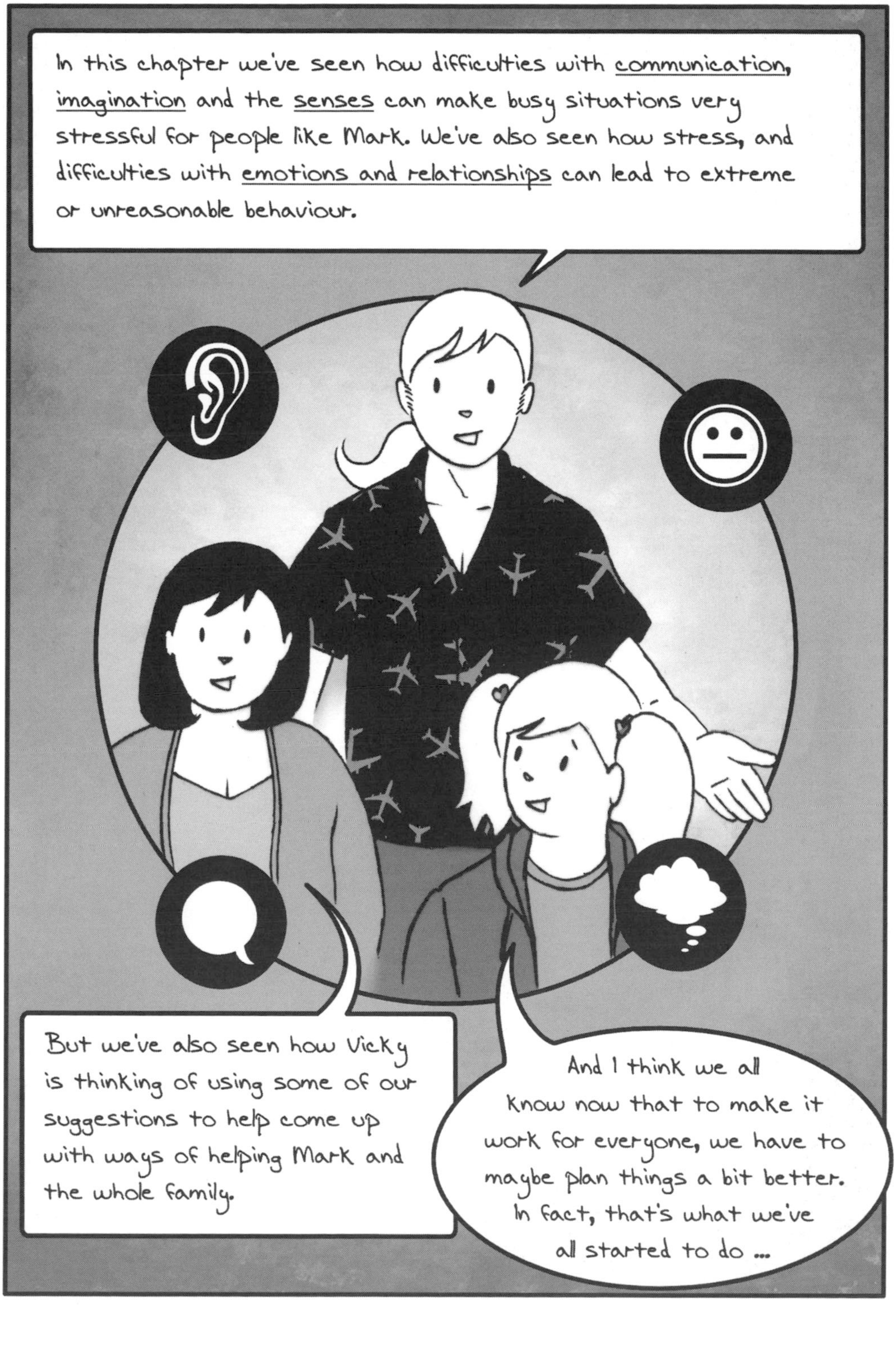
In this chapter we've seen how difficulties with communication, imagination and the senses can make busy situations very stressful for people like Mark. We've also seen how stress, and difficulties with emotions and relationships can lead to extreme or unreasonable behaviour.
But we've also seen how Vicky is thinking of using some of our suggestions to help come up with ways of helping Mark and the whole family.
And I think we all know now that to make it work for everyone, we have to maybe plan things a bit better. In fact, that's what we've all started to do ...

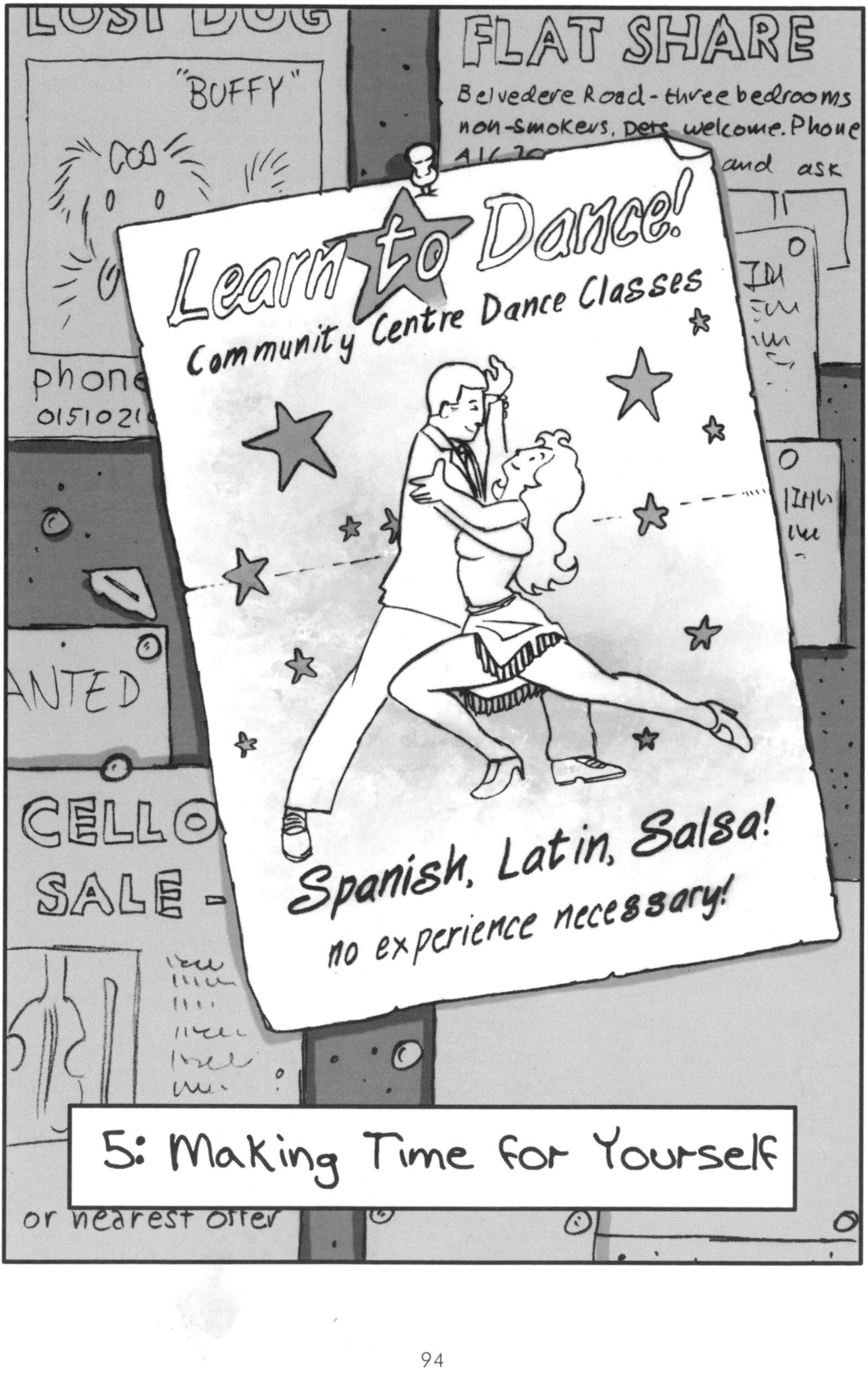
LOST DOG
"BUFFY"
phone
FLAT SHARE
Belvedere Road - three bedrooms
non-smokers, pets welcome. Phone
and ask
Learn to Dance!
Community Centre Dance Classes
Spanish, Latin, Salsa!
no experience necessary!
CELLO
SALE -
or nearest offer
5: Making Time for Yourself

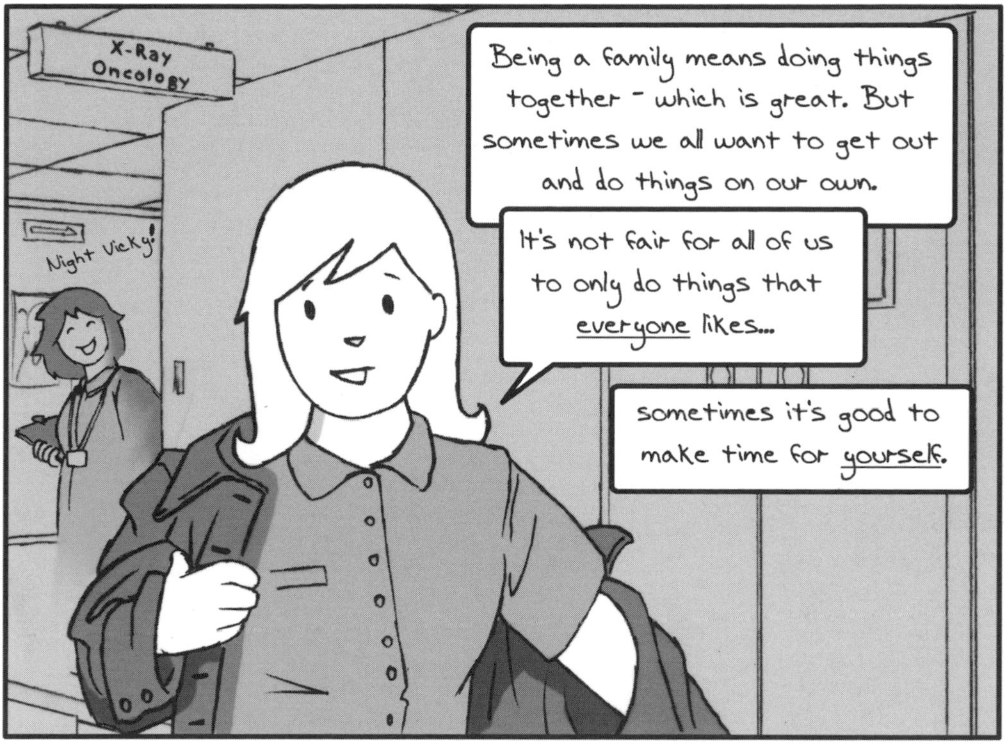
X-Ray
Oncology
Night Vicky!
Being a family means doing things together - which is great. But sometimes we all want to get out and do things on our own.
It's not fair for all of us to only do things that everyone likes...
sometimes it's good to make time for yourself.

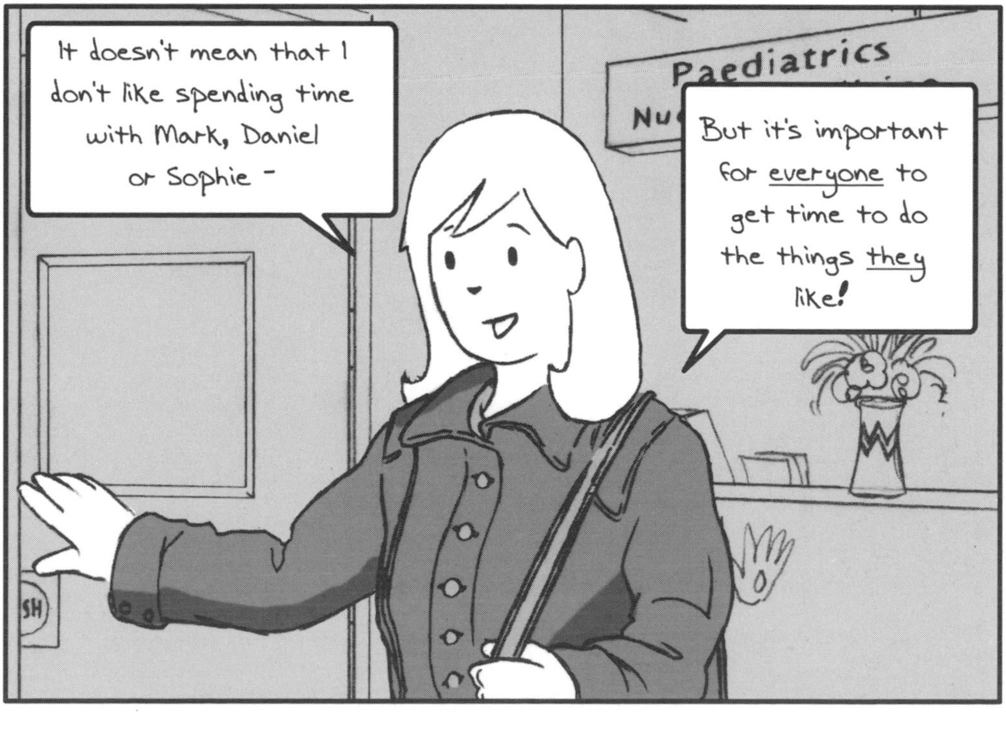
Paediatrics
It doesn't mean that I don't like spending time with Mark, Daniel or Sophie -
But it's important for everyone to get time to do the things they like!

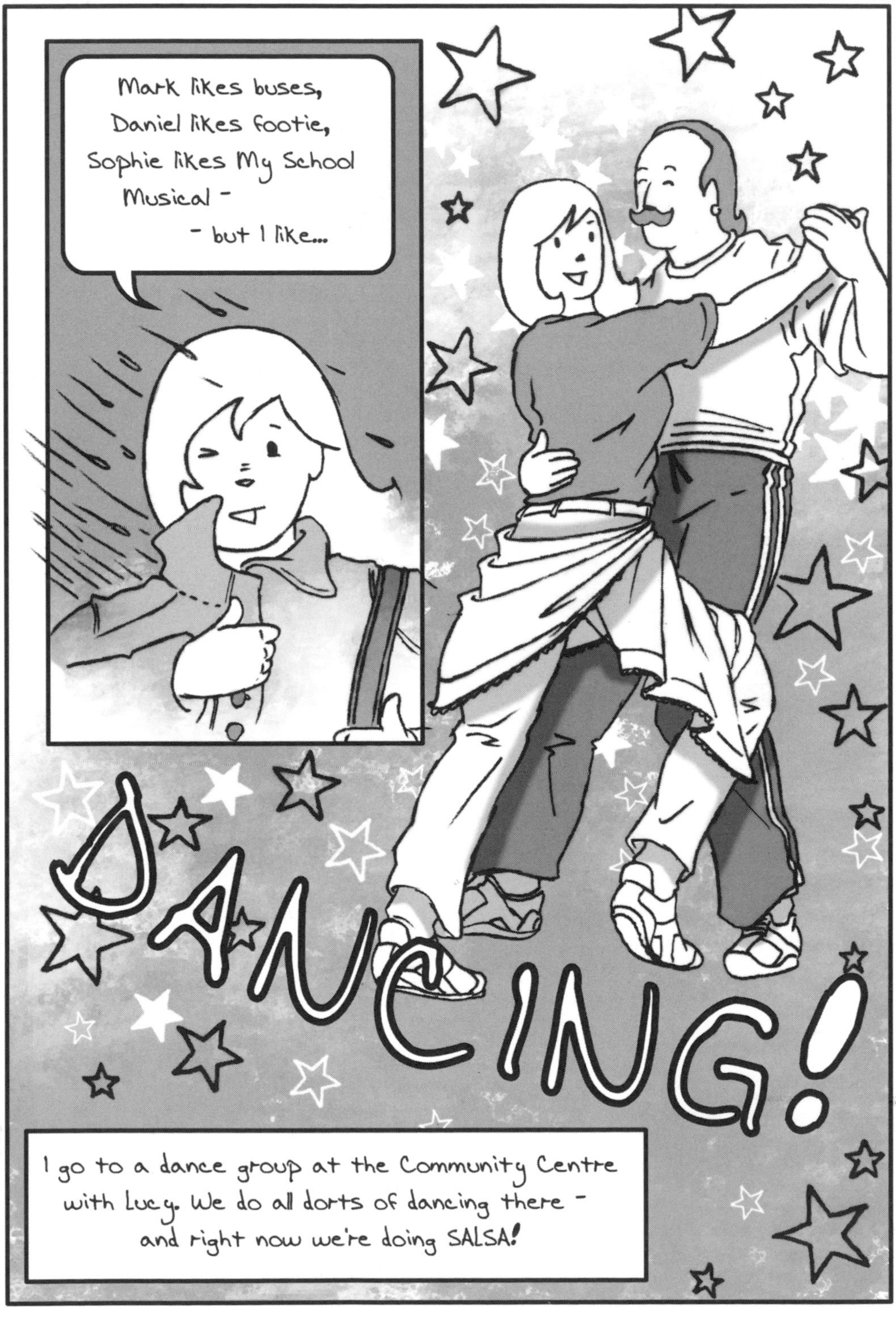
Mark likes buses, Daniel likes footie, Sophie likes My School Musical -
- but I like...
DANCING!
I go to a dance group at the Community Centre with Lucy. We do all dorts of dancing there - and right now we're doing SALSA!

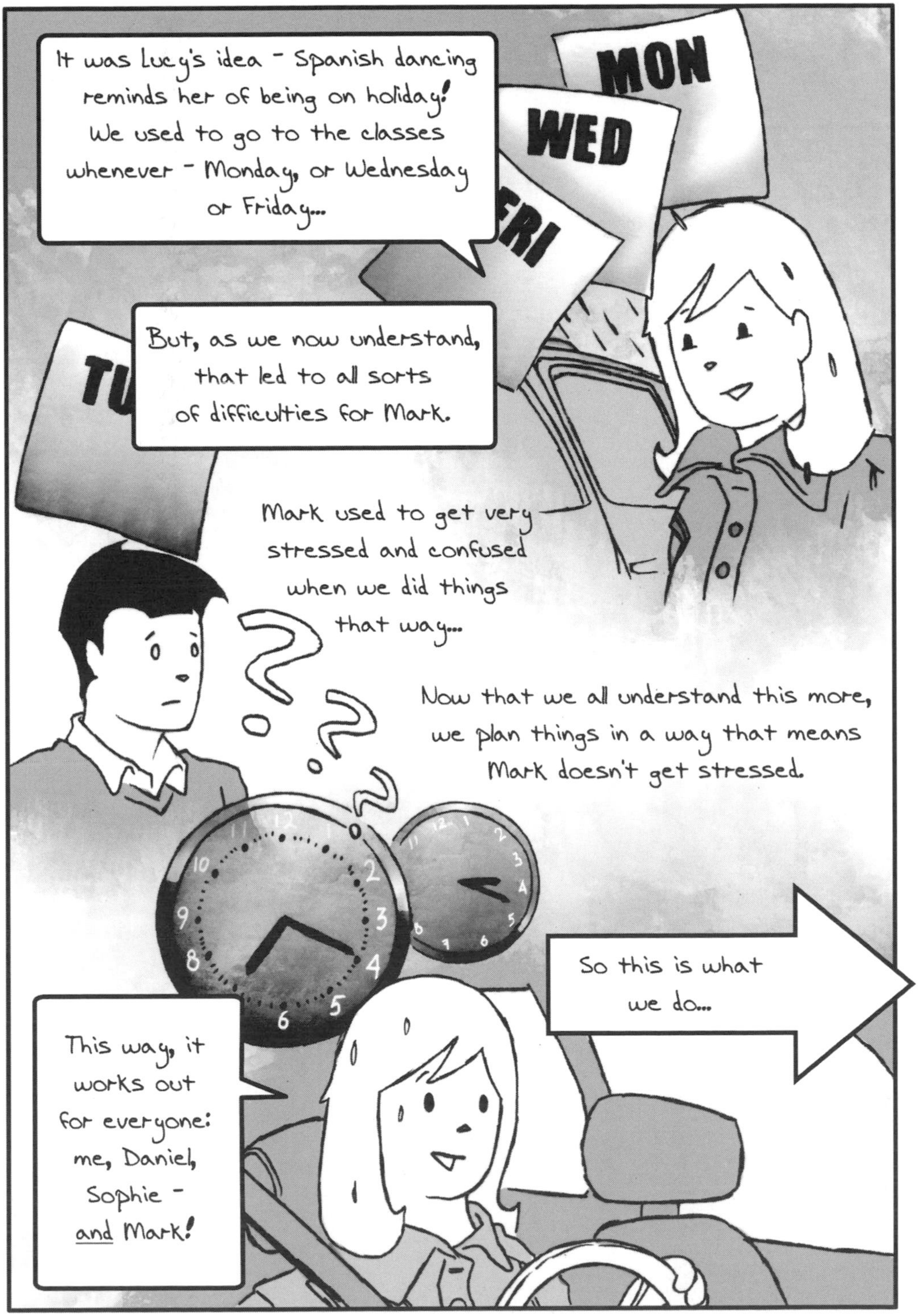
It was Lucy's idea - Spanish dancing reminds her of being on holiday! We used to go to the classes whenever - Monday, or Wednesday or Friday...
MON
WED
FRI
TU
But, as we now understand, that led to all sorts of difficulties for Mark.
Mark used to get very stressed and confused when we did things that way...
Now that we all understand this more, we plan things in a way that means Mark doesn't get stressed.
So this is what we do...
This way, it works out for everyone: me, Daniel, Sophie - and Mark!

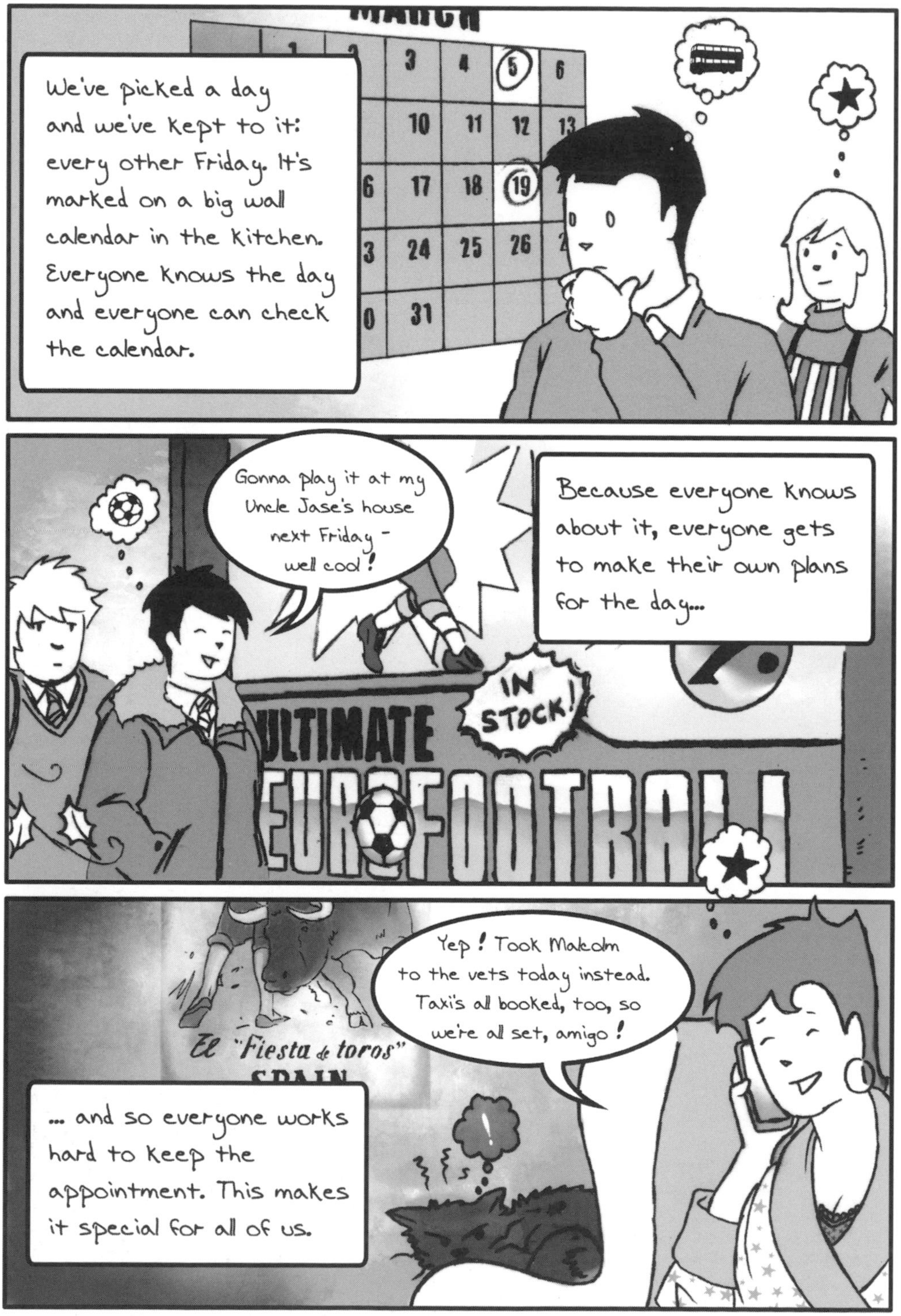
We've picked a day and we've kept to it: every other Friday. It's marked on a big wall calendar in the kitchen. Everyone knows the day and everyone can check the calendar.
Gonna play it at my Uncle Jase's house next Friday - well cool!
Because everyone knows about it, everyone gets to make their own plans for the day...
IN STOCK!
ULTIMATE
Yep! Took Malcolm to the vets today instead. Taxi's all booked, too, so we're all set, amigo!
El "Fiesta de toros"
... and so everyone works hard to keep the appointment. This makes it special for all of us.

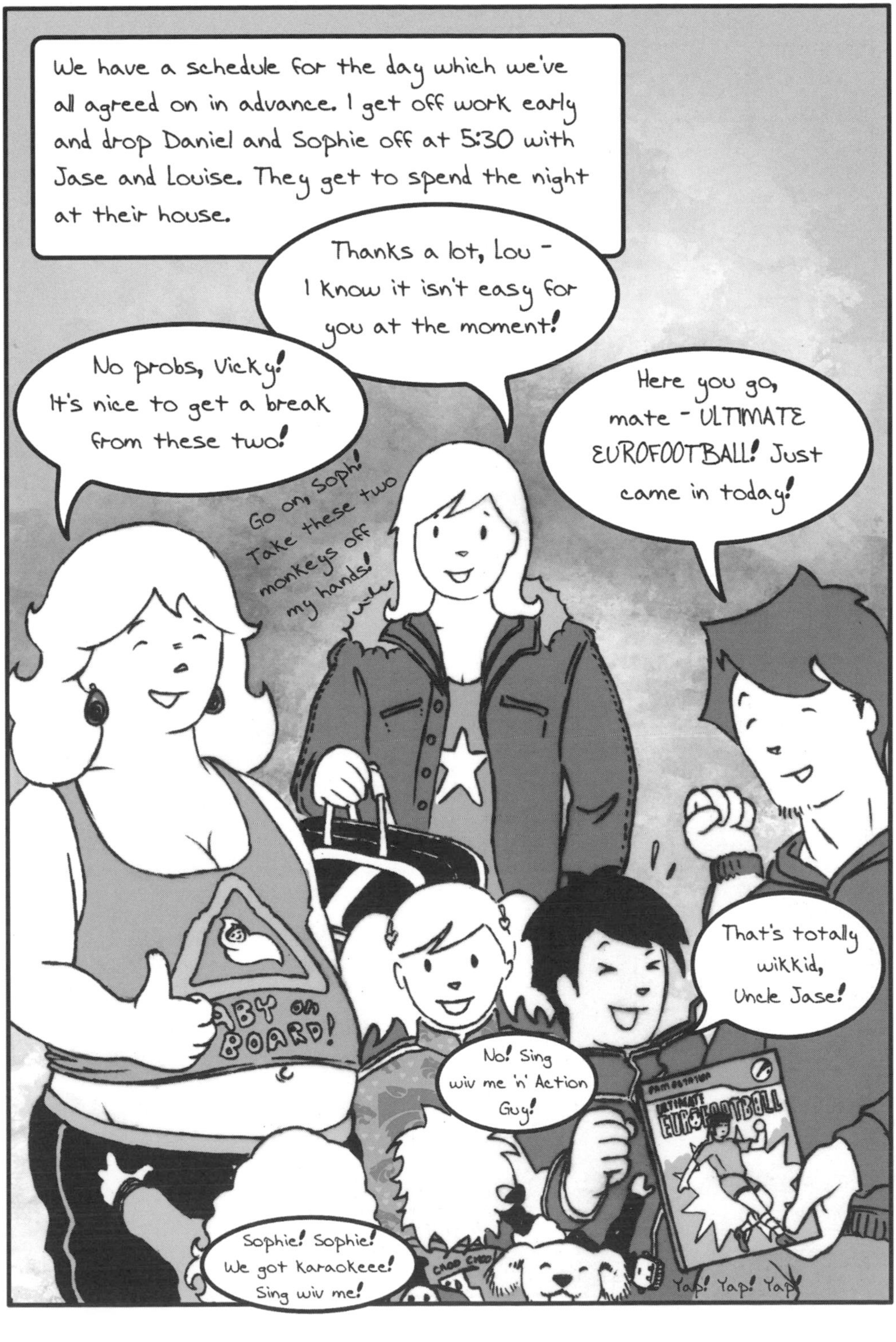
We have a schedule for the day which we've all agreed on in advance. I get off work early and drop Daniel and Sophie off at 5:30 with Jase and Louise. They get to spend the night at their house.
Thanks a lot, Lou - I know it isn't easy for you at the moment!
No probs, Vicky! It's nice to get a break from these two!
Here you go, mate - ULTIMATE EUROFOOTBALL! Just came in today!
Go on, Soph! Take these two monkeys off my hands!
BABY on BOARD!
That's totally wikkid, Uncle Jase!
No! Sing wiv me 'n' Action Guy!
Sophie! Sophie! We got Karaokeee! Sing wiv me!
Yap! Yap! Yap!

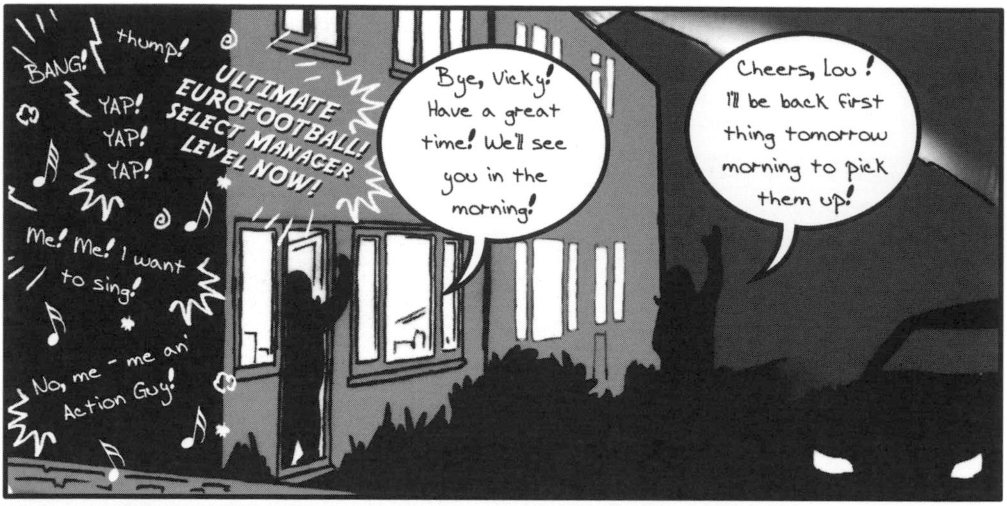
thump!
BANG!
ULTIMATE EUROFOOTBALL! SELECT MANAGER LEVEL NOW!
YAP!
YAP!
YAP!
Me! Me! I want to sing!
No, me - me an' Action Guy!
Bye, Vicky! Have a great time! We'll see you in the morning!
Cheers, Lou! I'll be back first thing tomorrow morning to pick them up!

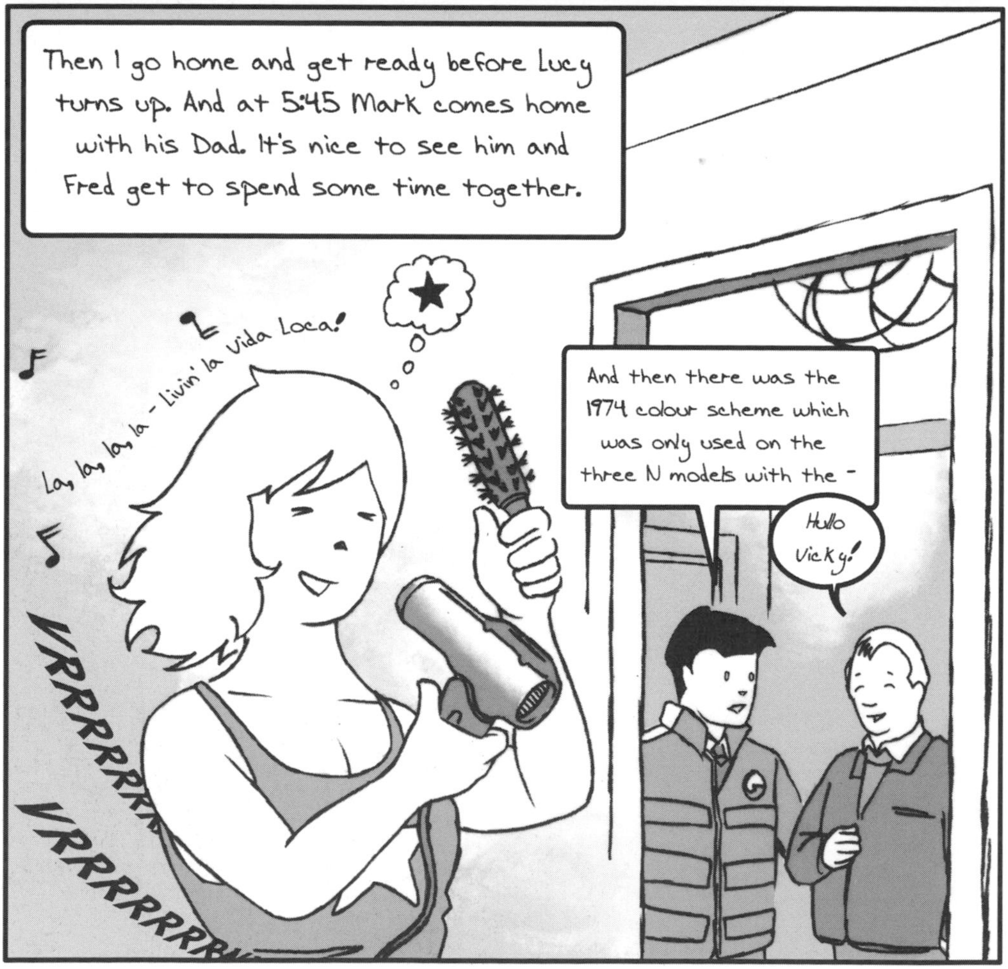
Then I go home and get ready before Lucy turns up. And at 5:45 Mark comes home with his Dad. It's nice to see him and Fred get to spend some time together.
La, la, la, la - Livin' la Vida Loca!
VRRRRRRR
VRRRRRRRR
And then there was the 1974 colour scheme which was only used on the three N models with the -
Hullo Vicky!

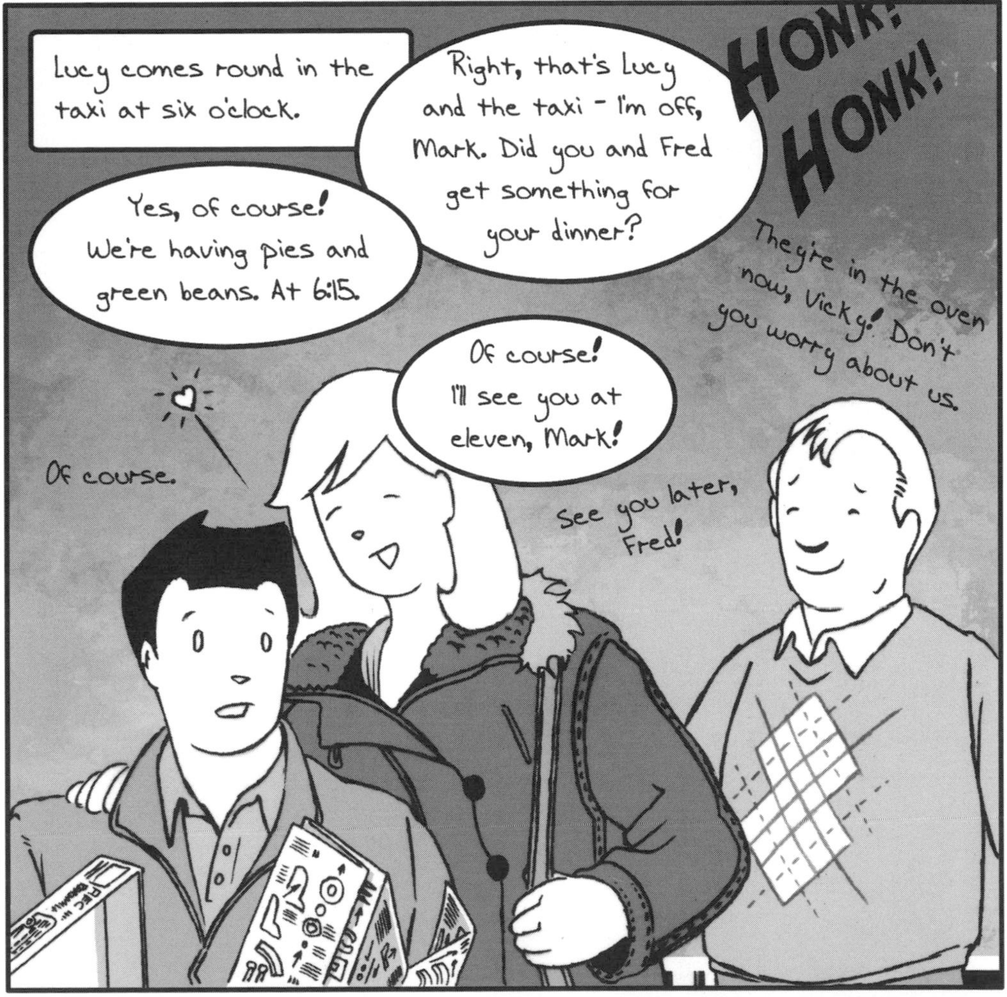
Lucy comes round in the taxi at six o'clock.
Right, that's Lucy and the taxi – I'm off, Mark. Did you and Fred get something for your dinner?
Yes, of course! We're having pies and green beans. At 6:15.
HONK! HONK!
They're in the oven now, Vicky! Don't you worry about us.
Of course! I'll see you at eleven, Mark!
Of course.
See you later, Fred!

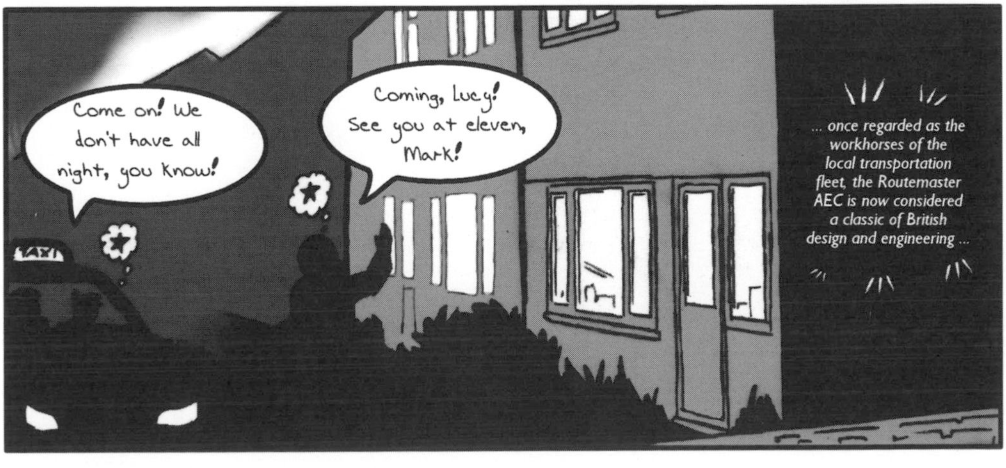
Come on! We don't have all night, you know!
Coming, Lucy! See you at eleven, Mark!
... once regarded as the workhorses of the local transportation fleet, the Routemaster AEC is now considered a classic of British design and engineering ...

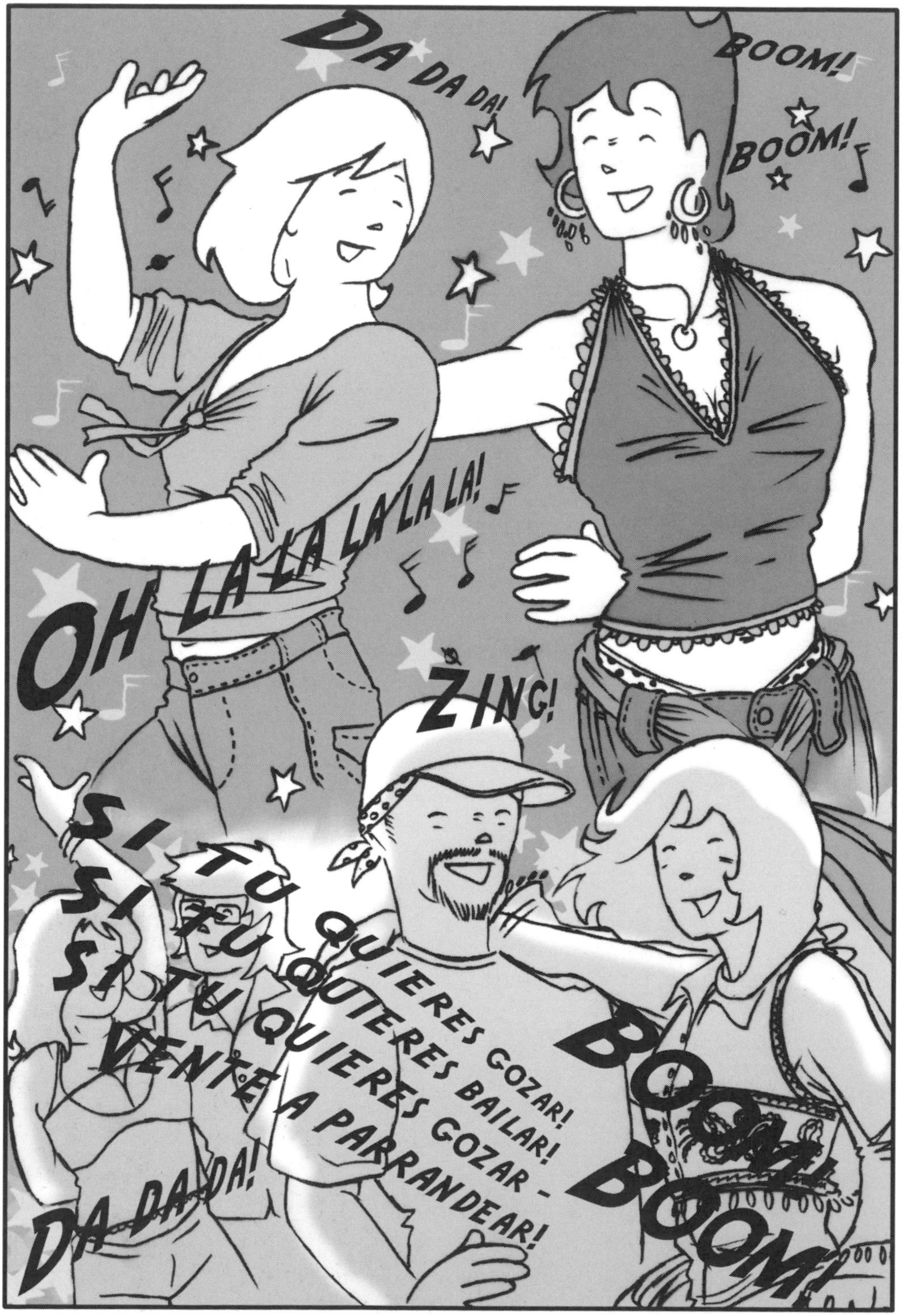
DA DA DA!
BOOM!
BOOM!
OH LA LA LA LA LA!
ZING!
SI TU QUIERES GOZAR!
SI TU QUIERES BAILAR!
SI TU QUIERES GOZAR -
VENTE A PARRANDEAR!
DA DA DA!
BOOM! BOOM!
BOOM!

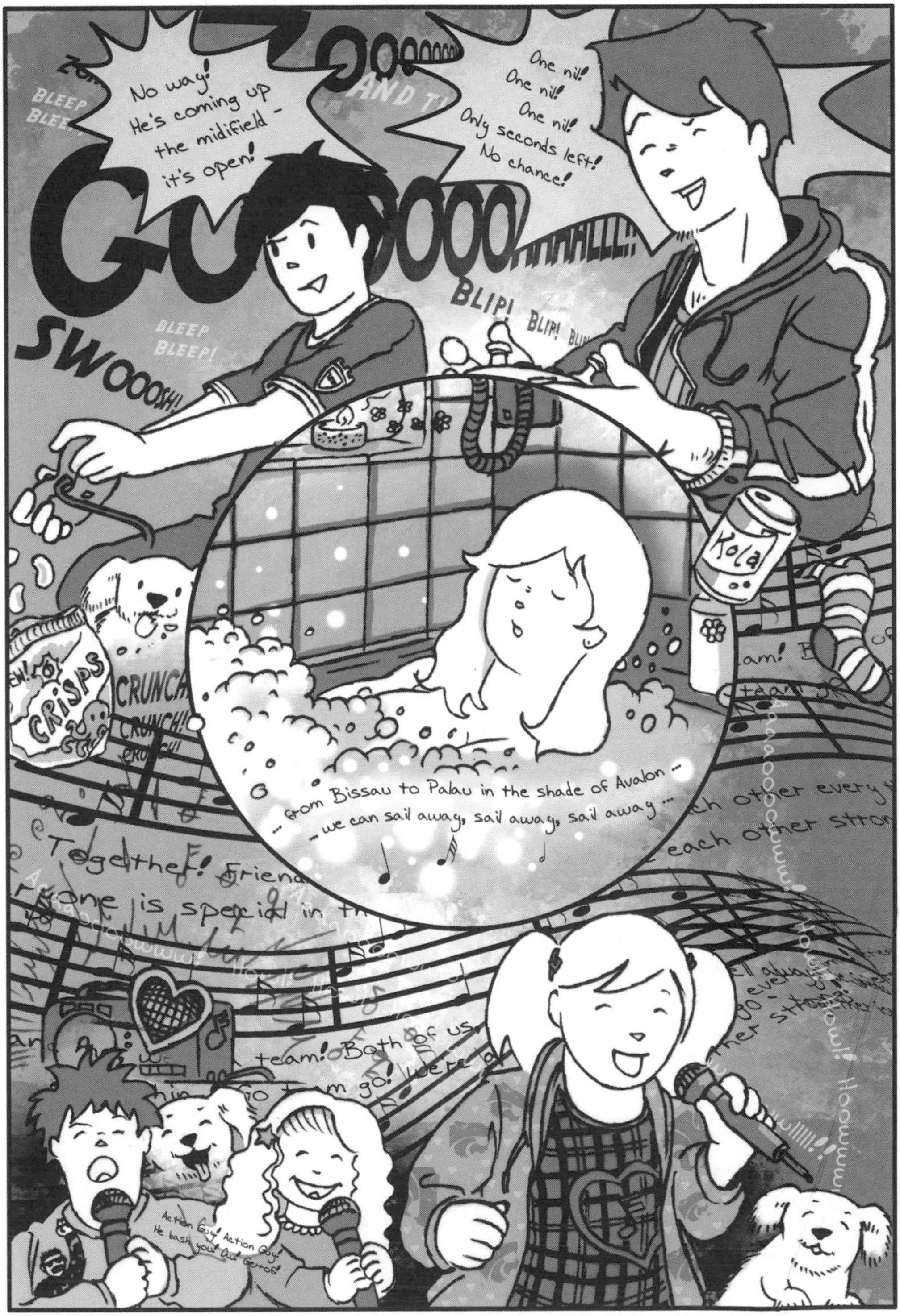
No way! He's coming up the midfield – it's open!
One nil! One nil! One nil! Only seconds left! No chance!
BLEEP BLEEP
BLEEP BLEEP!
SWOOOSH!
BLIP! BLIP!
Kola
CRISPS
... from Bissau to Palau in the shade of Avalon ...
... we can sail away, sail away, sail away ...
Together! Friend
team! Both of us
Action Guy! Action Guy! He bash you! Ou! Gerroff!

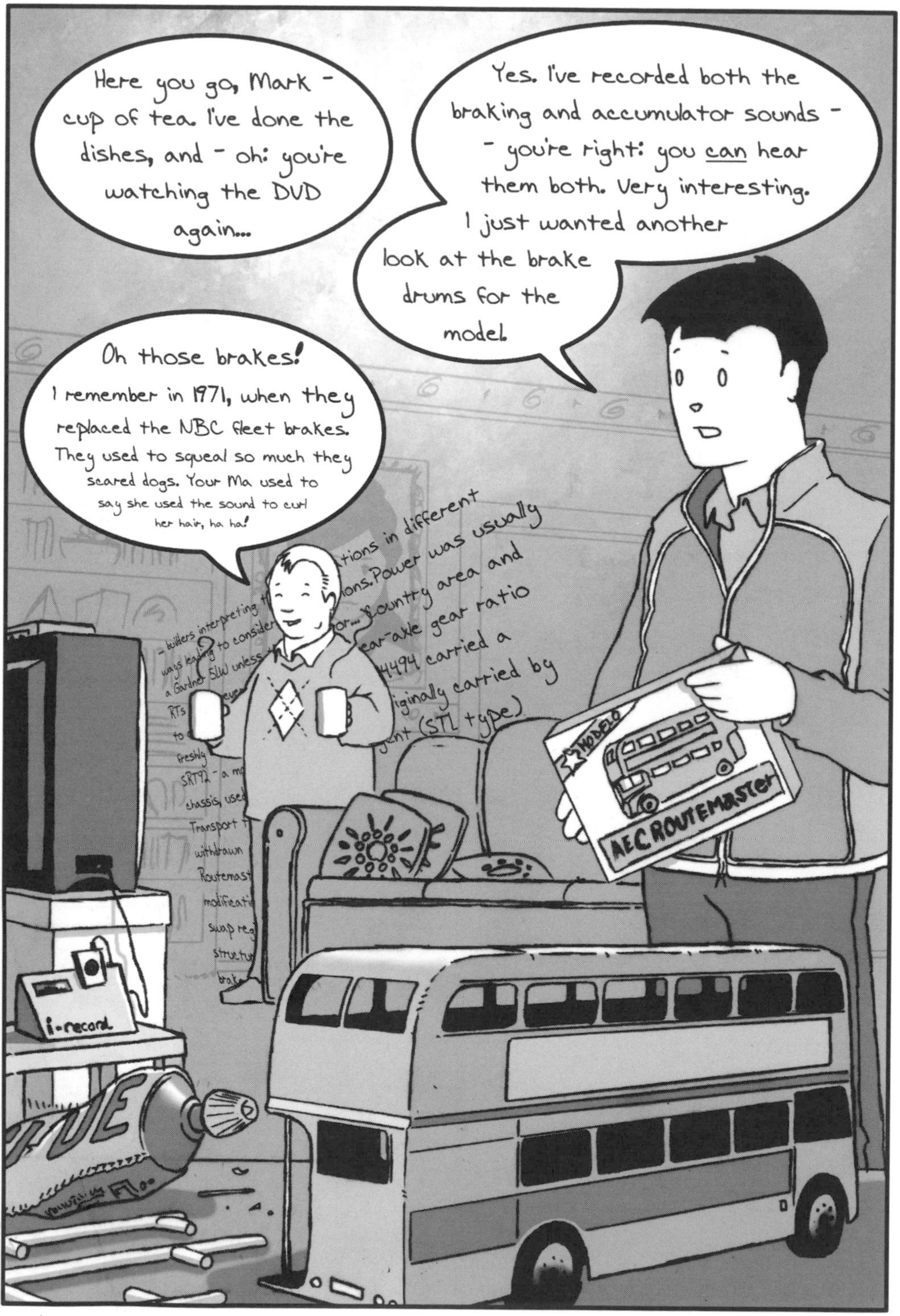
Here you go, Mark - cup of tea. I've done the dishes, and - oh: you're watching the DVD again...
Yes. I've recorded both the braking and accumulator sounds - - you're right: you can hear them both. Very interesting. I just wanted another look at the brake drums for the model.
Oh those brakes! I remember in 1971, when they replaced the NBC fleet brakes. They used to squeal so much they scared dogs. Your Ma used to say she used the sound to curl her hair, ha ha!
MODELO
AEC ROUTEMASTER
i-record

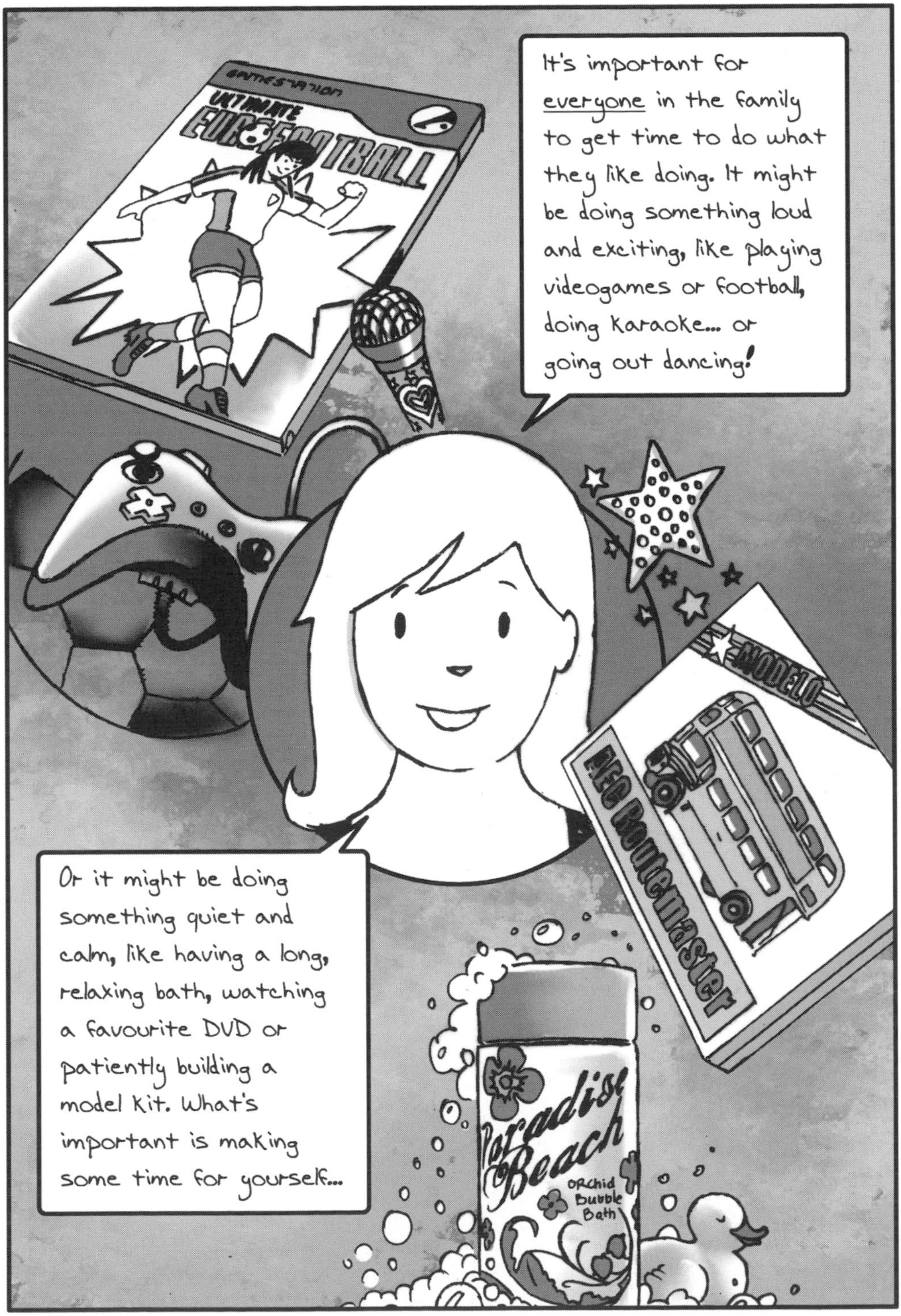

It's important for everyone in the family to get time to do what they like doing. It might be doing something loud and exciting, like playing videogames or football, doing karaoke... or going out dancing!
ULTIMATE EURO FOOTBALL
MODELO
Or it might be doing something quiet and calm, like having a long, relaxing bath, watching a favourite DVD or patiently building a model kit. What's important is making some time for yourself...
Paradise Beach
ORchid Bubble Bath

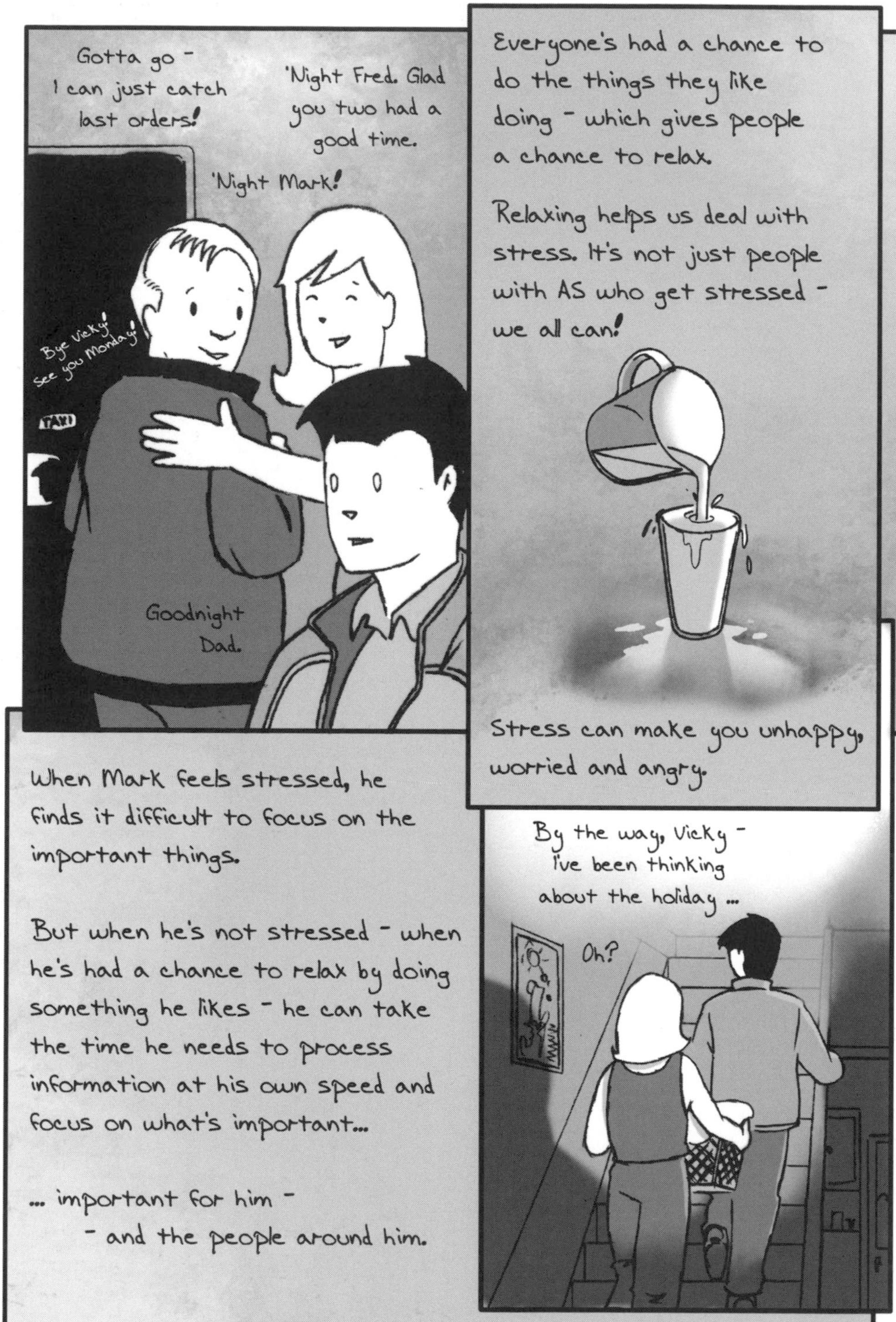
Gotta go - I can just catch last orders!
'Night Fred. Glad you two had a good time.
'Night Mark!
Bye Vicky! See you Monday!
TAXI
Goodnight Dad.
Everyone's had a chance to do the things they like doing - which gives people a chance to relax.
Relaxing helps us deal with stress. It's not just people with AS who get stressed - we all can!
Stress can make you unhappy, worried and angry.
When Mark feels stressed, he finds it difficult to focus on the important things.
But when he's not stressed - when he's had a chance to relax by doing something he likes - he can take the time he needs to process information at his own speed and focus on what's important...
... important for him -
- and the people around him.
By the way, Vicky - I've been thinking about the holiday ...
Oh?

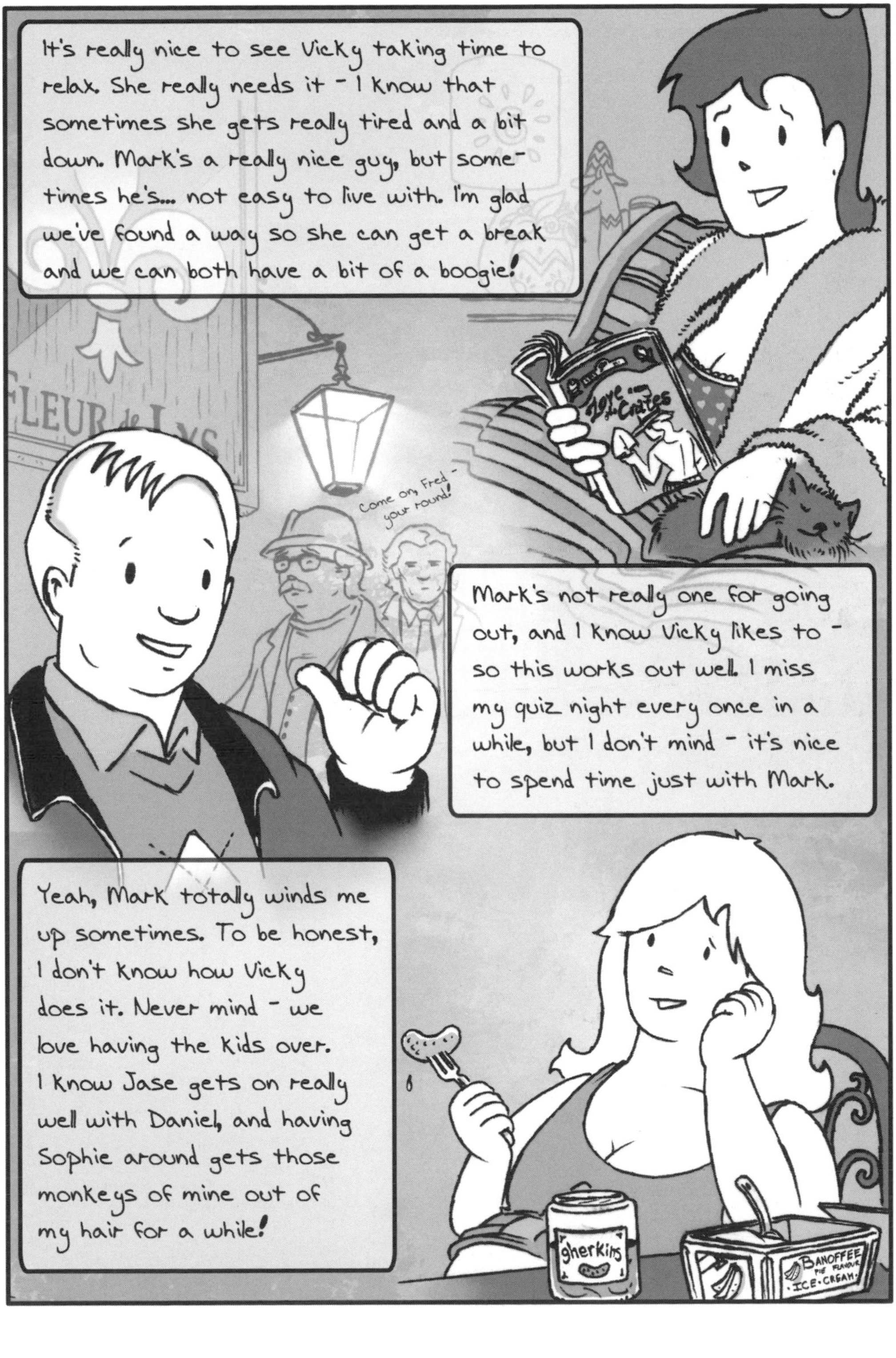
It's really nice to see Vicky taking time to relax. She really needs it - I know that sometimes she gets really tired and a bit down. Mark's a really nice guy, but sometimes he's... not easy to live with. I'm glad we've found a way so she can get a break and we can both have a bit of a boogie!
Come on, Fred - your round!
Mark's not really one for going out, and I know Vicky likes to - so this works out well. I miss my quiz night every once in a while, but I don't mind - it's nice to spend time just with Mark.
Yeah, Mark totally winds me up sometimes. To be honest, I don't know how Vicky does it. Never mind - we love having the kids over. I know Jase gets on really well with Daniel, and having Sophie around gets those monkeys of mine out of my hair for a while!
gherkins
BANOFFEE PIE FLAVOUR ICE-CREAM

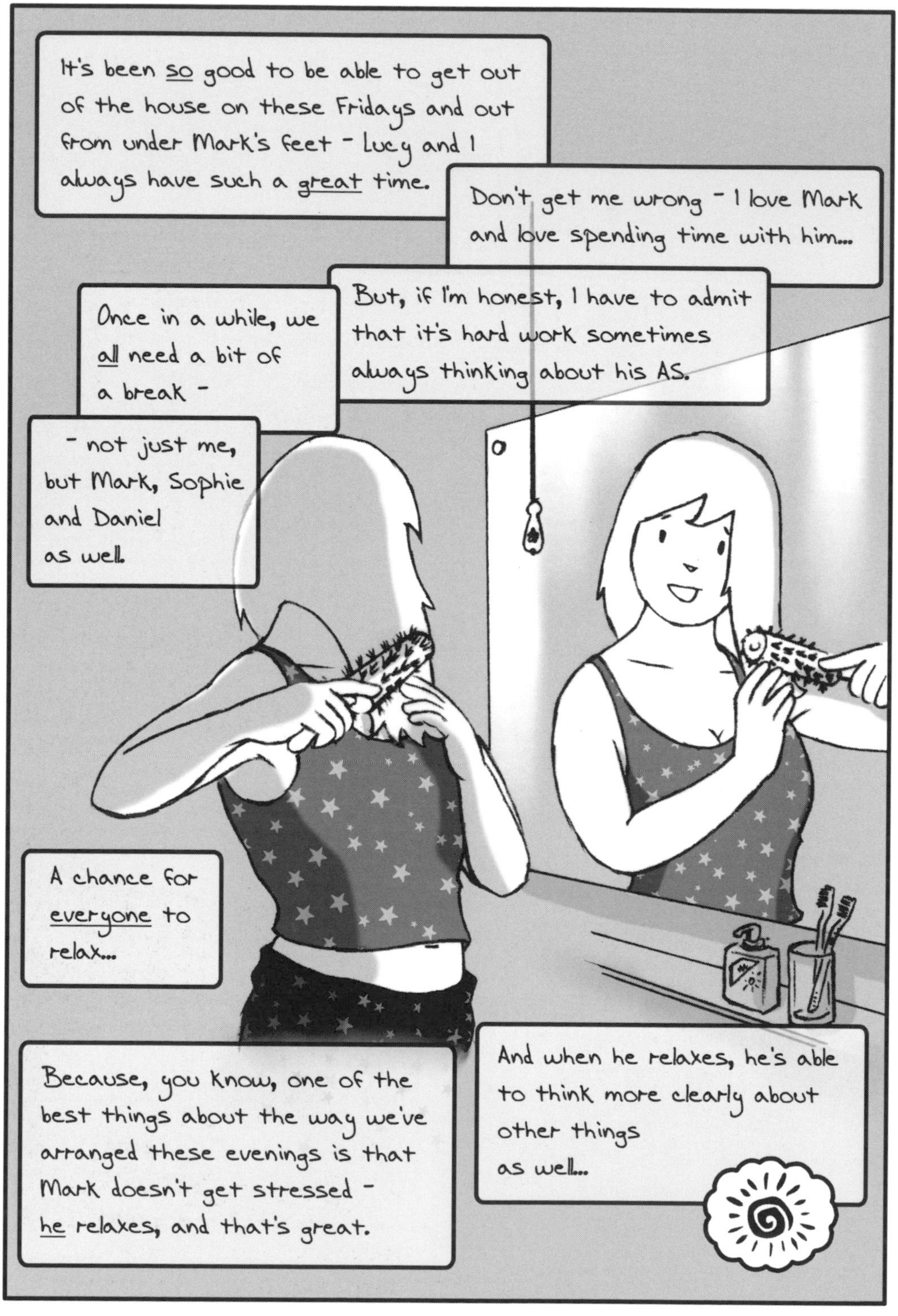
It's been so good to be able to get out of the house on these Fridays and out from under Mark's feet – Lucy and I always have such a great time.
Don't get me wrong – I love Mark and love spending time with him...
But, if I'm honest, I have to admit that it's hard work sometimes always thinking about his AS.
Once in a while, we all need a bit of a break –
– not just me, but Mark, Sophie and Daniel as well.
A chance for everyone to relax...
Because, you know, one of the best things about the way we've arranged these evenings is that Mark doesn't get stressed – he relaxes, and that's great.
And when he relaxes, he's able to think more clearly about other things as well...

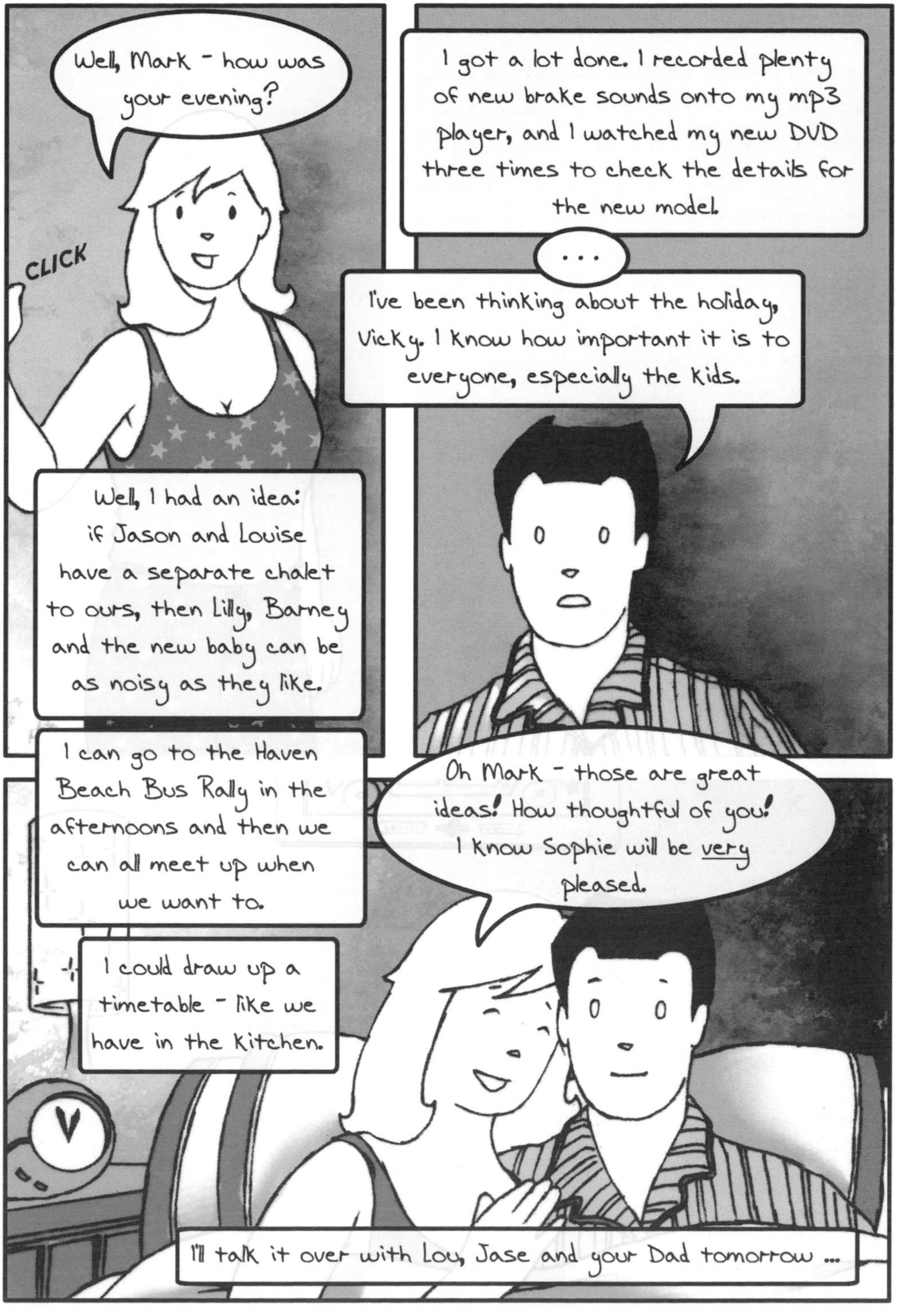
Well, Mark - how was your evening?
CLICK
I got a lot done. I recorded plenty of new brake sounds onto my mp3 player, and I watched my new DVD three times to check the details for the new model.
...
I've been thinking about the holiday, Vicky. I know how important it is to everyone, especially the kids.
Well, I had an idea: if Jason and Louise have a separate chalet to ours, then Lilly, Barney and the new baby can be as noisy as they like.
I can go to the Haven Beach Bus Rally in the afternoons and then we can all meet up when we want to.
I could draw up a timetable - like we have in the kitchen.
Oh Mark - those are great ideas! How thoughtful of you! I know Sophie will be very pleased.
I'll talk it over with Lou, Jase and your Dad tomorrow ...

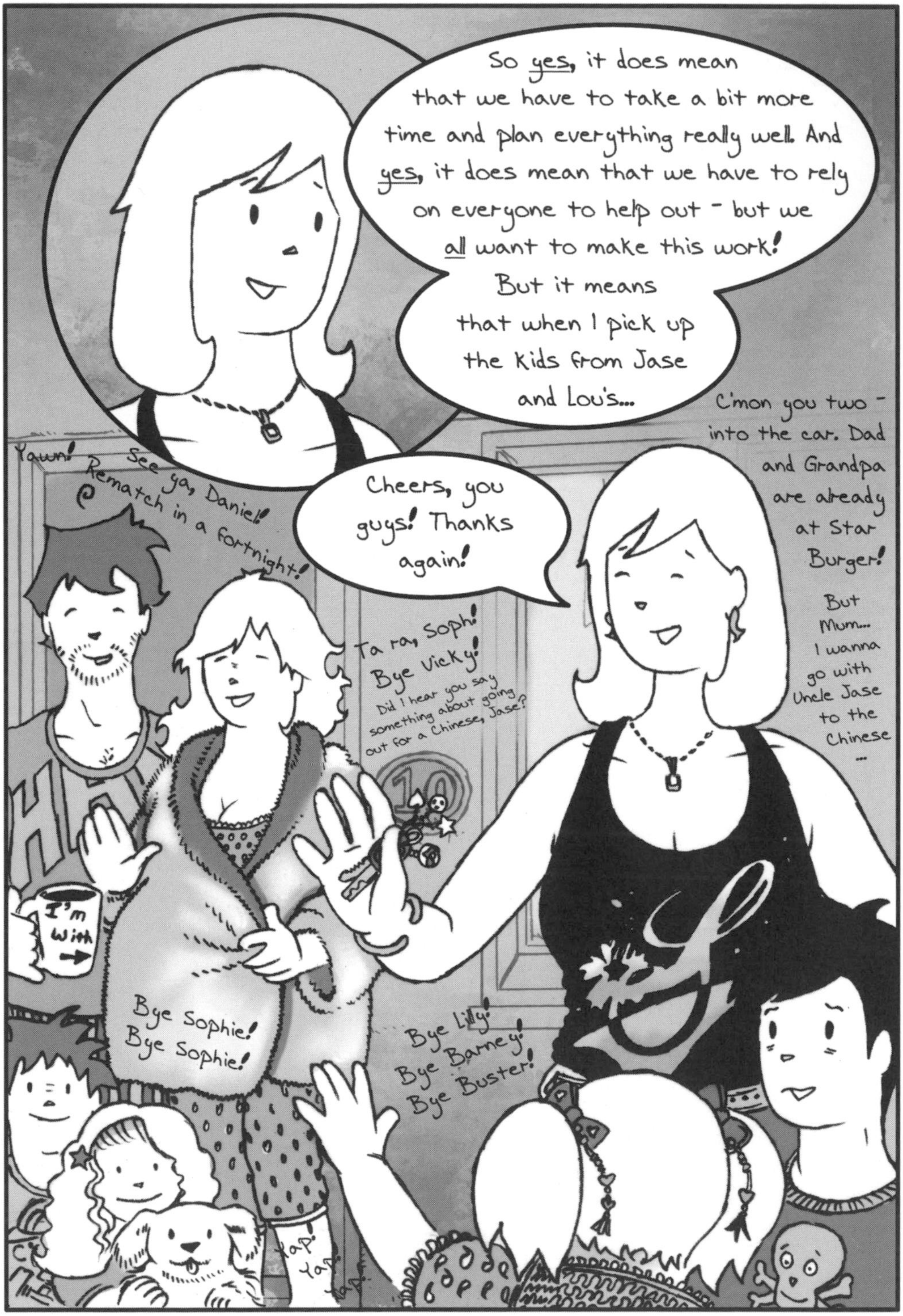
So yes, it does mean that we have to take a bit more time and plan everything really well. And yes, it does mean that we have to rely on everyone to help out – but we all want to make this work! But it means that when I pick up the kids from Jase and Lou's...
Yawn!
See ya, Daniel! Rematch in a fortnight!
Cheers, you guys! Thanks again!
C'mon you two – into the car. Dad and Grandpa are already at Star Burger!
But Mum... I wanna go with Uncle Jase to the Chinese ...
Ta ra, Soph! Bye Vicky!
Did I hear you say something about going out for a Chinese, Jase?
I'm with →
Bye Sophie! Bye Sophie!
Bye Lilly! Bye Barney! Bye Buster!
Yap! Yap! Yap!

What did you and Grandpa do, Dad?

Well, we watched – uh... Um, what did you do, Sophie?

Oh, it was so great! Me an' Lilly an' Ba... ...ng all the way... ...MSM !!! and... ...without... ...e words... ...o Hearts"...

Here, I'll get that, Fred.

Thanks, Vicky. Did you and Mark get a chance to talk it through?

Yep. It's all set. I'm making the bookings next week.

Fantastic!

STAR BURGER

STAR BURGER + cheese + bacon

New Burger + cheese

Chips
Onion...
Chilli...
Bacon...
Potato...
Chilli...

STAR...

Everyone's had a great time, no one's stressed –

Everyone's happy!

But I wanted to go to the Chinese with Jase... Why do we always have to do the exact same thing every Friday?

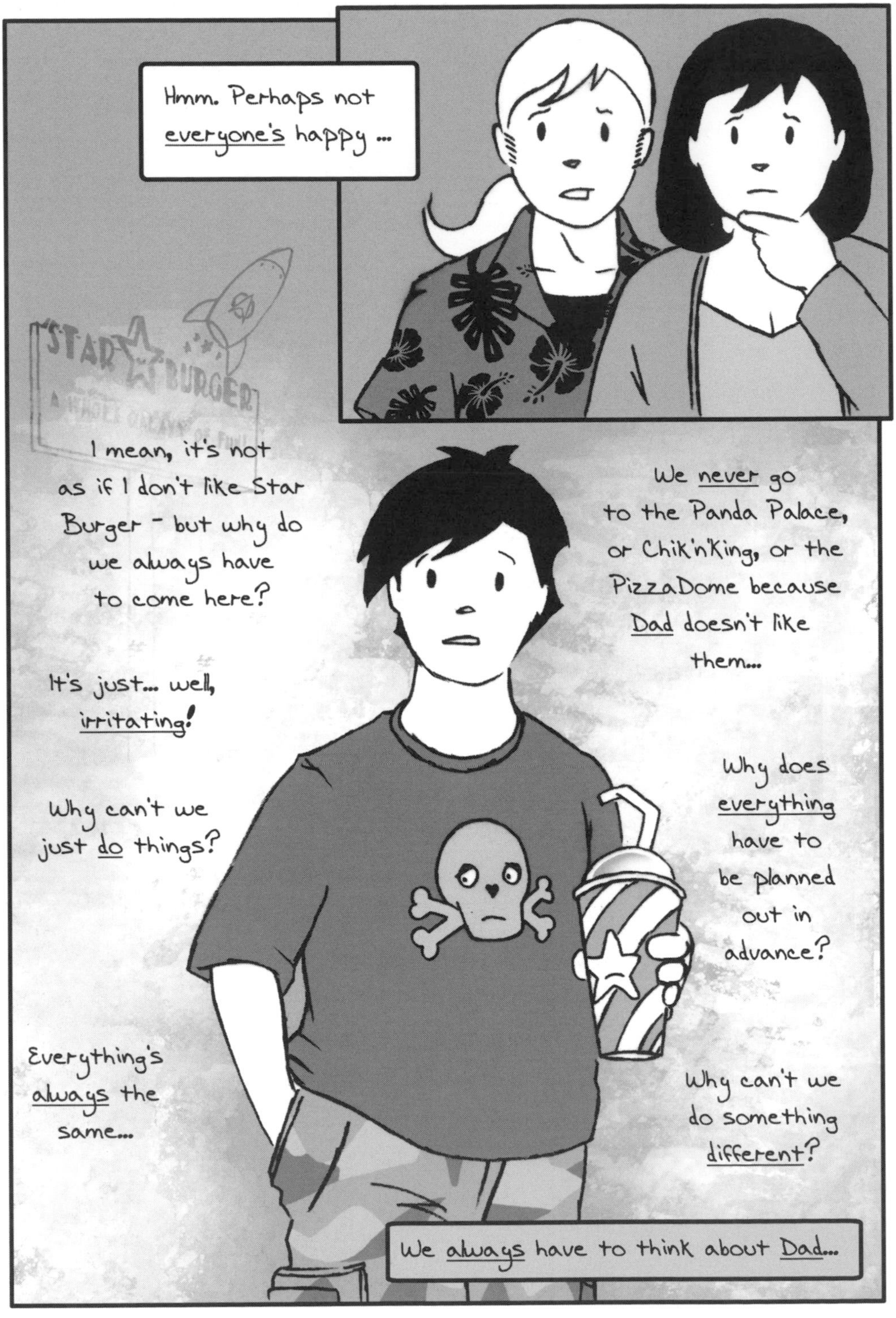
Hmm. Perhaps not everyone's happy ...
STAR BURGER
I mean, it's not as if I don't like Star Burger - but why do we always have to come here?
We never go to the Panda Palace, or Chik'n'King, or the PizzaDome because Dad doesn't like them...
It's just... well, irritating!
Why can't we just do things?
Why does everything have to be planned out in advance?
Everything's always the same...
Why can't we do something different?
We always have to think about Dad...

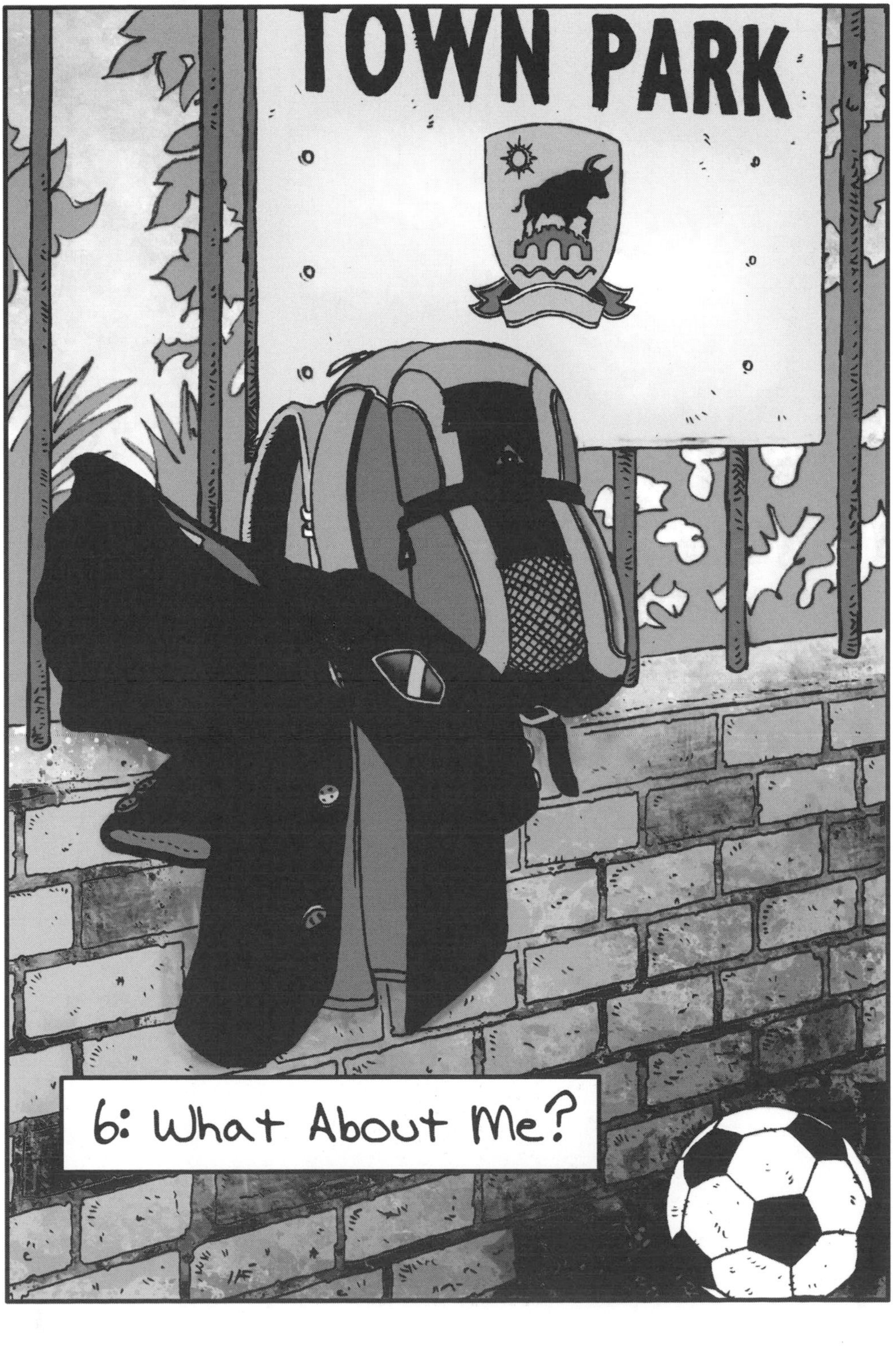
TOWN PARK
6: What About Me?

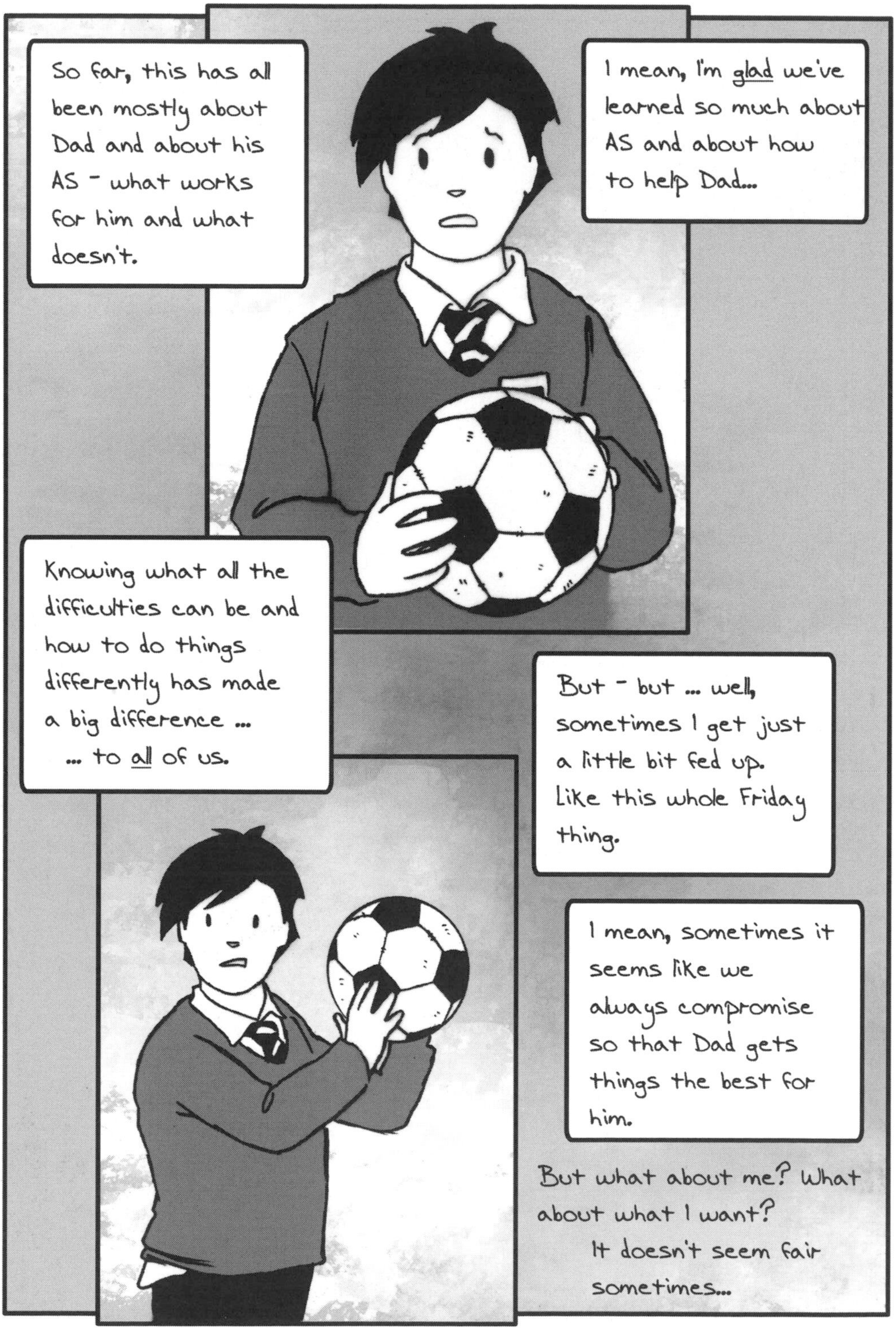
So far, this has all been mostly about Dad and about his AS - what works for him and what doesn't.
I mean, I'm glad we've learned so much about AS and about how to help Dad...
Knowing what all the difficulties can be and how to do things differently has made a big difference ...
... to all of us.
But - but ... well, sometimes I get just a little bit fed up. Like this whole Friday thing.
I mean, sometimes it seems like we always compromise so that Dad gets things the best for him.
But what about me? What about what I want?
It doesn't seem fair sometimes...

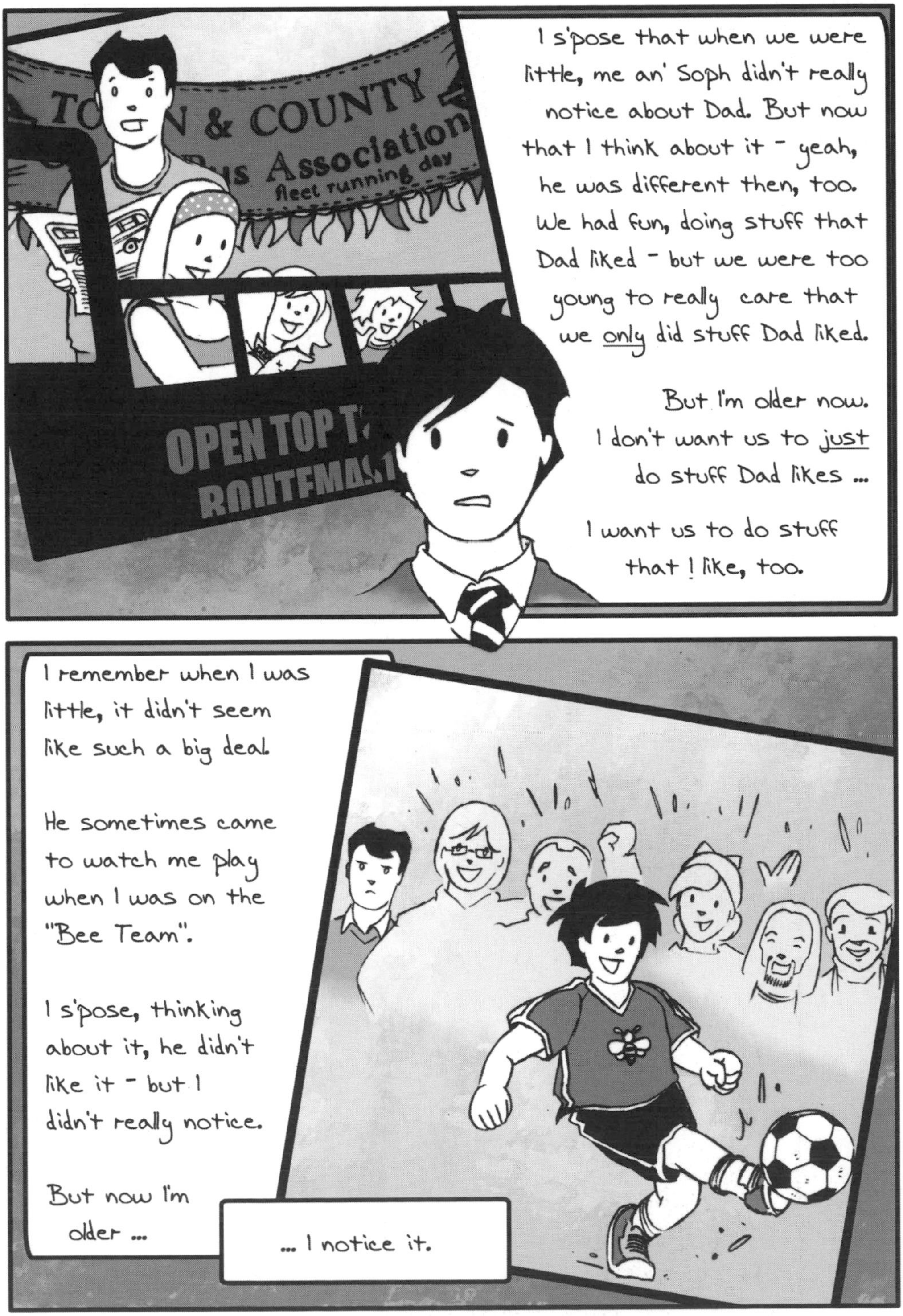
& COUNTY
Association
fleet running day
OPEN TOP
I s'pose that when we were little, me an' Soph didn't really notice about Dad. But now that I think about it – yeah, he was different then, too. We had fun, doing stuff that Dad liked – but we were too young to really care that we only did stuff Dad liked.
But I'm older now. I don't want us to just do stuff Dad likes ...
I want us to do stuff that I like, too.
I remember when I was little, it didn't seem like such a big deal.
He sometimes came to watch me play when I was on the "Bee Team".
I s'pose, thinking about it, he didn't like it – but I didn't really notice.
But now I'm older ...
... I notice it.

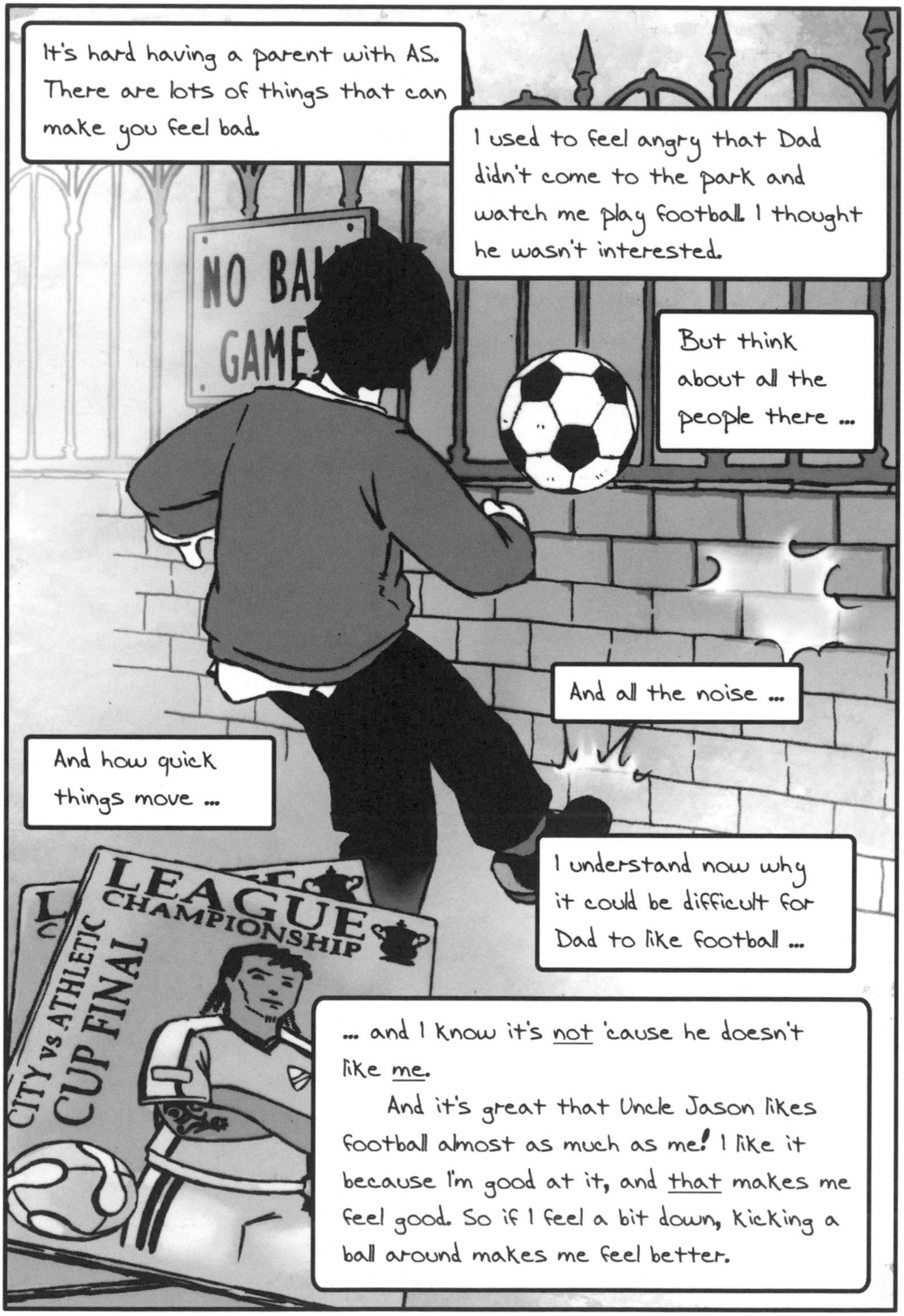
It's hard having a parent with AS. There are lots of things that can make you feel bad.
I used to feel angry that Dad didn't come to the park and watch me play football. I thought he wasn't interested.
NO BAL
GAME
But think about all the people there ...
And all the noise ...
And how quick things move ...
I understand now why it could be difficult for Dad to like football ...
LEAGUE CHAMPIONSHIP
CITY vs ATHLETIC CUP FINAL
... and I know it's not 'cause he doesn't like me.
And it's great that Uncle Jason likes football almost as much as me! I like it because I'm good at it, and that makes me feel good. So if I feel a bit down, kicking a ball around makes me feel better.

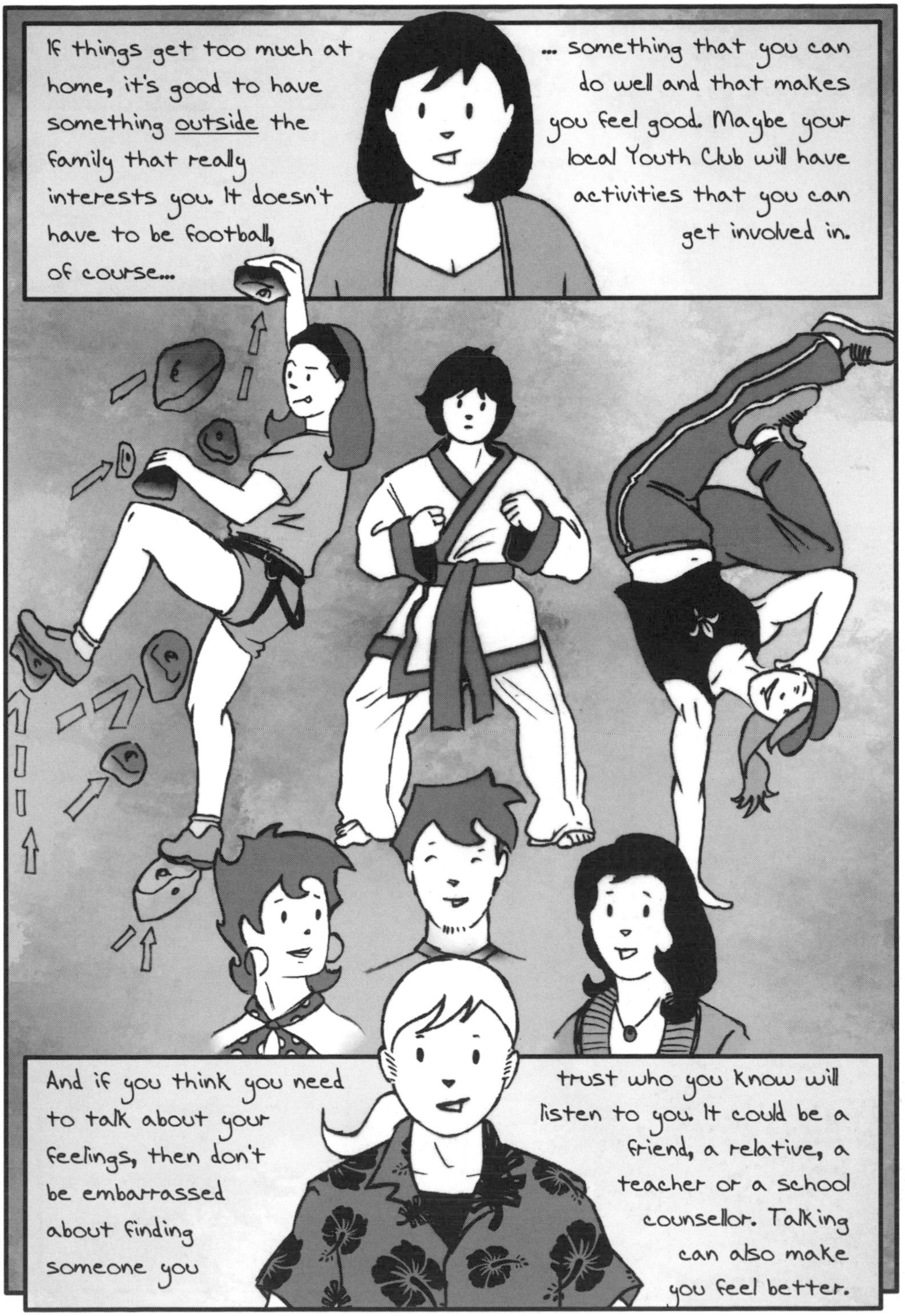
If things get too much at home, it's good to have something outside the family that really interests you. It doesn't have to be football, of course...
... something that you can do well and that makes you feel good. Maybe your local Youth Club will have activities that you can get involved in.
And if you think you need to talk about your feelings, then don't be embarrassed about finding someone you
trust who you know will listen to you. It could be a friend, a relative, a teacher or a school counsellor. Talking can also make you feel better.

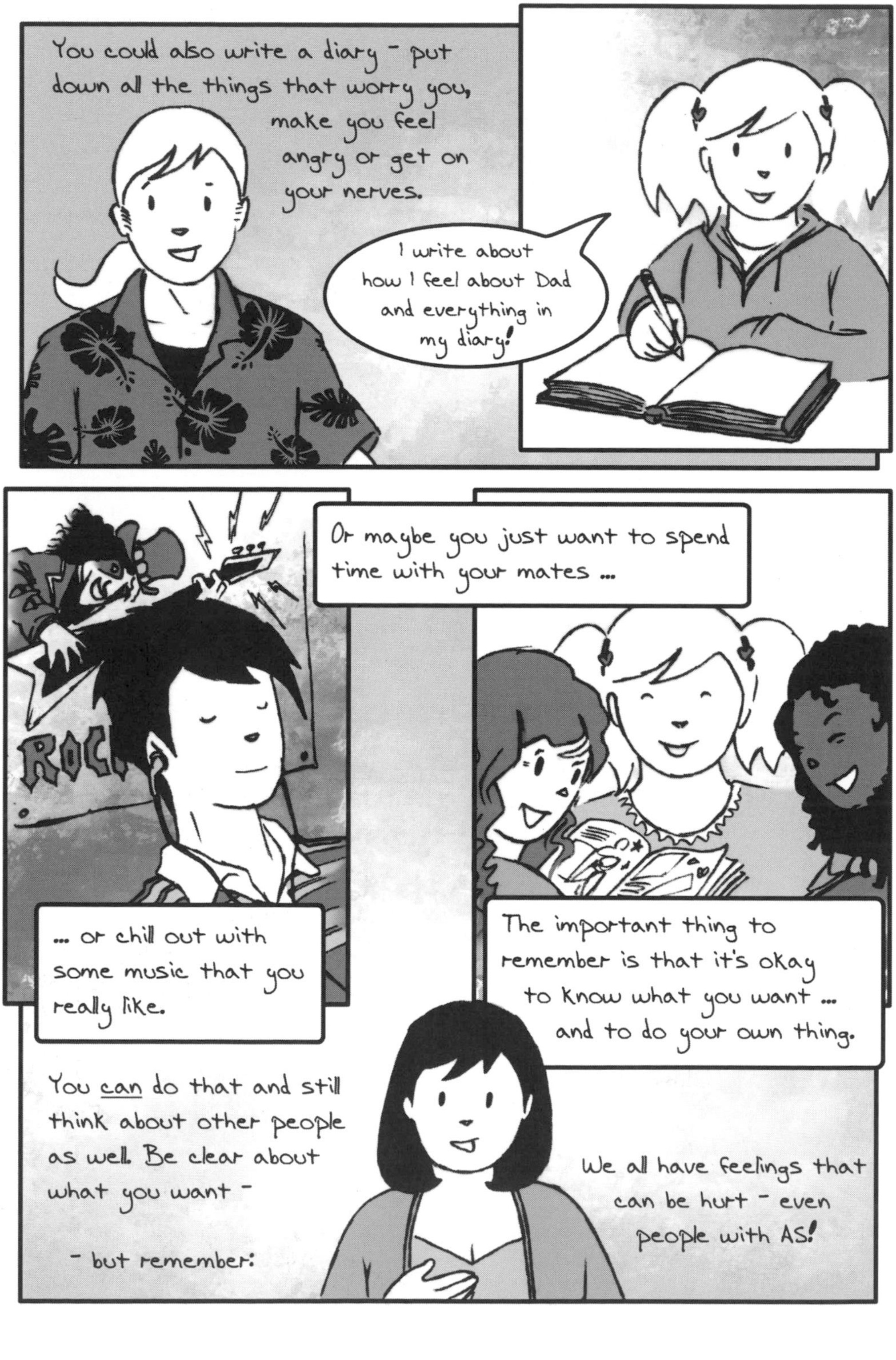
You could also write a diary - put down all the things that worry you, make you feel angry or get on your nerves.
I write about how I feel about Dad and everything in my diary!
Or maybe you just want to spend time with your mates ...
ROC
... or chill out with some music that you really like.
The important thing to remember is that it's okay to know what you want ... and to do your own thing.
You can do that and still think about other people as well. Be clear about what you want -
- but remember:
We all have feelings that can be hurt - even people with AS!

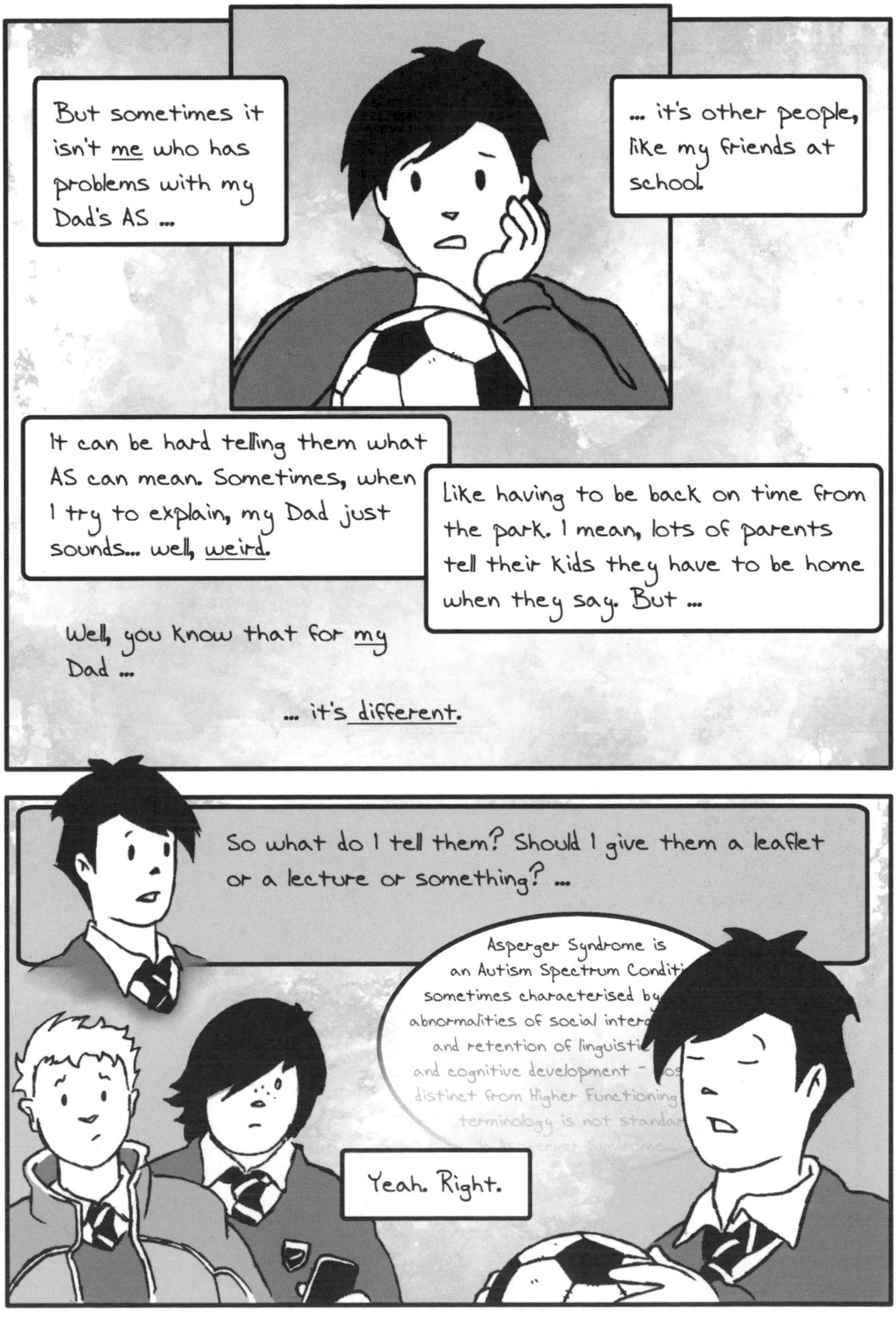
But sometimes it isn't me who has problems with my Dad's AS ...
... it's other people, like my friends at school.
It can be hard telling them what AS can mean. Sometimes, when I try to explain, my Dad just sounds... well, weird.
Like having to be back on time from the park. I mean, lots of parents tell their kids they have to be home when they say. But ...
Well, you know that for my Dad ...
... it's different.
So what do I tell them? Should I give them a leaflet or a lecture or something? ...
Asperger Syndrome is
an Autism Spectrum Conditi
sometimes characterised by
abnormalities of social intera
and retention of linguisti
and cognitive development –
distinct from Higher Functioning
terminology is not standar
Yeah. Right.

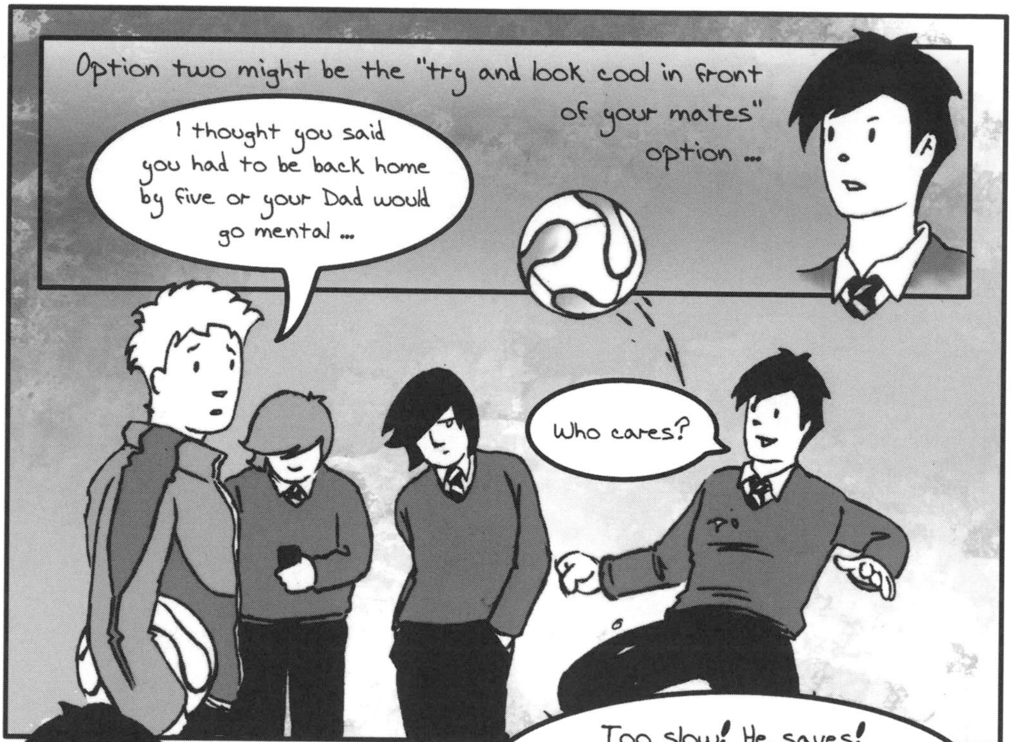
Option two might be the "try and look cool in front of your mates" option ...
I thought you said you had to be back home by five or your Dad would go mental ...
Who cares?

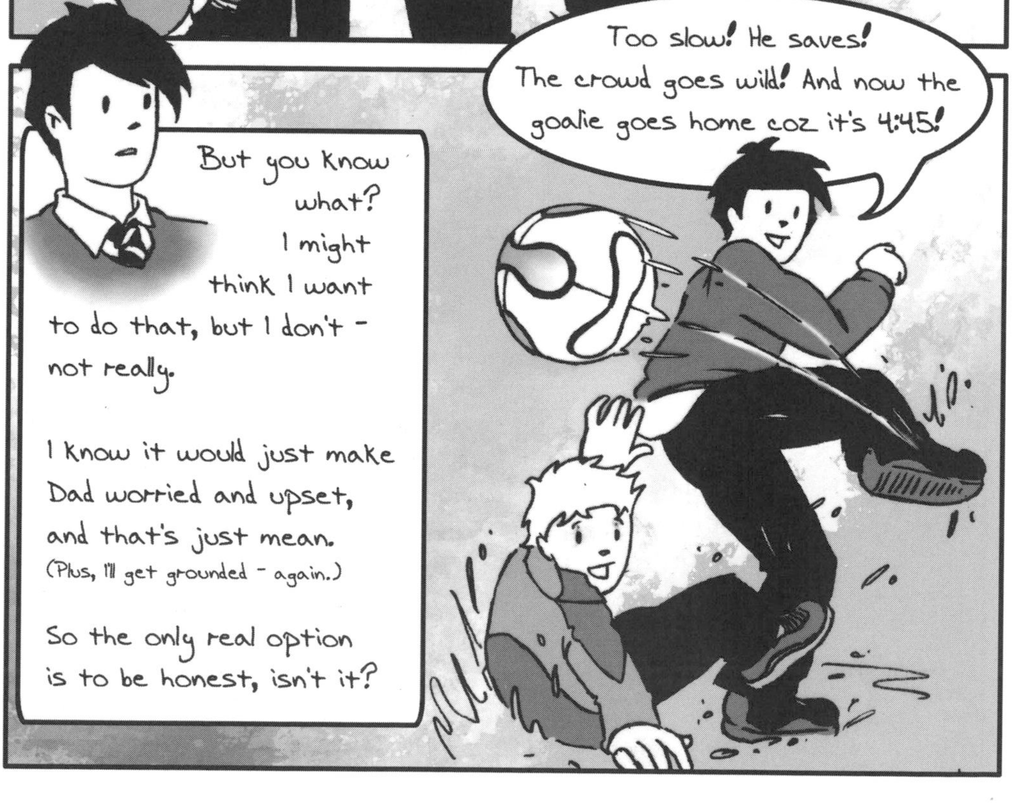
But you know what? I might think I want to do that, but I don't - not really.
I know it would just make Dad worried and upset, and that's just mean.
(Plus, I'll get grounded - again.)
So the only real option is to be honest, isn't it?
Too slow! He saves! The crowd goes wild! And now the goalie goes home coz it's 4:45!

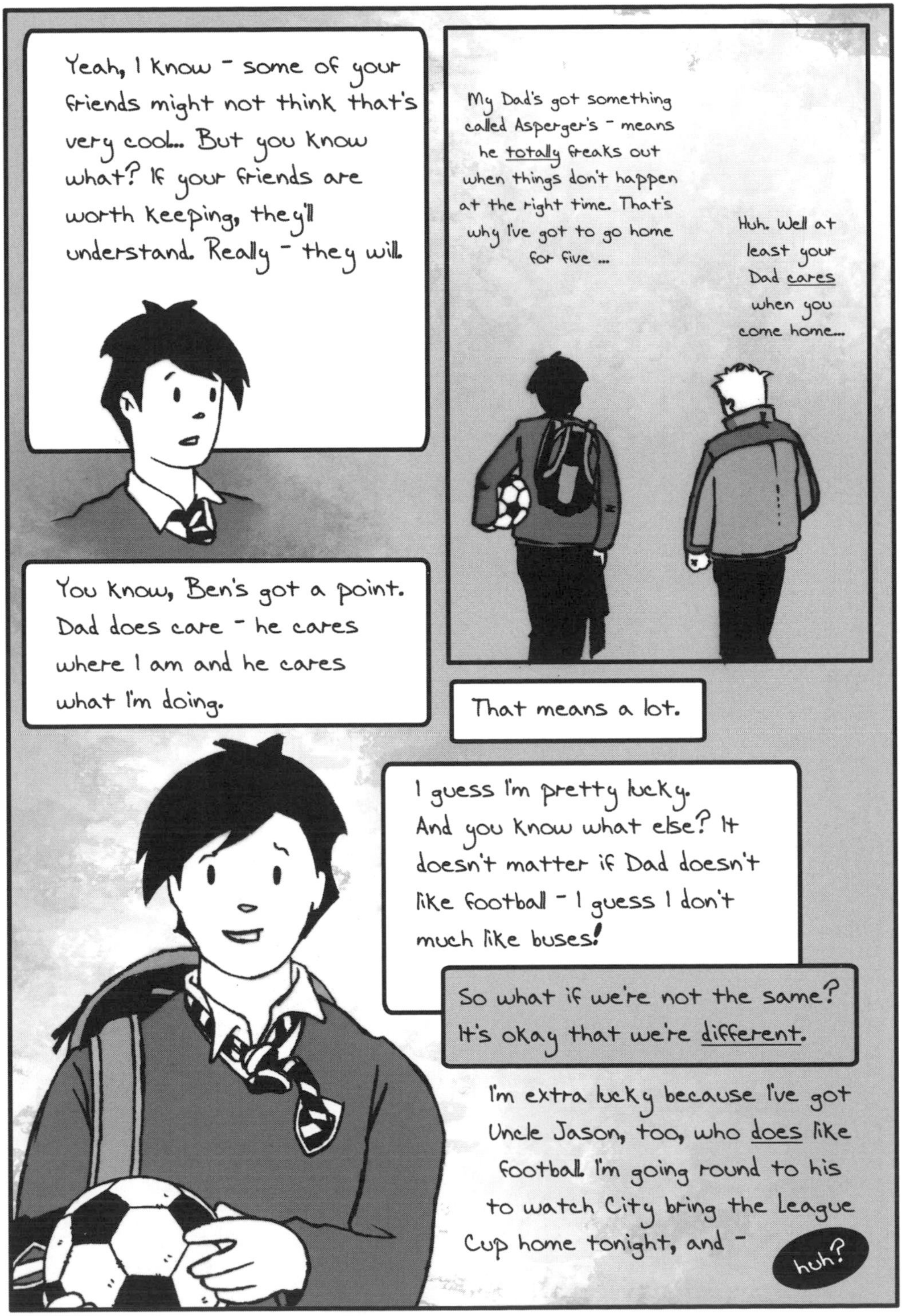
Yeah, I know – some of your friends might not think that's very cool... But you know what? If your friends are worth keeping, they'll understand. Really – they will.
My Dad's got something called Asperger's – means he totally freaks out when things don't happen at the right time. That's why I've got to go home for five ...
Huh. Well at least your Dad cares when you come home...
You know, Ben's got a point. Dad does care – he cares where I am and he cares what I'm doing.
That means a lot.
I guess I'm pretty lucky. And you know what else? It doesn't matter if Dad doesn't like football – I guess I don't much like buses!
So what if we're not the same? It's okay that we're different.
I'm extra lucky because I've got Uncle Jason, too, who does like football. I'm going round to his to watch City bring the League Cup home tonight, and –
huh?

Yes, just ten minutes ago. No, Fred's brought them round. Mrs C's going to cook, but I'm worried about – Would you, Lucy? You're a star!
YAP! YAP! YAP!
Puff, puff! Here I am! I found the tofu!
Wot's going on?
Auntie Louise just went into hospital – she's having the new baby!
Arrgh! Blinkin' dog!
WHINE WHINE
YAP! YAP!
Look what I brought, Sophie! My special
wok!
C'mere, dog! Ow!
Ow, my foot!
CRASH!
Give me a hand, Sophie – there's a good girl!
BARK! BARK! BARK! BARK!
I – uh, um...
Out into the
with you!
You okay, Grandpa?
Mark – I'm so sorry, but your Dad just can't handle those two on his own, so they've got to come here...
Unky Mark! Unky Mark! We're gettin' a new baby sister!
Bruvver! SISTER! Bruvver!

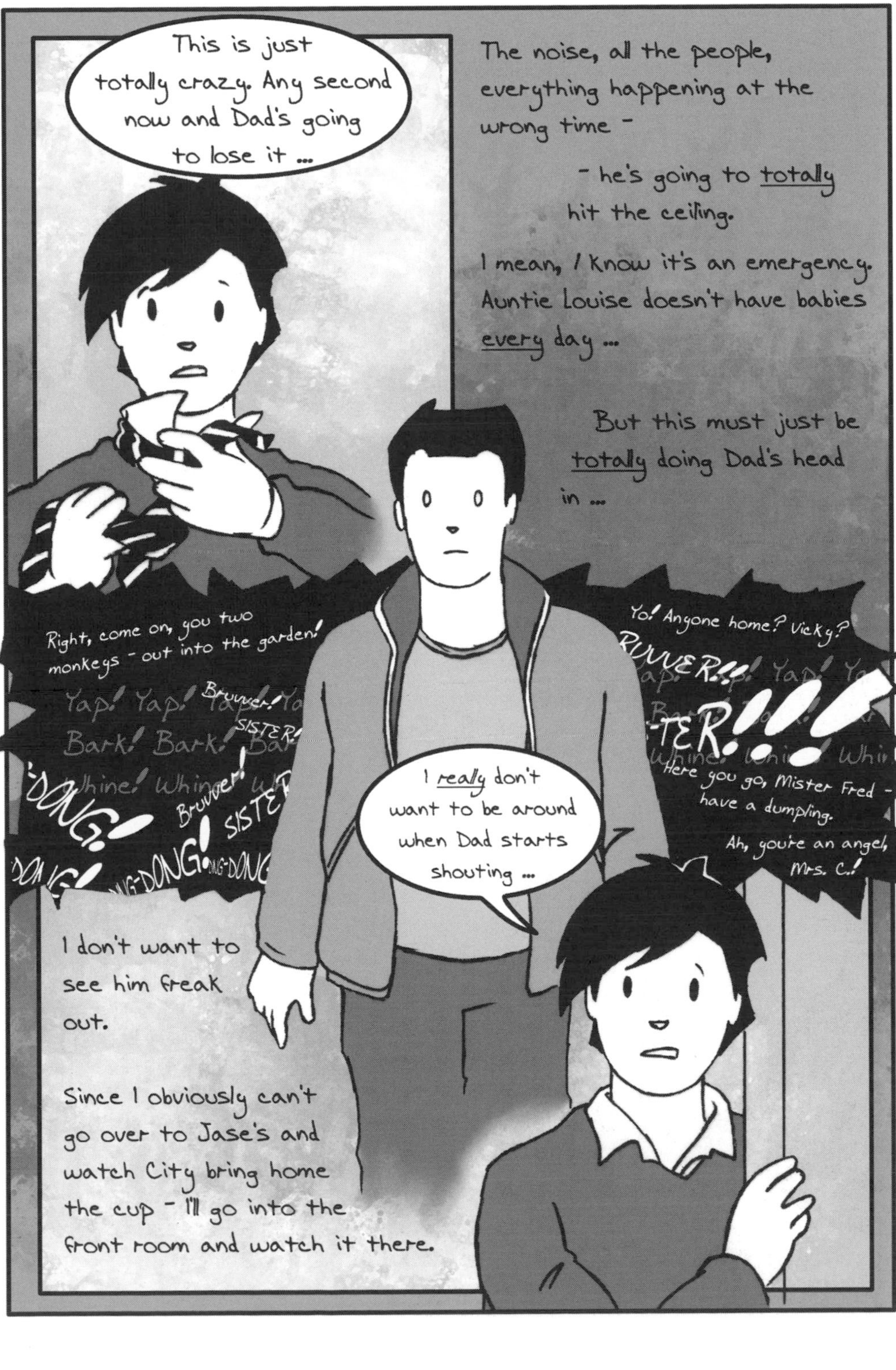
This is just totally crazy. Any second now and Dad's going to lose it ...
The noise, all the people, everything happening at the wrong time –
– he's going to totally hit the ceiling.
I mean, I know it's an emergency. Auntie Louise doesn't have babies every day ...
But this must just be totally doing Dad's head in ...
Right, come on, you two monkeys – out into the garden!
Yap! Yap!
Bark! Bark!
Bruvver!
SISTER!
Yo! Anyone home? Vicky?
Here you go, Mister Fred – have a dumpling.
Ah, you're an angel, Mrs. C.!
I really don't want to be around when Dad starts shouting ...
I don't want to see him freak out.
Since I obviously can't go over to Jase's and watch City bring home the cup – I'll go into the front room and watch it there.

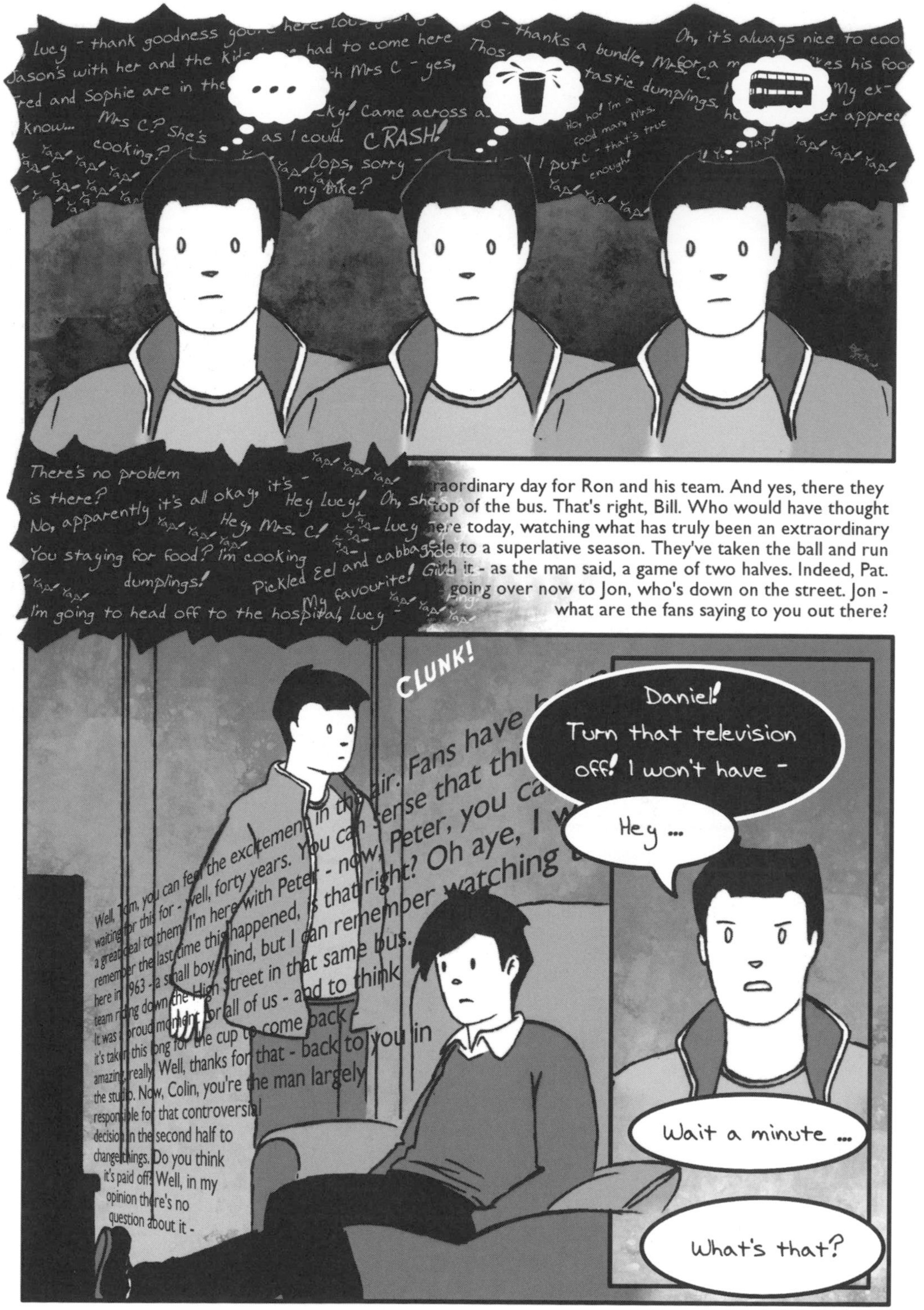
Lucy - thank goodness you're here.
had to come here
Jason's with her and the kids
Mrs C - yes,
Fred and Sophie are in the
Know...
Mrs C? She's cooking?
as I could.
Came across a
CRASH!
Oops, sorry -
my bike?
- thanks a bundle, Mrs C.
tastic dumplings.
Ho, ho! I'm a food man, Mrs. C - that's true enough!
Oh, it's always nice to coo
his foo
My ex-
appre
Yap! Yap! Yap!
There's no problem is there?
No, apparently it's all okay, it's -
Hey Lucy! Oh, she's
Hey, Mrs. C!
- Lucy
You staying for food? I'm cooking dumplings!
Pickled Eel and cabbage
My favourite!
I'm going to head off to the hospital, Lucy -
xtraordinary day for Ron and his team. And yes, there they top of the bus. That's right, Bill. Who would have thought here today, watching what has truly been an extraordinary ale to a superlative season. They've taken the ball and run with it - as the man said, a game of two halves. Indeed, Pat. going over now to Jon, who's down on the street. Jon - what are the fans saying to you out there?
CLUNK!
Well, Tom, you can feel the excitement in the air. Fans have been waiting for this for - well, forty years. You can sense that this means a great deal to them. I'm here with Peter - now, Peter, you can remember the last time this happened, is that right? Oh aye, I was here in 1963 - a small boy, mind, but I can remember watching the team riding down the High Street in that same bus. It was a proud moment for all of us - and to think it's taken this long for the cup to come back - amazing, really. Well, thanks for that - back to you in the studio. Now, Colin, you're the man largely responsible for that controversial decision in the second half to change things. Do you think it's paid off? Well, in my opinion there's no question about it -
Daniel! Turn that television off! I won't have -
Hey ...
Wait a minute ...
What's that?

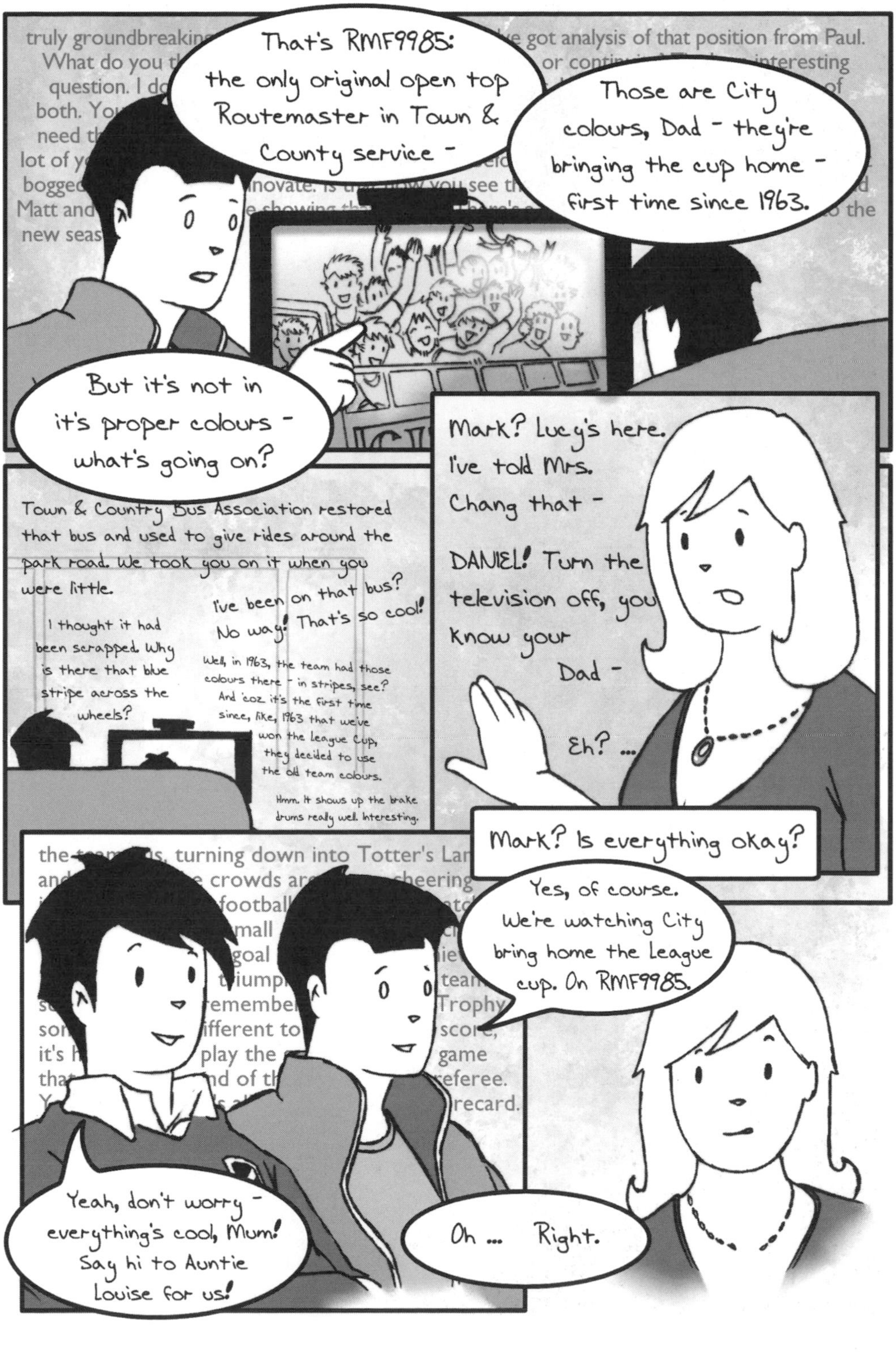
That's RMF9985: the only original open top Routemaster in Town & County service -
Those are City colours, Dad - they're bringing the cup home - first time since 1963.
But it's not in it's proper colours - what's going on?
Town & Country Bus Association restored that bus and used to give rides around the park road. We took you on it when you were little.
I thought it had been scrapped. Why is there that blue stripe across the wheels?
I've been on that bus? No way! That's so cool!
Well, in 1963, the team had those colours there - in stripes, see? And 'coz it's the first time since, like, 1963 that we've won the League Cup, they decided to use the old team colours.
Hmm. It shows up the brake drums really well. Interesting.
Mark? Lucy's here. I've told Mrs. Chang that -
DANIEL! Turn the television off, you know your Dad -
Eh? ...
Mark? Is everything okay?
Yes, of course. We're watching City bring home the League cup. On RMF9985.
Yeah, don't worry - everything's cool, Mum! Say hi to Auntie Louise for us!
Oh ... Right.

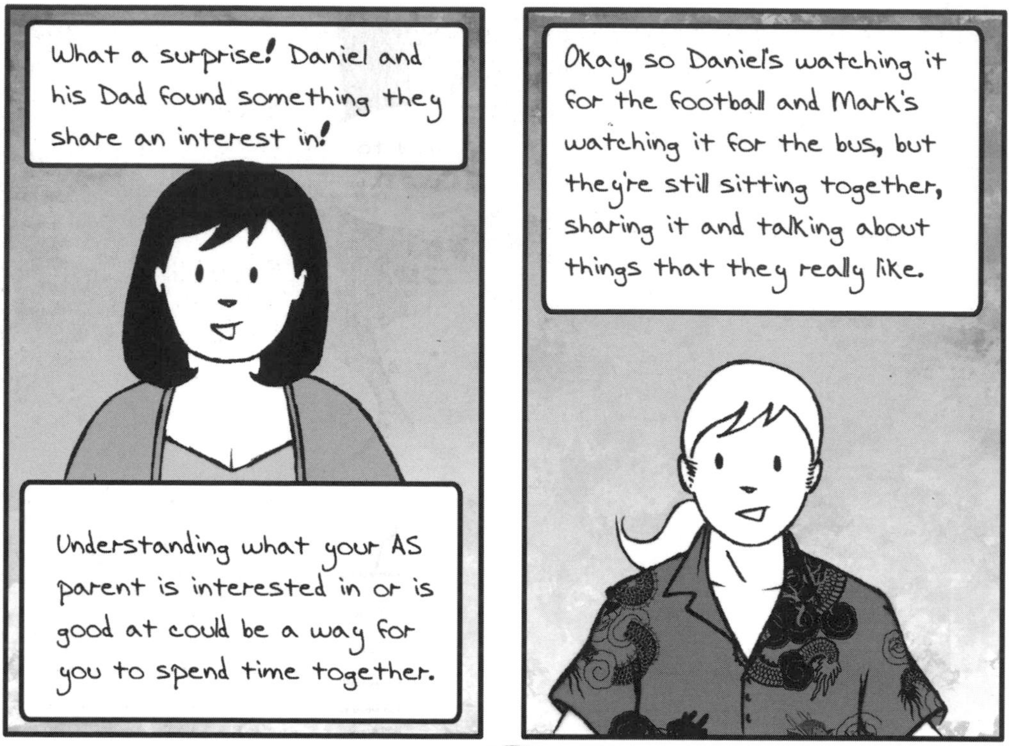
What a surprise! Daniel and his Dad found something they share an interest in!
Understanding what your AS parent is interested in or is good at could be a way for you to spend time together.
Okay, so Daniel's watching it for the football and Mark's watching it for the bus, but they're still sitting together, sharing it and talking about things that they really like.

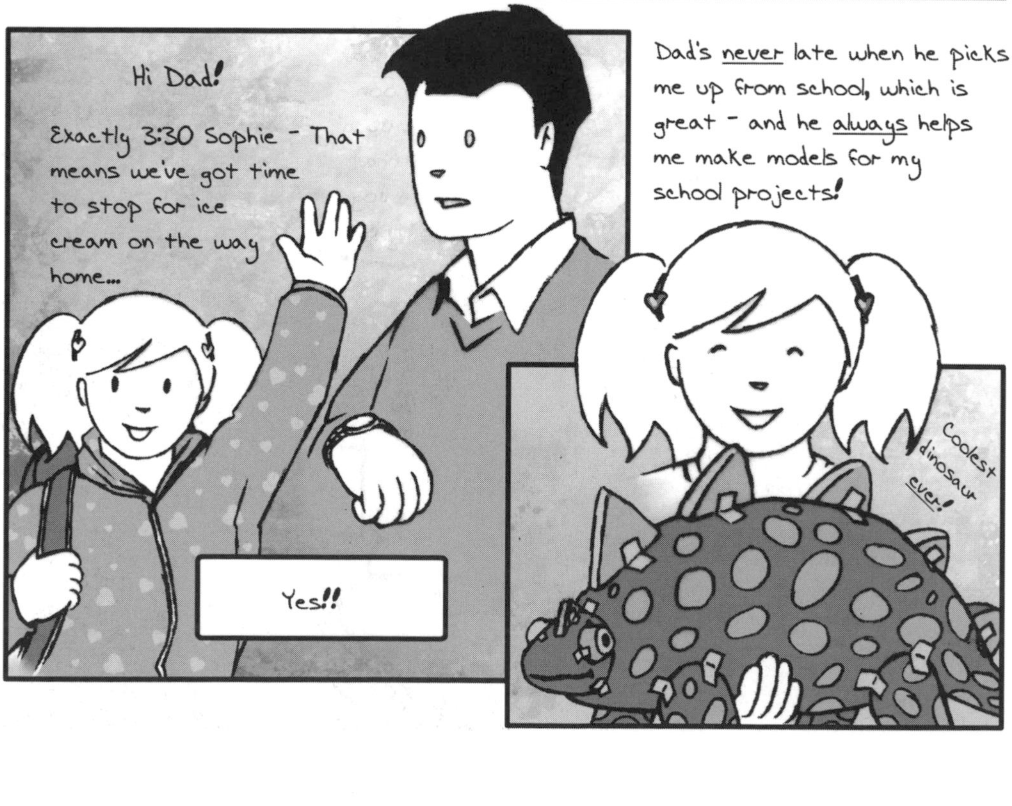
Hi Dad!
Exactly 3:30 Sophie - That means we've got time to stop for ice cream on the way home...
Yes!!
Dad's never late when he picks me up from school, which is great - and he always helps me make models for my school projects!
Coolest dinosaur ever!

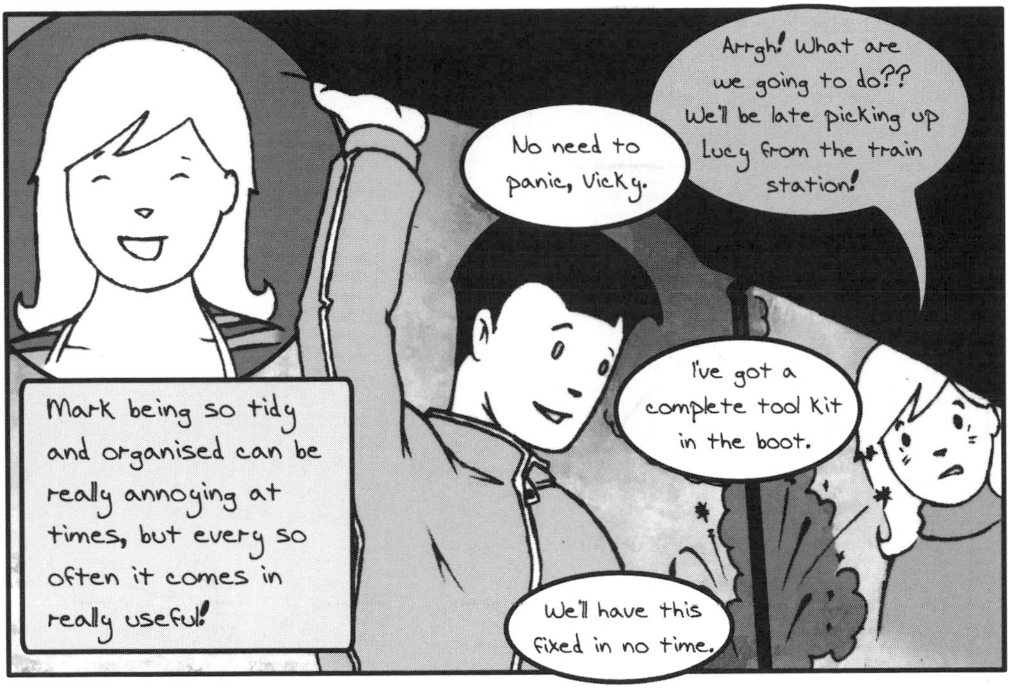
Mark being so tidy and organised can be really annoying at times, but every so often it comes in really useful!
Arrgh! What are we going to do?? We'll be late picking up Lucy from the train station!
No need to panic, Vicky.
I've got a complete tool kit in the boot.
We'll have this fixed in no time.

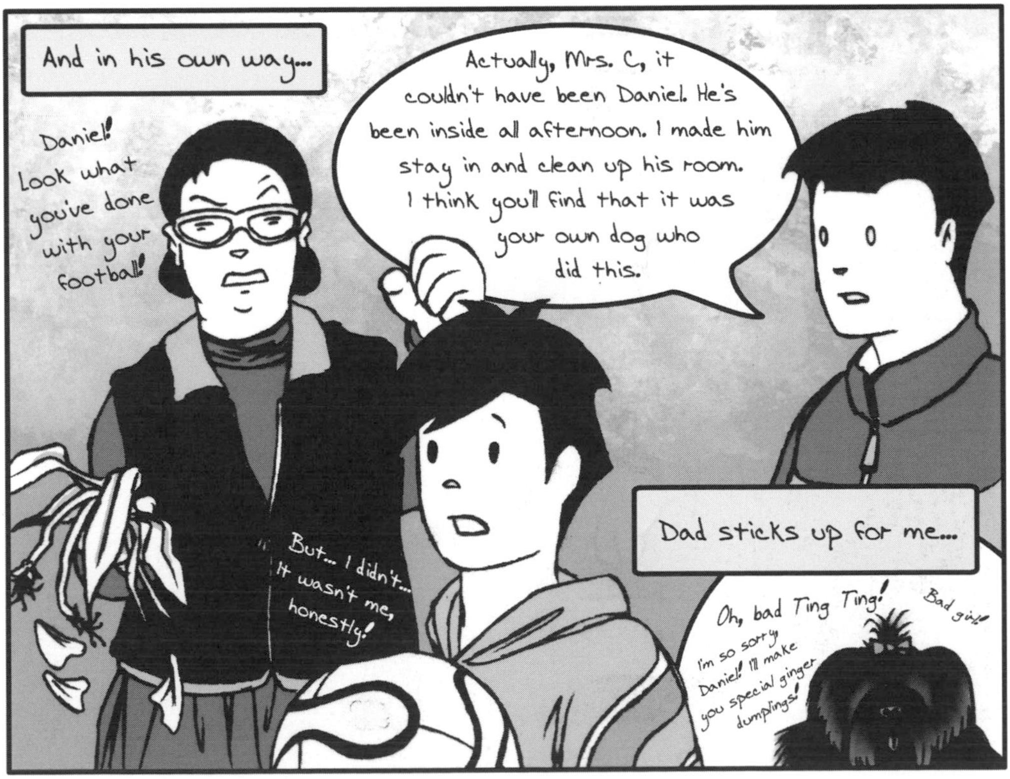
And in his own way...
Daniel! Look what you've done with your football!
Actually, Mrs. C, it couldn't have been Daniel. He's been inside all afternoon. I made him stay in and clean up his room. I think you'll find that it was your own dog who did this.
But... I didn't... It wasn't me, honestly!
Dad sticks up for me...
Oh, bad Ting Ting!
Bad girl!
I'm so sorry, Daniel! I'll make you special ginger dumplings!

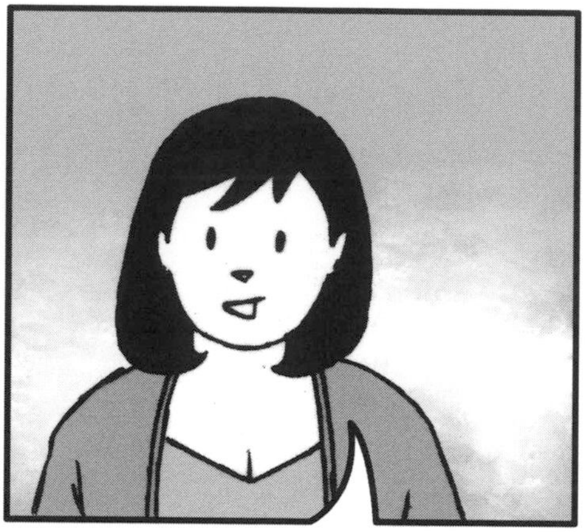

Part of understanding your AS parent is understanding that Asperger Syndrome isn't _just_ about problems.

As they've learned more about Asperger Syndrome, Sophie, Vicky and Daniel have started to see that Mark has talents as well as difficulties.

Punctuality, attention to detail, tidyness and interest in engines – all these make Mark reliable, loyal and good at fixing and making things.

Sophie and Daniel are starting to appreciate this side of their Dad. Perhaps it will help them find more ways of spending time with Mark and discovering more things that they might all be interested in.

All this helps the whole family learn to understand each other better – and perhaps accept that they're _all_ different!

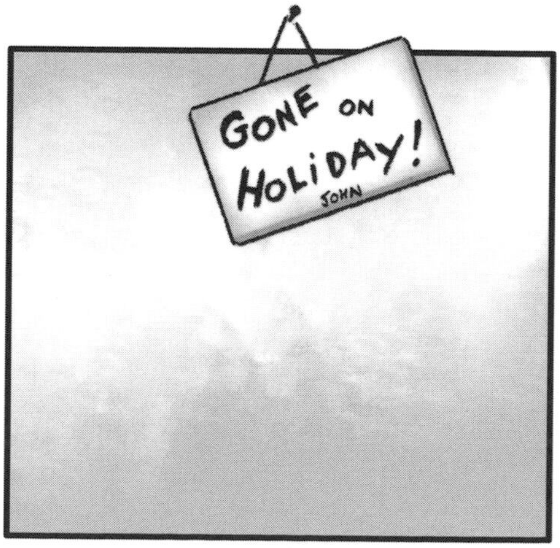
GONE ON HOLIDAY!
JOHN

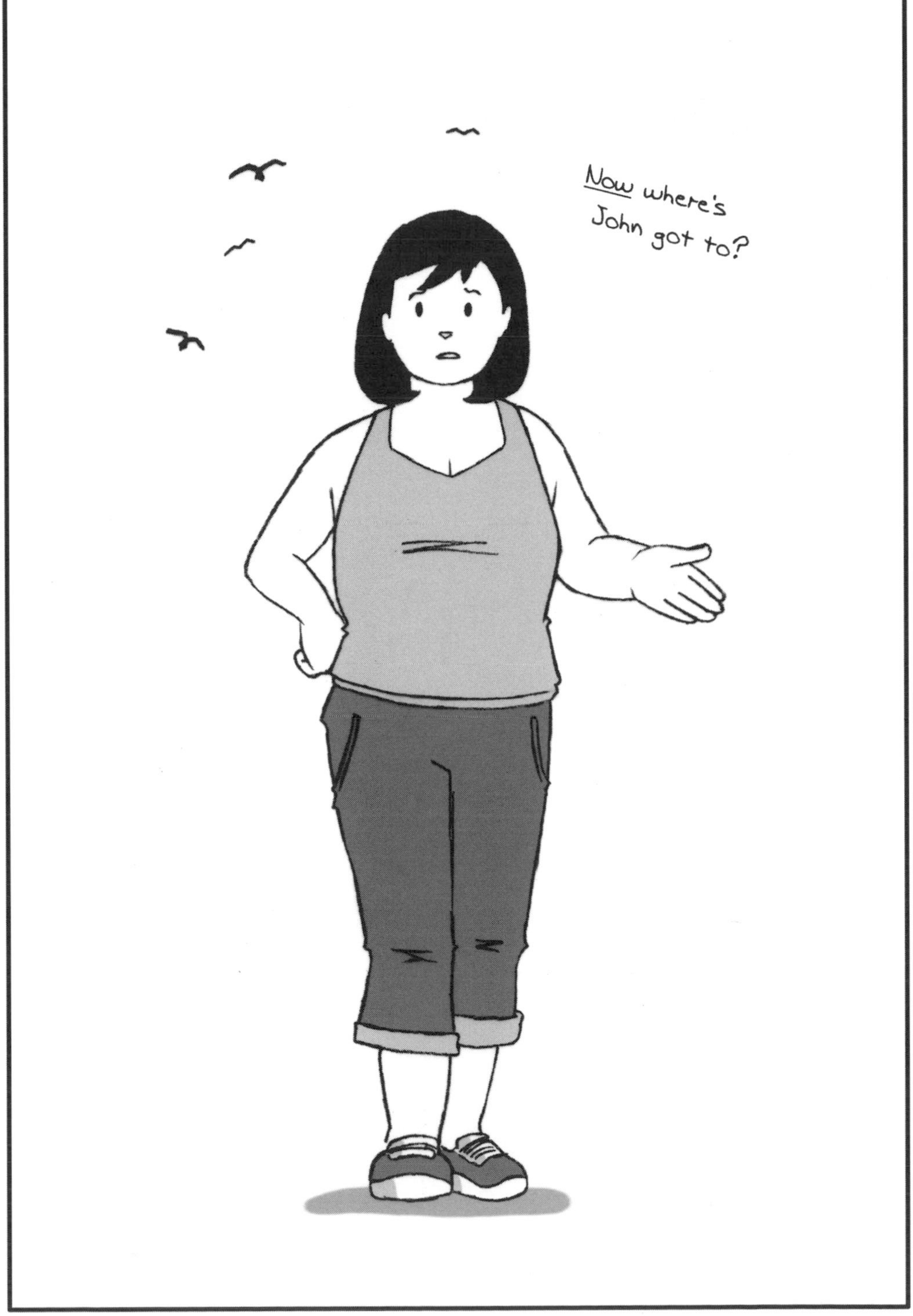
Now where's John got to?

7: Being Different

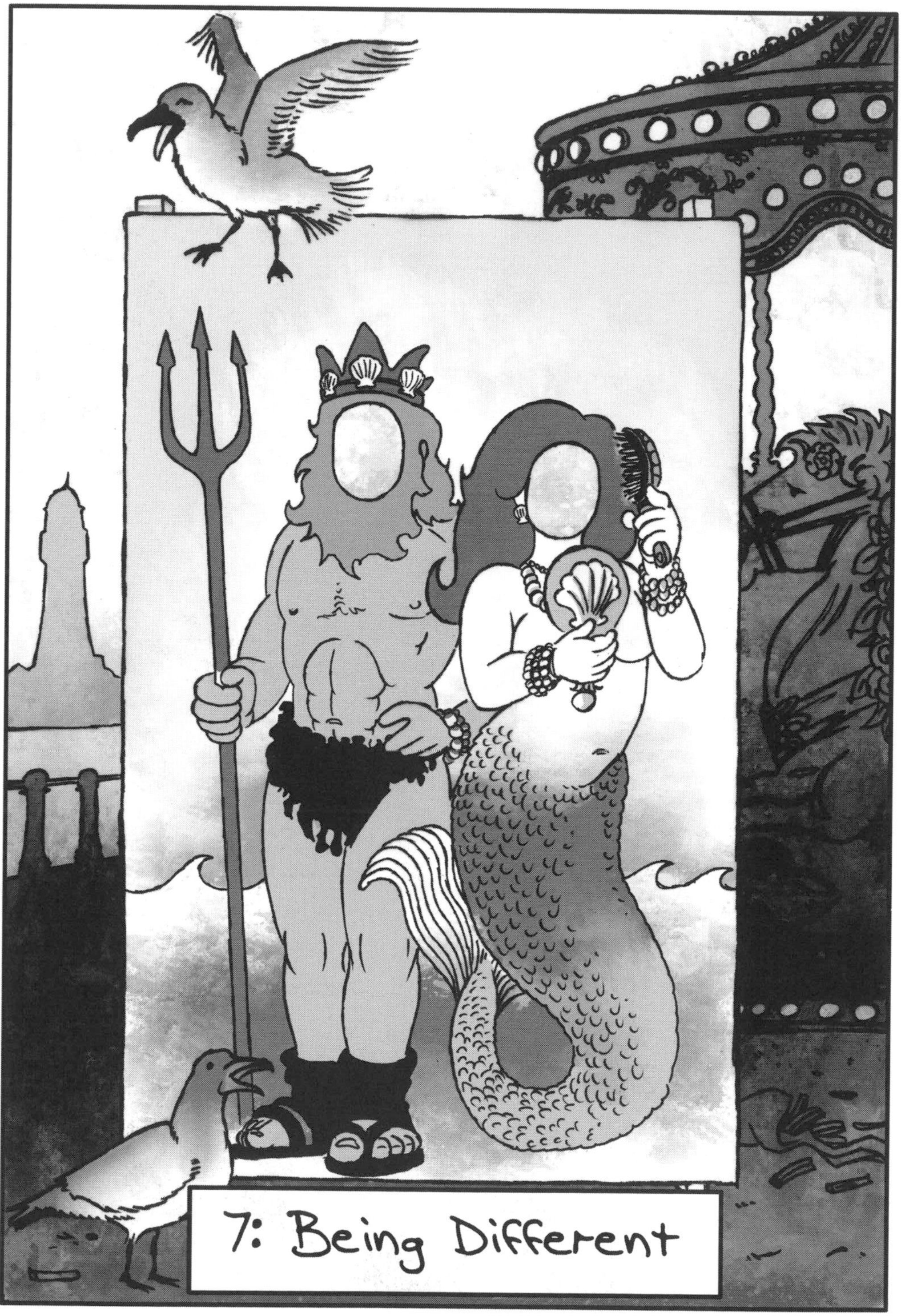

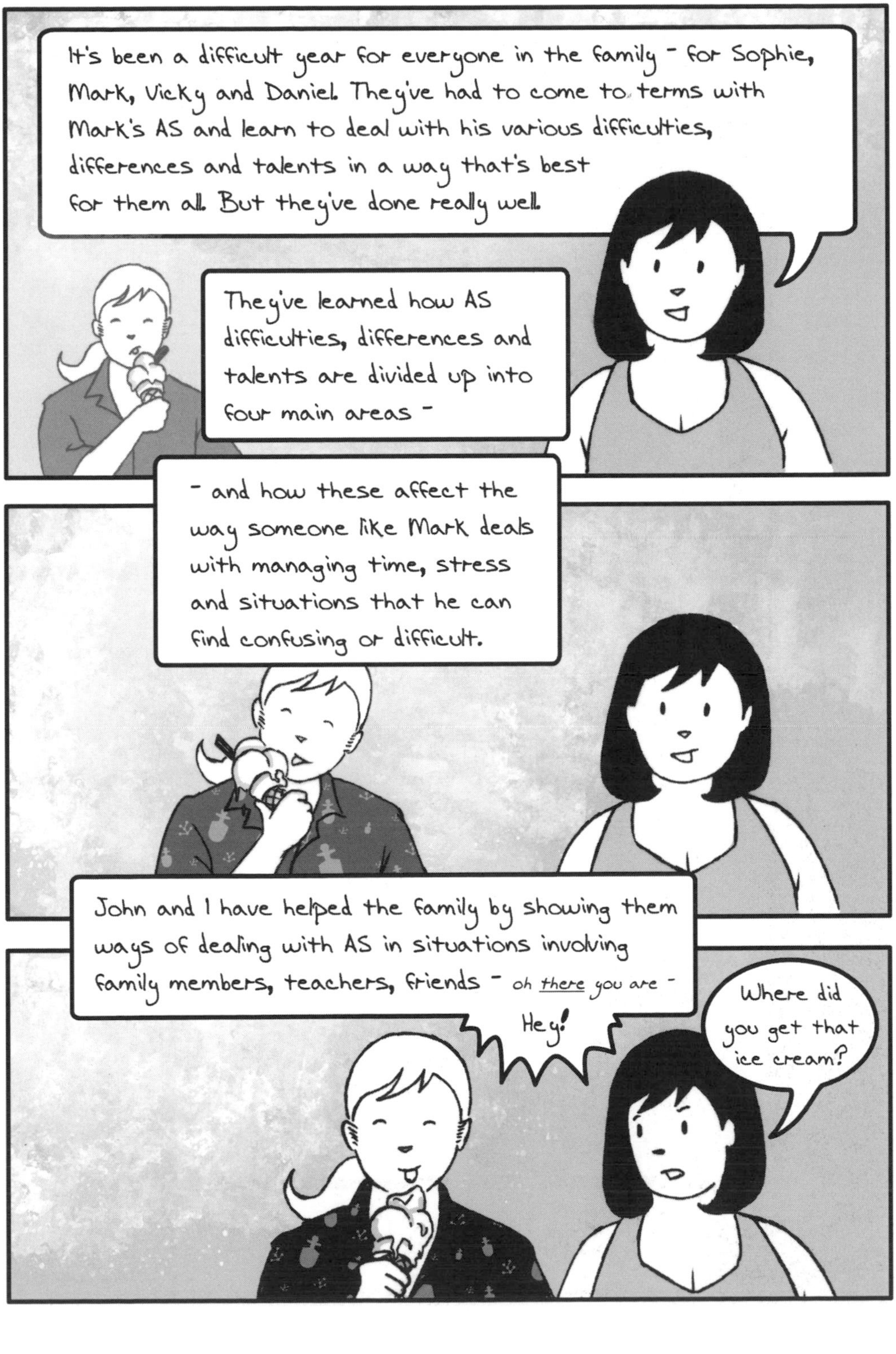
It's been a difficult year for everyone in the family - for Sophie, Mark, Vicky and Daniel. They've had to come to terms with Mark's AS and learn to deal with his various difficulties, differences and talents in a way that's best for them all. But they've done really well.
They've learned how AS difficulties, differences and talents are divided up into four main areas -
- and how these affect the way someone like Mark deals with managing time, stress and situations that he can find confusing or difficult.
John and I have helped the family by showing them ways of dealing with AS in situations involving family members, teachers, friends - oh there you are -
Hey!
Where did you get that ice cream?

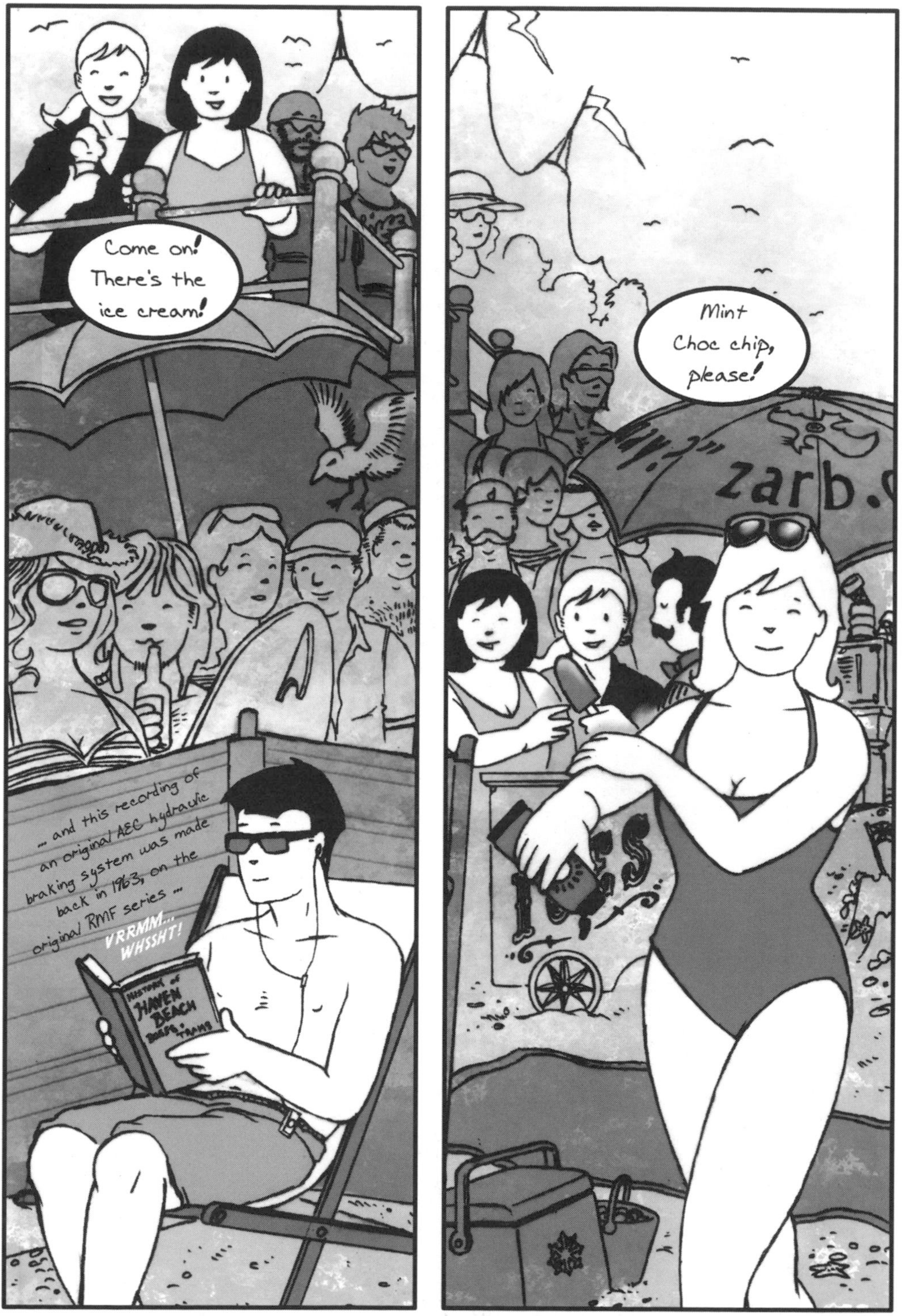
Come on! There's the ice cream!
... and this recording of an original AEC hydraulic braking system was made back in 1963, on the original RMF series ...
VRRMM... WHSSHT!
HAVEN BEACH
Mint Choc chip, please!
zarb.

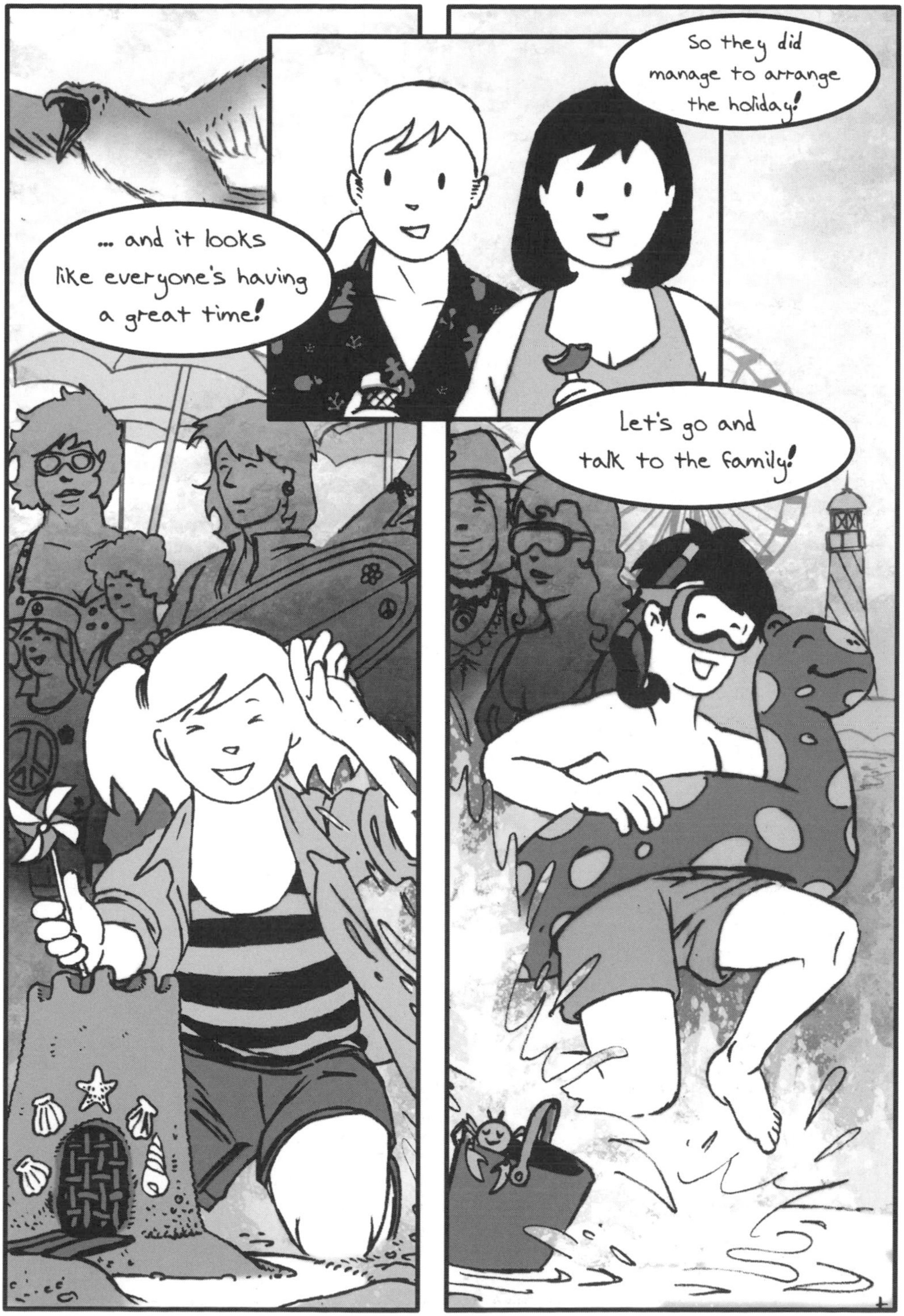
So they did manage to arrange the holiday!
... and it looks like everyone's having a great time!
Let's go and talk to the family!

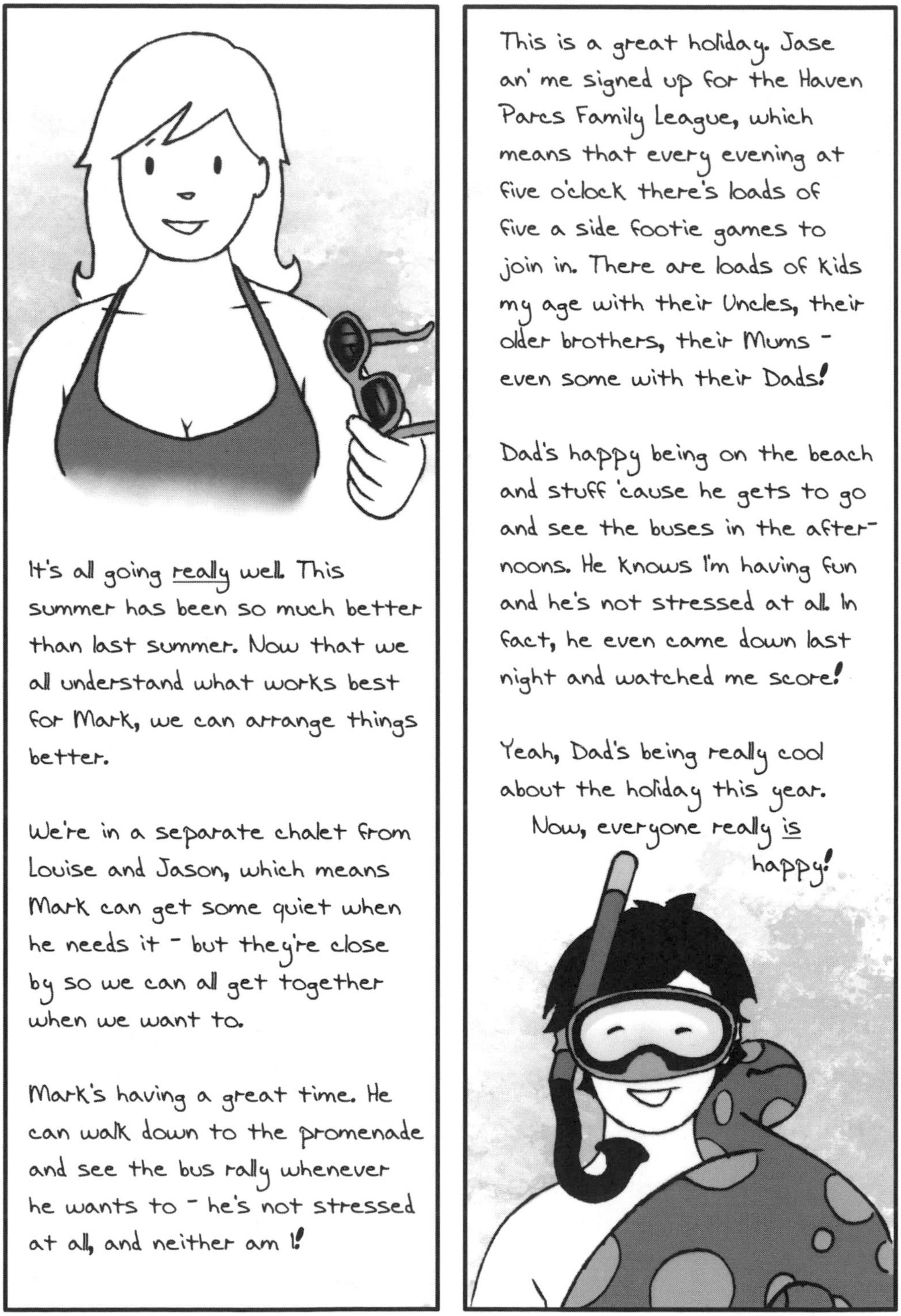
It's all going really well. This summer has been so much better than last summer. Now that we all understand what works best for Mark, we can arrange things better.
We're in a separate chalet from Louise and Jason, which means Mark can get some quiet when he needs it – but they're close by so we can all get together when we want to.
Mark's having a great time. He can walk down to the promenade and see the bus rally whenever he wants to – he's not stressed at all, and neither am I!
This is a great holiday. Jase an' me signed up for the Haven Parcs Family League, which means that every evening at five o'clock there's loads of five a side footie games to join in. There are loads of kids my age with their Uncles, their older brothers, their Mums – even some with their Dads!
Dad's happy being on the beach and stuff 'cause he gets to go and see the buses in the after-noons. He knows I'm having fun and he's not stressed at all. In fact, he even came down last night and watched me score!
Yeah, Dad's being really cool about the holiday this year.
Now, everyone really is happy!

I'm having a great time. Haven Parcs is just so cool. This year, because I'm old enough, I'm in the Junior Activity Club which means I get to ride bikes through the woods and go on the rope course! And you know what? Dad said that he'll take me on the pony rides! Did you know he really likes horses? No, I didn't either!

Dad's so much happier this year. Lilly and Barney don't get on his nerves like they did last year coz they're in the other chalet most of the time.

I'm so glad Dad's not stressed. It makes it better for everyone!

Well, yes - I suppose it has been a difficult year. Things are better now - everything's planned and I know what's going on. I don't mind being on the beach with everyone: I can listen to my mp3 player and read behind the windbreak. And the way we've organised our time means I can spend my afternoons at the Haven Bus Rally, which is good.

I still don't really understand why people think I'm different - but I do understand now that it can affect people I love: Vicky, Daniel and Sophie. I want to help make things better for them as well as me.

I think everyone's enjoying this holiday more than last year's ... and yes, I am too.

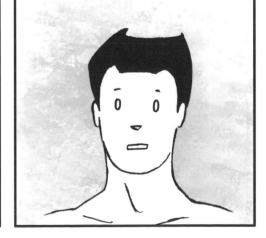

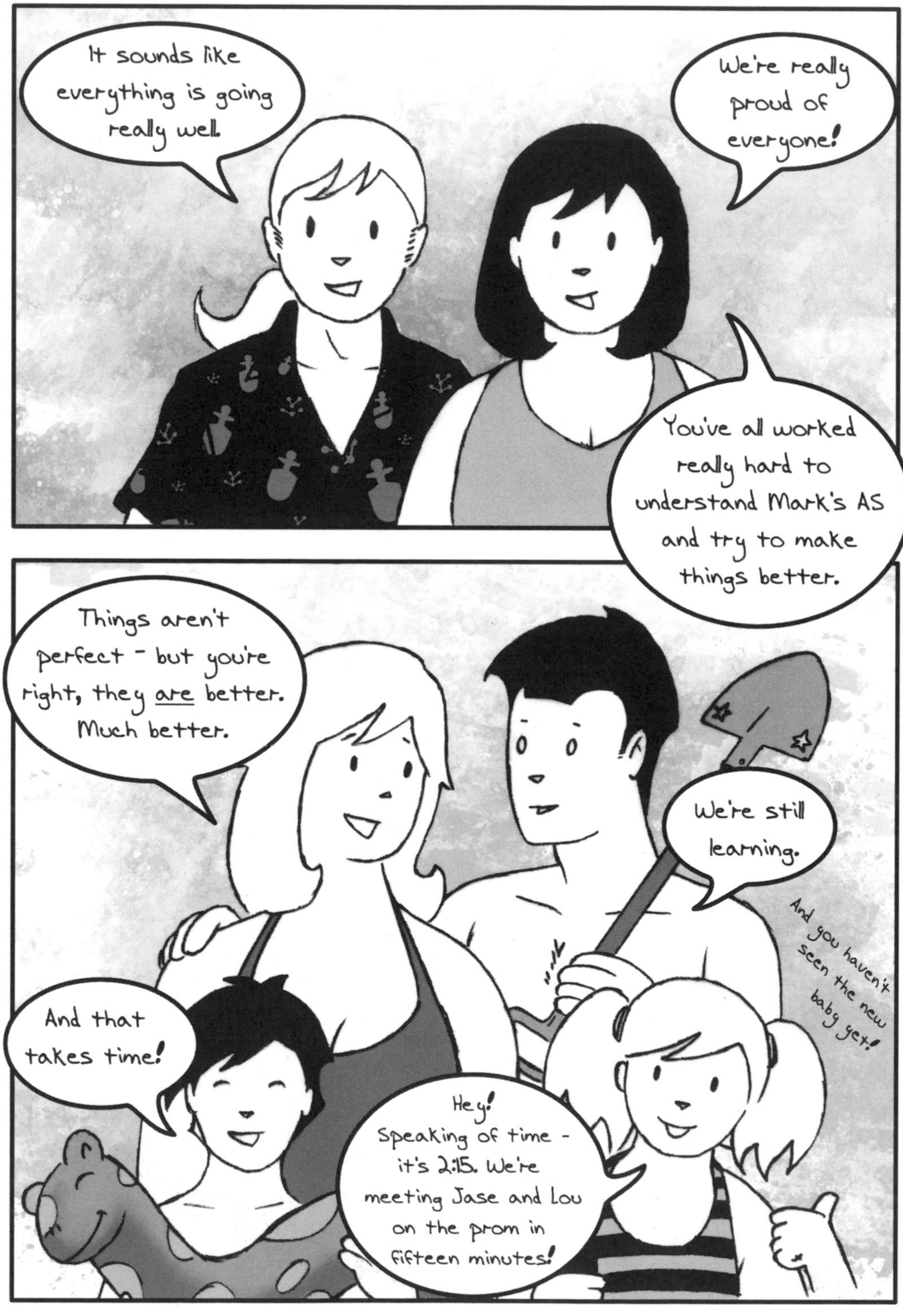
It sounds like everything is going really well.
We're really proud of everyone!
You've all worked really hard to understand Mark's AS and try to make things better.
Things aren't perfect - but you're right, they are better. Much better.
We're still learning.
And you haven't seen the new baby yet!
And that takes time!
Hey! Speaking of time - it's 2:15. We're meeting Jase and Lou on the prom in fifteen minutes!

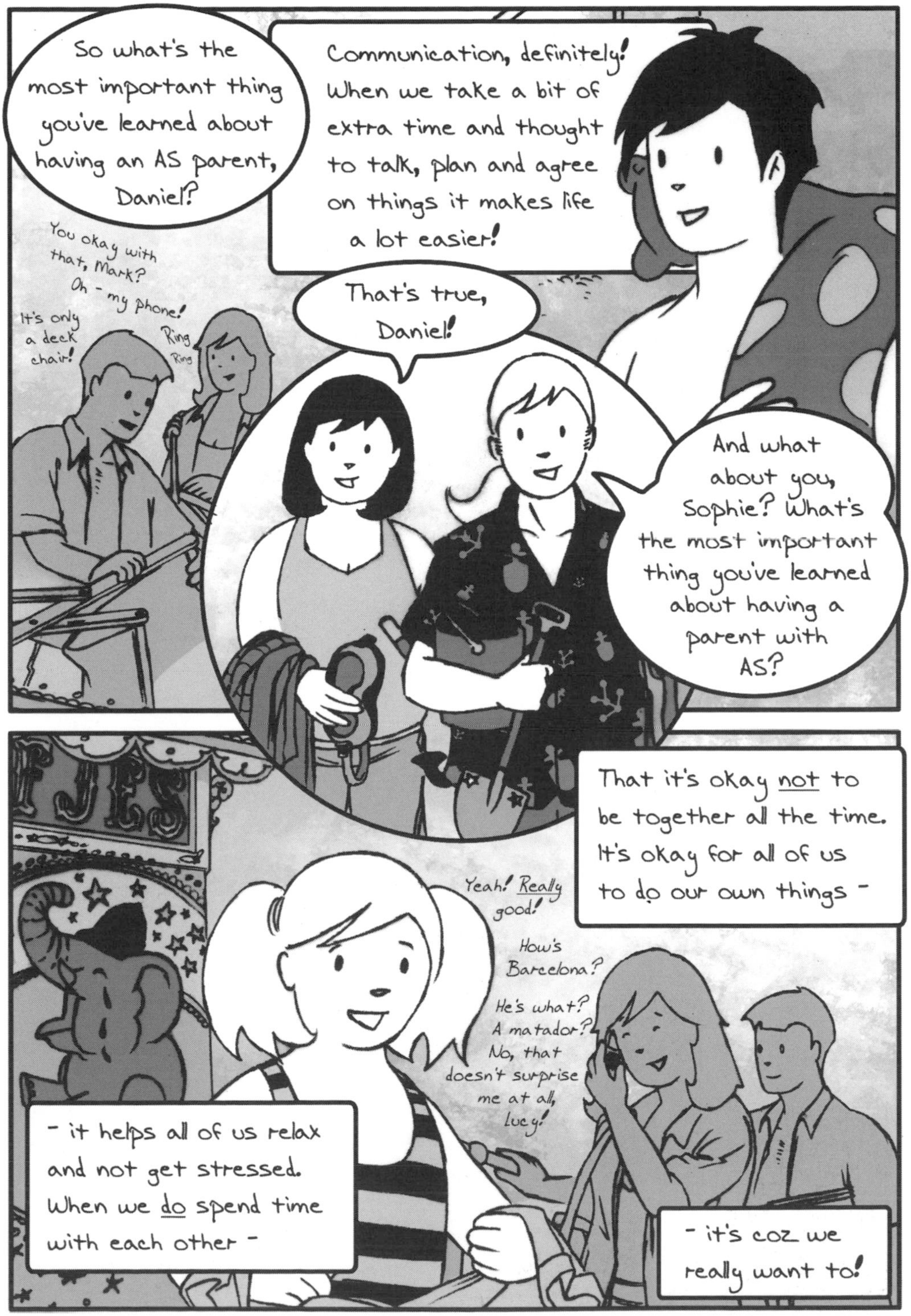
So what's the most important thing you've learned about having an AS parent, Daniel?
Communication, definitely! When we take a bit of extra time and thought to talk, plan and agree on things it makes life a lot easier!
You okay with that, Mark?
Oh - my phone!
It's only a deck chair!
Ring Ring
That's true, Daniel!
And what about you, Sophie? What's the most important thing you've learned about having a parent with AS?
That it's okay not to be together all the time. It's okay for all of us to do our own things -
Yeah! Really good!
How's Barcelona?
He's what? A matador? No, that doesn't surprise me at all, Lucy!
- it helps all of us relax and not get stressed. When we do spend time with each other -
- it's coz we really want to!

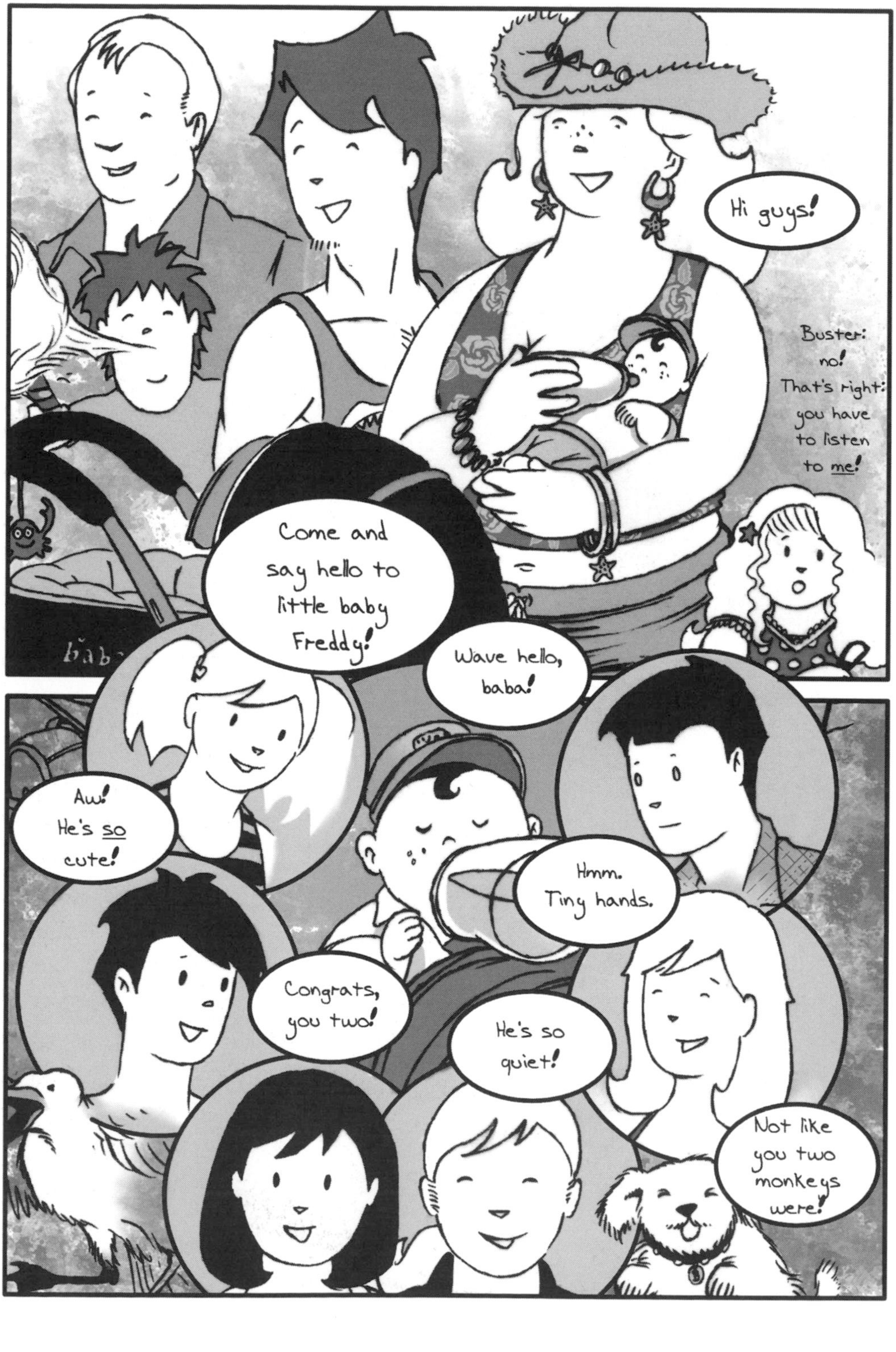
Hi guys!
Buster: no! That's right: you have to listen to me!
Come and say hello to little baby Freddy!
Wave hello, baba!
Aw! He's so cute!
Hmm. Tiny hands.
Congrats, you two!
He's so quiet!
Not like you two monkeys were!

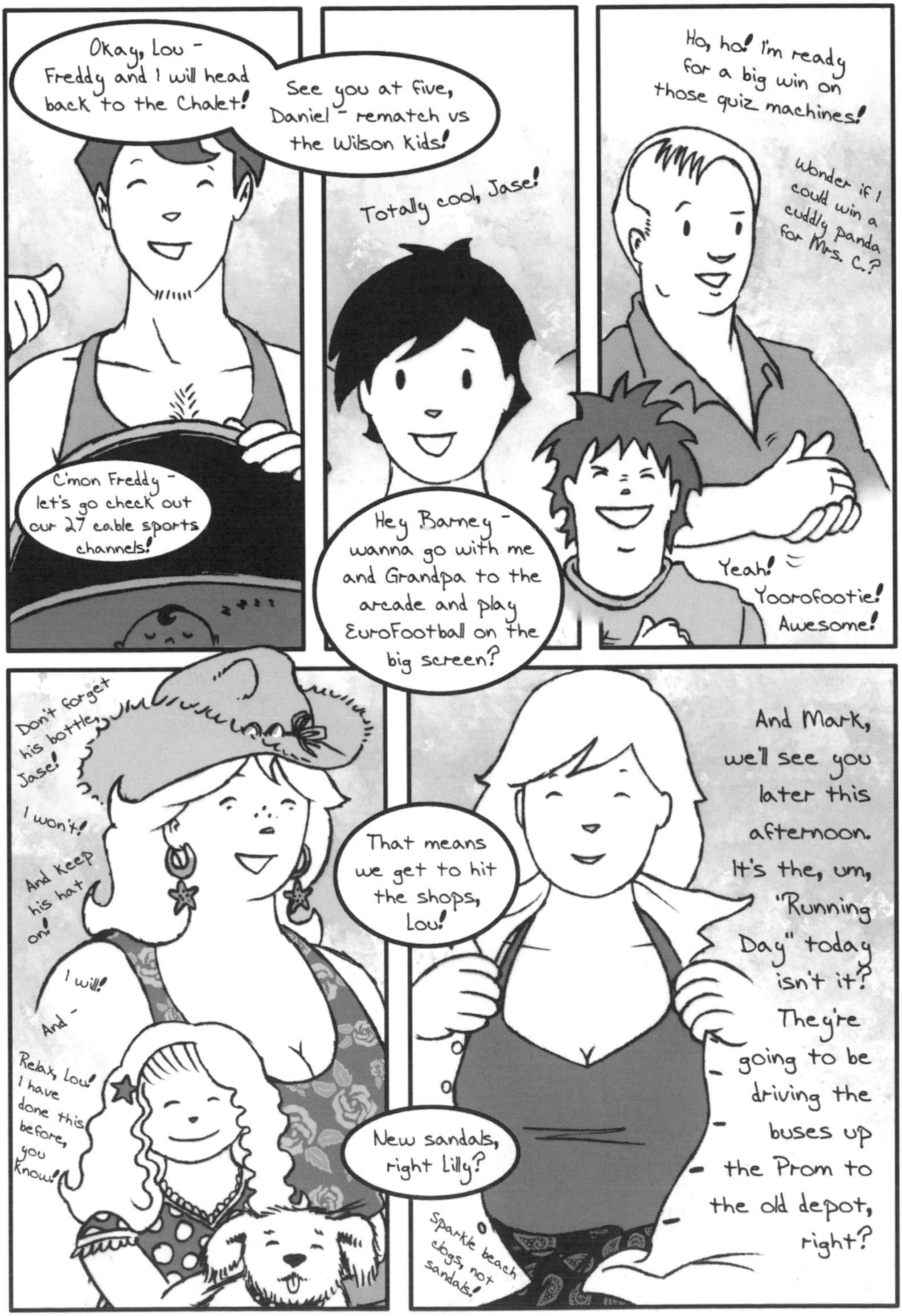
Okay, Lou - Freddy and I will head back to the Chalet!
C'mon Freddy - let's go check out our 27 cable sports channels!
See you at five, Daniel - rematch vs the Wilson Kids!
Totally cool, Jase!
Hey Barney - wanna go with me and Grandpa to the arcade and play EuroFootball on the big screen?
Ho, ho! I'm ready for a big win on those quiz machines!
Wonder if I could win a cuddly panda for Mrs. C.?
Yeah! Yoorofootie! Awesome!
Don't forget his bottle, Jase!
I won't!
And keep his hat on!
I will!
And -
Relax, Lou! I have done this before, you know!
That means we get to hit the shops, Lou!
New sandals, right Lilly?
Sparkle beach clogs, not sandals!
And Mark, we'll see you later this afternoon. It's the, um, "Running Day" today isn't it? They're going to be driving the buses up the Prom to the old depot, right?

It's the most important day of the rally. I've got my camera and my mp3 recorder – I don't want to miss anything!
I bet you don't!
And what about you, Sophie? You coming down the shops with me and Lou? There's a Hollywoodland MSM store!
Hmm ...
Actually, you know what Mum? I think I'd like to go and watch the buses with Dad – if you don't mind, Dad!
Of course not! Are you sure? I'll be there all afternoon ...
Yeah! I'm sure!
I don't know why ...
... but I just fancy doing – Something Different!

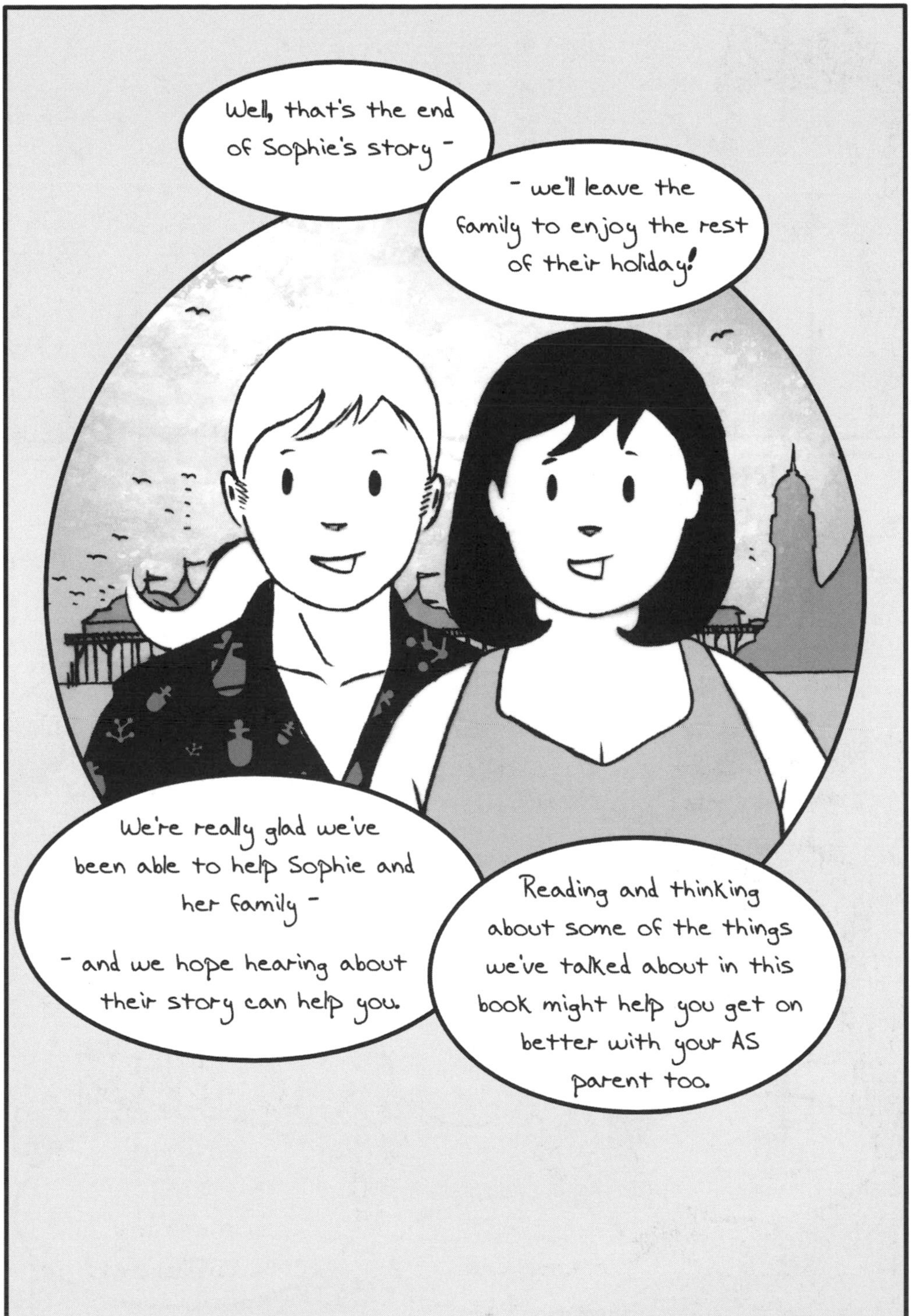
Well, that's the end of Sophie's story -
- we'll leave the family to enjoy the rest of their holiday!
We're really glad we've been able to help Sophie and her family -
- and we hope hearing about their story can help you.
Reading and thinking about some of the things we've talked about in this book might help you get on better with your AS parent too.

Glossary

Anxious, anxiety: feeling worried and scared.

Apologise: say sorry.

Apparent, apparently: what you can see.

Appointment: a fixed time for a meeting with someone.

Asperger Syndrome: Asperger Syndrome is an Autism Spectrum Condition. A Syndrome is a collection of certain differences and difficulties. This one is named after Hans Asperger, a Hungarian doctor who lived from 1906 until 1980. He was the first person to see this collection of differences and difficulties in the children he worked with.

Awkward: difficult, uncomfortable.

Certain: sure, particular (see below).

Comfortable: feeling okay, relaxed, not worried.

Uncomfortable is the opposite of this.

Communicate, communication: talking and listening, reading and writing – any way of giving and getting information.

Compromise: meet halfway, give and take.

Criticise, criticism: say negative and unhelpful things to and about someone or something.

Embarrassed: a feeling of shame and discomfort.

Emotion, emotions: feelings, like happiness, sadness, anger, fear, worry etc.

Empathy: understanding other people's emotions. Being able to see things from another person's point of view.

Encourage, encouragement: say helpful, positive things to someone.

Expected: what you thought would happen, what you had planned. Unexpected is the opposite of this.

Extreme: a lot, an unusual amount of something.

Flexibility: being able to change plans and cope when things turn out differently.

Frustrated: feeling angry and upset, usually because something is stopping you from doing or having what you want.

Imagine, imagination: how our brains think about things.

In advance: before something happens

Inconsiderate: not thinking about other people's needs or feelings. Considerate is the opposite of this.

Organise: put in order, sort.

Particular, particularly: especially, even more.

Patient, patiently: being able to wait for something, or do something that takes a long time.

Process: to think about something and understand what it means.

Reasonable: fair, sensible.

Reassure: remind someone to feel that things are okay

Routine: a set way or order of doing something.

Schedule: a plan or timetable. To reschedule is to change your plan, or to decide to do something at a different time.

Senses, sensory: things to do with hearing, seeing, smelling, tasting, touching, plus feelings of balance and space.

Stress: a feeling of anxiety, worry and fear.

Suggest, suggestion: giving someone an idea, or something to try.

Taking things literally: this is about not understanding that things people say sometimes mean something else – like if someone says 'it's raining cats and dogs'. This means that it's raining a lot, not that cats and dogs are falling out of the sky!